Bernard Taylor was bor[...]
studied fine arts in Swi[...]
ham. He is an actor as w[...]
has been a teacher, a pain[...], and a commercial artist.
He has published eight novels, the latest of which is
Charmed Life, and has had plays produced on stage
and on television. His non-fiction book written with
Stephen Knight, *Perfect Murder*: A Century of
Unsolved Homicides, won the Crime Writers' Association Gold Dagger Award. He lives in London.

Kate Clarke, who like Bernard Taylor has a degree in
Fine Arts, worked as a schoolteacher in London for
many years before moving to Hay-on-Wye, Here-
fordshire, where she now lives. *Murder at The Priory* is
her first book. She is at present working on a fresh
assessment of the case of Adelaide Bartlett, a young
woman who in 1886 was tried for murder after her
husband died with a stomach full of liquid chloroform.

Other works by Bernard Taylor

NOVELS
The Godsend
Sweetheart, Sweetheart
The Reaping
The Moorstone Sickness
The Kindness of Strangers
Madeleine
Mother's Boys
Charmed Life

NON-FICTION
Cruelly Murdered: Constance Kent and the Killing at Road Hill House
Perfect Murder: A Century of Unsolved Homicides (with Stephen Knight)

BERNARD TAYLOR
and
KATE CLARKE

Murder at The Priory

The Mysterious Poisoning of Charles Bravo

GRAFTON BOOKS

A Division of the Collins Publishing Group

LONDON GLASGOW
TORONTO SYDNEY AUCKLAND

Grafton Books
A Division of the Collins Publishing Group
8 Grafton Street, London W1X 3LA

Published in paperback by Grafton Books 1989

First published in Great Britain by
Grafton Books 1988

Copyright © Bernard Taylor and Kate Clarke 1988

ISBN 0-586-20651-5

Printed and bound in Great Britain by
Collins, Glasgow

Set in Bembo

For Sasha and for Douglas and Audrey

CONTENTS

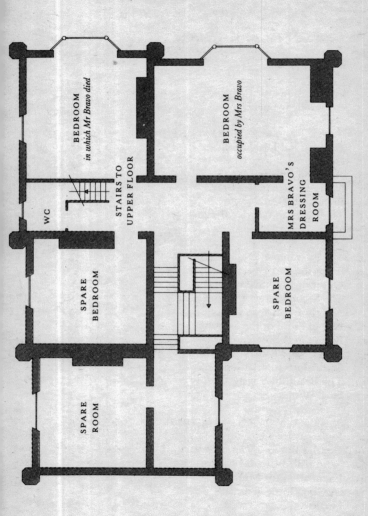

THE PRIORY: *First Floor Plan*

Labels within the plan:

BEDROOM *in which Mr Bravo died*

BEDROOM *occupied by Mrs Bravo*

WC

STAIRS TO UPPER FLOOR

MRS BRAVO'S DRESSING ROOM

SPARE BEDROOM

SPARE BEDROOM

SPARE ROOM

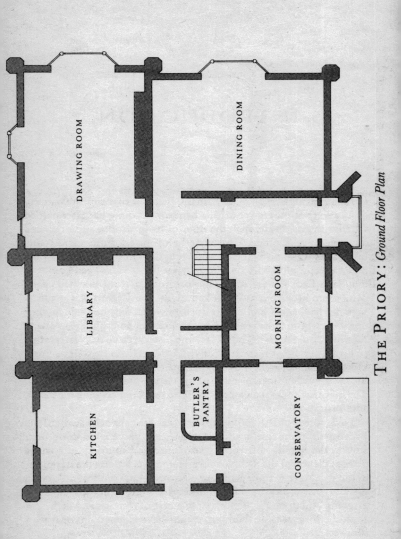

THE PRIORY: *Ground Floor Plan*

INTRODUCTION

On an April night in 1876, in Balham, then one of the most far-flung of London's southern suburbs, a handsome young barrister named Charles Bravo threw open the door of his bedroom and screamed out, 'Florence! Florence! Hot water! Hot water!' In the next room his beautiful young wife of less than five months lay in bed seemingly asleep, while in a chair nearby sat her middle-aged companion, Jane Cox. Later, with Florence roused from her bed, pandemonium broke out as – so it appeared – every effort was made to save her husband's life. Seven doctors were consulted – including one with whom Florence had had a scandalous and adulterous affair. Nothing could be done, however, and just over two days later, after suffering the most terrible agony, Charles Bravo died. The post-mortem that followed showed that he had swallowed enough antimony, a virulent irritant poison, to – as it was said – 'kill a horse'. The question to be answered was: Who had been responsible for its administration?

To devotees of Britain's history of real-life crime the story of the Bravo poisoning case is a familiar one, and there is no doubt that among the handful of truly classic 'unsolved murders' it owns a place at the top of the list. Not surprisingly; set among the trappings of the wealthier members of mid-Victorian England's middle class, the Bravo mystery has all the necessary ingredients for the most gripping and dramatic fiction, with a cast of characters which, one could be forgiven for thinking, might have stepped down from a film set.

In truth, however, no dramatist could quite have invented the characters who, between them, unfold the Bravo story through its theme of love, treachery and violent death to its inexorable conclusion of scandal, public humiliation, degradation, and death again.

There is Florence Bravo, the young wife: beautiful, wealthy, sensual – and with a growing taste for the bottle – a young woman with a past which, when exposed, was variously to shock and titillate a nation. There too is her young barrister husband, Charles, handsome, charismatic, ambitious and jealous. There also is the 'other man', James Gully, a much respected doctor: an old man besotted with a girl young enough to be his granddaughter. And there too, to make up the quartet, is Florence's enigmatic companion, Jane Cox, a woman with her own share of particular hopes and fears.

A fit setting for the drama was The Priory, a beautiful Victorian Gothic house set in its own grounds. Here it was that the poisoning took place.

There are degrees of cruelty and despicableness even in murder, and surely the use of poison is more despicable than most. One might even say that in comparison with poison there is a certain honesty about the straightforward use of a gun or a knife. The poisoner, who works in secret, relies first and foremost on trust; not for him the angry words, the threats, the acts of physical violence. Which is why, of course, practically all evidence in a poisoning case is circumstantial. It must be. The poisoner will never be seen sprinkling the arsenic into the soup or the strychnine into the cocoa, for if suspected of being observed he will desist and wait until a more propitious time when he can act in secret. The poisoner's course is the most subtle and secret of all, so it is hardly surprising that murders by the means of poison have created some of crime's most enduring mysteries.

The Bravo mystery has been made more impenetrable by the rumours that spread at the time and which have distorted the truth increasingly over the intervening years. While researching the case one of the present authors spoke to a publican living very close to Buscot Park (one-time home of Florence Bravo's family) who, hearing Florence's name, said: 'Ah, yes – she murdered her husband and was the first woman to be tried at the Old Bailey' – which illustrates the wildness of the rumour that has developed over the years. Florence Bravo was never charged with the murder of her husband, so she was never tried. And neither was anybody else. The investigations never got further than an inquest, so any notion of a trial having taken place at the Old Bailey is pure fantasy – like so much else that has come down to the present day in relation to the case and which, one must say, has in some cases been perpetuated by writers who should have known better.

Many brief accounts of the Bravo poisoning case have been written over the years, while the mystery has also inspired at least one novel (*Dr Gully* by Elizabeth Jenkins, 1972) and two full-length non-fiction works — *How Charles Bravo Died* (1956) by Yseult Bridges, and *Suddenly at The Priory* by John Williams (1957). These non-fiction works will be referred to later; for now it is enough to say that in many respects they have only served to cast the mystery into even deeper shadow – by presenting rumour as fact, and by doing it so persuasively that the veracity of much of that rumour has never been questioned.

The present authors do not believe that these two writers came anywhere near the truth, and therefore have set out to research the facts for themselves, using all the contemporary evidence that could be found. Apart from studying the newspapers of the time (including a well-known seven-part broadsheet, *The Balham Mystery*) the authors have also consulted the files of the Metropolitan Police and the Treasury. A careful study of these papers in addition to research among other records has produced a picture quite at odds with so many of the rumour-based accounts that have come from other sources.

In 1928 that fine Scottish writer on real-life crime, William Roughead, wrote of the Bravo poisoning case that it 'keeps its proud position as the prize puzzle of British criminal jurisprudence'. It is the belief of the present authors that their book will solve that puzzle; that it will dispel the mystery once and for all.

ACKNOWLEDGEMENTS

In our researches into the truth behind the Bravo mystery we have been helped by a number of people. The limitation of space does not allow us to specify the nature of the valuable assistance given in each case, but nevertheless we wish to acknowledge our great gratitude to those who so willingly gave their help. They are: Clive Alexander, Kay Brunger, Detective Superintendent Douglas Campbell, John Campling, Nel Cantle, Sasha Clarke, Barbara Cow, Norma Diack, B. Graham, Ethel Isles, Elizabeth Jenkins, Jeremiah Johnson, Barbara and Sean Phelan, Kevin Poulter, Roy Purkess, Dr Richard Shepherd of the Department of Forensic Medicine, Guy's Hospital, the Reverend Robert Swanborough, Detective Superintendent John Troon, Hugo Vickers, Tom Watt, Nicky Willets, and David Williamson.

We would also like to thank John Farquharson Ltd for permission to quote from *How Charles Bravo Died* by the late Yseult Bridges, and to state that the essay *Who Poisoned Charles Bravo* by the late Mrs Belloc Lowndes – and quoted herein – comes from the book *Great Unsolved Crimes*, published by Hutchinson in 1938.

To anyone who gave help which has not been acknowledged we apologise and offer our thanks now.

Bernard Taylor and Kate Clarke

'The manner of Mr Bravo's poisoning was so strange and inexplicable that it tempted the mind to fashion hypotheses which might provisionally account for it, and, in fact, the matter had the air of a problem in fiction rather than of a calamity in fact.'

The Daily News, 12 August 1876

I

Promise and Disillusion

In looking at the drama of the Bravo poisoning mystery there is no question but that centre stage must be taken by Florence Bravo, the beautiful woman who became Charles Bravo's wife – and who, with his death, was widowed for the second time in her young life.

She was born Florence Campbell on 5 September 1845 in the Sydney suburb of Darlinghurst, New South Wales, Australia. Her parents, wealthy merchant Robert Campbell and his wife Anne (*née* Orr), who had married in 1835, had altogether three daughters and six sons, of whom Florence was the second child and eldest daughter.

Robert Campbell's courageous and enterprising father – also Robert – had left Scotland for Australia in 1825 and made a fortune from wool and gold. Consequently his son was promised a most comfortable future. In the 1850s Robert and Anne Campbell and their children left Australia to make their lives in England, where in 1859 Robert Campbell bought Buscot Park, an estate of 3500 acres near the ancient town of Faringdon in Berkshire.

Robert Campbell was a remarkable man. Under his design Buscot became the most highly industrialized farm in the country, his innovations including the creation of a twenty-acre reservoir as part of a huge drainage and irrigation system in connection with a scheme for the production of sugar beet and alcohol. In addition he erected a distillery, had the estate ringed with six miles of narrow-gauge railway to facilitate the collection of beet, established a gas works and had a telegraph system installed. He is said to have overreached himself later in his financial commitments, but nevertheless when he died in 1887 he left a fortune in excess of £617,000.

Beside the farming industry of Buscot lay the formal green swards and long sweeping avenues of the estate with its centrepiece, a late eighteenth-century mansion which Campbell had transformed from a state of dereliction into a magnificent showplace. (At the present time, apart from being one of the assets of the National Trust, the house is the home of Lord Faringdon.)

This then was Buscot Park, home of the Campbells; they also enjoyed a fine house in London's Lowndes Square, in the fashionable area of Knightsbridge, and another in Brunswick Terrace, Brighton.

In such a position the Campbells must have anticipated a good marriage for their eldest daughter. And they had every reason to. Apart from the wealth of her background Florence was physically very attractive. She had wide blue eyes, chestnut hair that was striking in its abundance, and a small-boned figure possessing that roundness so much in keeping with the ideal beauty of the day. In addition she was said to be accomplished at the pianoforte, and an extremely fine horsewoman.

The Campbells did not have to wait long before finding a young man whom they regarded as a good match. In the spring of 1864, whilst on a trip to Canada, Florence was introduced to a young officer attached to the Grenadier Guards stationed in Montreal. He was Alexander Louis Ricardo, only child of the late John Lewis Ricardo, MP for Stoke-on-Trent, and the Right Honourable (known as Lady) Catherine, née Duff, who was sister to the fifth Earl of Fife.

The young couple were immediately attracted to one another and with their parents' blessing the wedding took place in the small, narrow church of St Mary's in the tiny village of Buscot on 21 September of that same year, 1864. It was a grand affair with the Bishop of Oxford officiating and many local dignitaries present along with a large circle of family friends. The latter, resplendent in their London fashions, must have provided a lively spectacle for the village folk as they clustered at a respectful distance beyond the lych gate.

Alexander was twenty-one and his bride nineteen, and it must have seemed that their future happiness was assured. Apart from

their affection for one another they also had the promise of financial
security. Alexander had been left at least £13,000 in his father's will
two years before, and now, on the marriage, his mother made a
settlement on the young couple, giving them a life interest on
£40,000. This was an arrangement whereby the capital sum was
held in trust, the interest from which would give to the couple a
yearly income for the rest of their married lives; on the death of the
surviving partner the capital being divided between any children of
the marriage. On his part, Robert Campbell entered a similar bond
where Florence would receive a life interest on the sum of £20,000.
At the going rate of interest at the time, approximately four per
cent, the interest on these two settlements would bring to the young
couple £2400 a year – which was in addition to that realized from
any capital brought to the union by themselves. In the knowledge
that the average labourer at that time was expected to raise a family
on about £28 a year, one can appreciate the wealth that came to
Florence and Alexander on their marriage.

After enjoying a honeymoon on the Rhine, the young couple
returned to England where Alexander took a lease on Hockham
Hall, a very large, impressive house in Norfolk. After that, when
Alexander's army commitments allowed, they seem to have spent
their time going from one vacation to the next, either to their
parents, to Florence's brother William in Sudbury, Suffolk, on trips
abroad or on long visits to friends.

Those carefree times, however, such as they were, were soon to
end. In 1867 Alexander retired from the army, and very soon
afterwards the inadequacies of the couple's domestic lives together
became apparent. For one thing they found that they were living
beyond their means – to the extent that in 1868 they could not afford
to renew the lease of Hockham Hall and were forced to leave,
moving to a smaller place, Shute House in Axminster, Devonshire.
Money was not the only problem, however. Alexander, who had
demonstrated a weakness for alcohol early in the marriage, was now
habitually drinking to excess. When Florence remonstrated with
him he abstained for short periods and showed signs of remorse, but
his periods of sobriety were becoming less and less frequent as time
went by.

Following an accident Alexander's mother died on 6 December
1869 at her house in Chester Square, Belgravia. Her death made the

young Ricardos solvent again, which in other circumstances might well have ended their difficulties; by that time, however, the marriage was past saving. Alexander's drinking had increased to an alarming degree, and any promises he gave to reform quickly dissolved into repeated bouts of drunkenness.

With his drinking making Florence's life increasingly intolerable, to the extent where her own health was failing, she sought the advice of her mother and uncle who suggested that she go away on her own for a while to recover her health and strength. The venue recommended by Mrs Campbell was the small Worcestershire town of Malvern, a salubrious spa at the foot of the Malvern Hills, near the Welsh border, renowned for its curative waters. It was further suggested that if Florence remained apart from Alexander for a period it might bring him to his senses and lead to a reform in his behaviour.

This course Florence determined to follow, and on 28 April 1870, accompanied by two maids, she set off for Malvern, leaving her husband at the St James's Hotel, Piccadilly, in the care of Field, his valet – a man who had proved invaluable, not only in attending to Alexander's everyday needs, but also in dealing with the violent outbursts and despondent moods created by his addiction.

Florence had reserved rooms for herself and her maids at Malvern House, a lodging house, and on her arrival, being close to a state of collapse, she wasted no time in seeking medical attention. She was first attended by the hydropathic physician Dr Fernie, but soon afterwards, on 2 May, she consulted his partner, Dr James Gully, the most famous of Malvern's resident doctors and a family acquaintance of some years.

Florence's meeting with the doctor was not her first; she had previously met him when she and her sister Alice were pupils at a boarding school in the town. Florence, at twelve years old, had been treated by him for a childhood malady and, on another occasion, at the age of fourteen, had accompanied her sister to his house where, probably out of friendship for the girls' parents, he had entertained the young sisters to tea.

By means of his homeopathic and hydropathic treatments Dr James Manby Gully had gained an enviable reputation for relieving many forms of suffering, and by the time of Florence's arrival in Malvern in 1870 his practice was an extremely lucrative and successful one.

Apart from his work as a doctor he was well travelled and widely read and was interested in phrenology and spiritualism. He had had success as a writer, too; in 1839 a play he had written had been presented at London's Drury Lane Theatre, while in his more recent years he had produced several works for publication, the best known being a book entitled *The Water Cure in Chronic Disease*.

He had been born in Jamaica in 1808, the son of a wealthy coffee planter. Sent to Europe for his education, he eventually progressed to France, to L'Ecole de St Barbe in Paris. Later, deciding on a scientific career, he went to Edinburgh University to study medicine, afterwards returning to Paris for a further year's study at L'Ecole de Médecine. It was in 1842, when he was in his mid-thirties, that he became strongly influenced by the Austrian Vincenz Priessnitz, an early advocate of the water-cure, and as a result totally rejected orthodox medicine. With another doctor, James Wilson, he established the hydropathic centre at Malvern, a venture partly financed by Gully's second wife, seventeen years his senior, whom he had married in 1841.

Over a period of nearly thirty years Dr Gully worked with pioneering determination and, despite much opposition from the orthodox medical profession, firmly established himself and his methods which, in accordance with the notion that a certain amount of supervised suffering must be beneficial, appear to have been truly punishing. Patients were encased in wet sheets, subjected to cold-water douches and persuaded to perch in sitz-baths, maintaining positions that were anything but elegant. The diets prescribed were extremely rigid, and, water being the optimum beverage, wine, and even hot tea, were much frowned upon. Nevertheless, so respected were Dr Gully and his methods that he listed among his patients such people as Dickens, George Eliot, Florence Nightingale and Tennyson. The latter, who was treated at Malvern for 'morbid depression' when he was thirty-eight, said of the treatment that it 'half-cured, half-destroyed' him.

In spite of the discomforts, however, a steady flow of patients went for the treatment, and praise for the water-cure spread, its popularity increasing throughout the 1850s and 1860s and the small town of Malvern expanding to accommodate the pilgrims. By 1870 hydropathic treatments were very much in vogue and the curative

waters of Malvern were being widely advertised. Clearly, Dr Gully
and his kind fulfilled a need among the moneyed members of
Victorian society, a society that had adopted the word 'stress' and
could afford to suffer from it and pay well for its banishment.

It was certainly a very stressed Florence Ricardo who entered Dr
Gully's consulting room on 2 May 1870.

At the time of the meeting James Gully was sixty-two years old
and living the life of a respectable bachelor. Although his wife was
still alive she had been confined for many years in a mental home. In
her absence the doctor's comforts and fine house in Malvern were
cared for by his two unmarried sisters.

A powerful man through his wealth and eminence, Dr Gully
made up in charisma what he might have lacked in physical appeal.
He was bald – save for the neatly trimmed side-pieces which,
contrasting with his florid complexion, appeared almost white –
and small in stature. However, he had an upright carriage and very
handsome features. In addition he exuded an air of wisdom and
quiet confidence, kindness, and authoritative calm.

In contrast, the young woman who faced him that day was
distraught, insecure and very much in need of help. To her frayed
constitution, however, Dr Gully's kind, understanding attention
must have been balm, for further appointments were made over the
days that followed.

With Gully's help Florence's nervous tension faded as she found
relief in the comfort he offered and in the wet-packings and spinal
washes he prescribed. As a result she soon lost her dependence on
opiates for a good night's rest and became accustomed to natural
sleep once more.

As the meetings continued – socially as well as for Florence's
hydropathic treatments – their relationship progressed. Florence
realized that in many ways Dr Gully was a liberal thinker, one who
did not subscribe to society's view that her marriage vows were
irreversible – despite her husband's addiction and its attendant
humiliation – and in her desperate state these were the views she
wished to hear.

To certain women such power as was Gully's is a compelling
aphrodisiac, and Florence may be counted among them. Also,
being extremely egocentric, she would have relished the attention

that her delicacy demanded. All things considered, it was perhaps inevitable that she should find herself drawn to James Gully's warmth, sympathy and understanding of her situation.

For his part, notwithstanding that he had led a full and satisfying life in many respects, he had been forced to live for many years without the affection and the approval of an attractive woman. Here before him was a woman who was beautiful, elegant and, it appeared, in need of him. And if the maxim is true that there is no fool like an old fool, then Gully exemplified it, for he in turn was equally drawn to Florence.

The pleasant and diverting time in one another's company had to come to an end, however, for from the St James's Hotel in Piccadilly, Alexander, swearing that he had given up alcohol and would not return to it, was writing to Florence in the hope of being reunited with her. Consequently it was arranged that he should join her and in preparation for his arrival she rented Orwell Lodge, a furnished house in the area. When he finally got there, however, with his valet Field in attendance, he was far from well. Whatever happened then between Florence and Alexander did nothing for the relationship, for two or three weeks later, on 7 June, he had given Florence and Field the slip and left the town.

Field was at once sent to London to search for him, eventually running him to ground in rooms in Wigmore Street where his alcoholic excesses had reduced him to a wretched state. Mrs Campbell, arriving in London in response to Florence's cry for help, had her son-in-law taken to his late mother's ex-butler in Westminster. By this time Florence, with her maid (she had dismissed the other, Laundon, for impertinence), had arrived in the capital and joined her mother at the family house in Lowndes Square. There, a few days later, Alexander lurched onto the doorstep.

The doctor who attended him diagnosed delirium tremens. After a few days, however, Alexander seemed a little better and asked to be moved to his house in Chester Square. Florence and her mother were only too glad to comply.

When Alexander had recovered further, Florence, in another effort to bring him to his senses, threatened to leave him for good, with the result that he remained sober for several weeks. Then, in August, she managed to persuade him to return to Malvern with her. If she hoped, however, that Dr Gully would be able to impose sobriety on him, she was mistaken, for once having arrived in the town Alexander resumed his drinking with alarming effects. His behaviour now became totally unpredictable. Sometimes he was aggressive, at other times he was sullenly silent. He would beg Florence to forgive him and soon afterwards would lock himself in his room and refuse to allow her anywhere near him. Those about him were baffled as to how to deal with his irrational behaviour.

His condition deteriorated even further. In November of that year, while Florence's sister was staying with them at Orwell Lodge, he became so violent that Field had forcibly to restrain him. Very much frightened, Florence, her sister and her maid hurriedly left to take refuge in Dr Gully's house.

Not knowing how to cope, Florence telegraphed her mother who came immediately to Malvern and escorted her two daughters back to Buscot. Shortly after arriving there Florence received a letter from Alexander begging for her forgiveness and the resumption of their life together. Now, however, she was indifferent to his pleading, and to the great displeasure of her parents made it clear that she no longer had any hopes of her husband's recovery and had no intention of returning to him.

In her bid for freedom Florence seems to have been encouraged throughout by Dr Gully who at some stage had discussed with her the possibility of her obtaining a legal separation from her husband. Subsequently, the doctor consulted a solicitor on her behalf – a Mr Henry Brooks of Streatham – who agreed to draw up the necessary documents.

When Florence's father heard of her intentions he was outraged, for in accordance with the social climate of the time his belief in the sanctity and permanence of marriage was absolute. Florence, though, refused to return to Alexander, and as a result her father threatened to withhold the interest on her marriage settlement. If he imagined, however, that this would coerce her into complying with his wishes he was mistaken, for she responded by immediately leaving Buscot for London.

Once in the capital, Florence settled herself into a suite of rooms at the Crystal Palace Hotel and then allowed her indignation to direct her to the office of Mr Brooks. There she told him of her predicament, following which he offered her, as a paying guest, three rooms in his own house. Florence readily accepted and, taking her maid with her, moved into Brooklands, the solicitor's comfortable Streatham villa.

Besides making frequent trips to see Florence in Streatham during the winter of 1870, James Gully had been making some sweeping changes at his home – for one thing notifying his partner, Dr Fernie, that he would retire in December of the following year, a little earlier than he had originally planned. The news which most disturbed his family, however – his two sisters and his son William and daughter Susanna – was that instead of spending a tranquil old age in Malvern, he now intended to retire to London.

On 31 March 1871 he went to see Henry Brooks again, this time, as trustee, to sign the Deed of Separation between Florence and Alexander. Brooks signed as a co-trustee, having drawn up an agreement whereby Florence would receive an allowance from her husband of £1200 a year.

Three weeks later, on 19 April, at 6/8 Frankenplatz, Cologne, Alexander died.

At Brooklands Florence received a telegram notifying her of his demise. No official cause of death was given but the evident rapid deterioration of his health left no doubt that he had died as the result of his alcoholic excesses. Any grief Florence might have felt on learning of her young husband's death was tempered by the news that when he died he had been living with a woman, obviously a mistress. As a result, she indignantly refused to pay his debts – though she later relented.

Alexander's death was tragic and sordid – yet also very convenient, for Florence's Deed of Separation had not yet become effective and the terms of the huge settlement made by Lady Ricardo on the couple only six years before had therefore remained unchanged. Consequently, and with there being no children of the marriage, the whole amount of the capital became Florence's. Not only was she a widow at the age of twenty-six, but, in addition to her youth and beauty and the money she owned in her own right, she had now come into a fortune of over £40,000.

2

Changes

Florence looked charming in her widow's weeds, courtesy of Jay's, suppliers of mourning to the more fashionably bereaved. Thinking it unnecessary to disappear completely under folds of heavy crape, however, she settled instead for a simple dress of black silk, added to which she dressed her chestnut hair in an elaborate style, topped, almost as if by an afterthought, by a tiny widow's cap of black lace.

Although Dr Gully was still resident in Malvern at this time he frequently took the long journey to see the young widow at Streatham. The visits caused little comment at first; indeed, it seemed perhaps only fitting that the doctor should make regular calls on a lady in delicate health who was suffering from a tragic bereavement. Florence's mother, however, did not view Dr Gully's concern quite so naïvely. She felt that local gossips might misconstrue his visits, and it was little comfort to her that he was a man of renown, a family acquaintance and so much older than her daughter. Five years later Mrs Campbell was to say that she had remonstrated with her daughter over her infatuation for Dr Gully, but that all her words had been 'to no purpose'.

Florence's father, however, was not content with remonstrations and, carrying out his earlier threat, proceeded to withhold the interest payments on her marriage settlement. As a result Florence took the surprising step of entering a charge against him in the Court of Chancery and he was forced to capitulate.

Meanwhile the relationship between herself and Dr Gully developed still further during his visits to Brooklands, and they became lovers. Apparently considering themselves 'privately engaged', they had an understanding that they would marry when

Gully's elderly wife died. She was over eighty at the time, so the couple must have felt that their freedom was imminent – a matter of a few months, or a year perhaps, during which time they could consolidate their attachment. ·

In June of that year, when Mrs Brooks was confined with the birth of her second daughter, Florence visited Malvern in the company of Dr Gully's son William, and William's wife and small daughter, also taking along with her Georgina, the eleven-year-old daughter of Mr and Mrs Brooks. In her absence the latter were informed by a family friend that while visiting them at Brooklands she had 'surprised Mrs Ricardo and Dr Gully cuddling together on a sofa'. On Florence's return to Streatham she was informed by Henry Brooks and his wife that they could no longer tolerate the 'private engagement' between herself and Dr Gully, and in the heated scene that ensued Mrs Brooks used such strong words that Dr Gully later threatened to defend Florence's good name with an action for slander.

Clearly the time had come for Florence to become the mistress of her own household, and without further delay she took a two-year lease on a semi-detached villa – Stokefield – in Leigham Court Road, Streatham. This arrangement rendered her free to conduct her affairs as she saw fit and to entertain her elderly lover whenever it pleased her.

In December of that year, 1871, James Gully retired from his thirty-year medical practice in Malvern. His departure was marked by a ceremony during which he received many formal tributes and citations. A large number of friends and colleagues gathered in the town to mark the occasion – though many were not a little puzzled by his intention to leave Malvern. Furthermore, they could not understand that, while he planned to take his butler with him, he would no longer require his sisters to keep house for him – something the two women had done for many years.

Before long, however, the rumours of his affair with Mrs Ricardo had reached the town, and it became common knowledge that Gully's coachman, Griffiths, had already gone to work for her in Streatham. Gully's friends and patients alike began to wonder if the dignified doctor was about to let a pretty young widow make a fool out of him.

Following Dr Gully's move to his newly leased house in Streatham – like Florence's, in Leigham Court Road – he and Florence flouted convention still further by spending six weeks together in Italy – accompanied only by Pritchard, Gully's butler, and Fanny Plascot, Florence's maid. Despite their claim that the relationship was an innocent one during this winter sojourn, however, the fact that they travelled abroad together was extremely damaging to Florence's already shaken reputation.

Eventually Florence herself had to admit that she was not entirely happy with her way of life. Through her relationship with Dr Gully she had sacrificed not only the affections of those close to her, but also the pleasures of society. Being shunned by parents and friends alike – only her brother William and his wife continued to call on her – and with all the fashionable drawing rooms of the area closed to her she had begun to feel her isolation. She still had the pleasures of the doctor's daily visits from his own house nearby, but as he made a point of leaving her by nine-thirty each evening – in order to present some semblance of respectability – she was alone for much of the time.

As a result of her loneliness, and her segregation from the company of friends and neighbours, she decided to employ a companion, someone who would be company and who would lend her life a degree of respectability which at present it was lacking.

In her search for a suitable candidate, Florence recalled that at Brooklands, the home of her solicitor, there was a daily governess, a Mrs Cox.

The woman, a widow, appeared a little threadbare and weighed down with responsibilities. Nevertheless, in their meetings Florence had noted a canny intelligence and a willingness to please. Also the woman had demonstrated discretion with regard to Dr Gully's visits. In the event, Florence felt sure that Mrs Cox would suit her very well.

Consequently in May 1872 Florence suggested to the governess that she leave Brooklands and become her resident companion. Mrs Cox accepted the invitation, and the following July, after taking her three sons to Malvern for their summer holidays, she moved to Stokefield to take up her new position.

And so the third player took her place in the developing drama.

*

According to her own statements Mrs Cox was born Jane Cannon Edouard in the East Indies. Her father, a Frenchman, had been a merchant in the East India Company. After his death she worked as a governess, first for a few months teaching the children of the Rev. Robert Leslie, curate of the parish of Bingham, Nottinghamshire, then for a little over a year for the Rev. John Papillon, rector of Lexden, Essex. After leaving the service of Mr Papillon in 1858 she married Philip Cox and, following the birth of her son, John Leslie Clarke (known as Leslie), in 1860, went the next year with her husband to Jamaica where he was employed by the government as a civil engineer. There in 1862 she bore twins, Henry and Sarah (Sarah dying in infancy), and in 1864 a third son, Charles.

Her husband's death in 1867 placed Mrs Cox in a desperate predicament. Left with very little money and with three small sons to rear, and having no breadwinner but herself, she decided in 1868 to return to England and support herself and her family by teaching.

Following her return she opened a dame school in Woodbridge, Suffolk, but the project failed and she was faced once again with the question of survival. In the event she travelled to London to seek the help of a Mr Joseph Bravo who lived with his family in Lancaster Road, Notting Hill. Mr Bravo, a merchant, had come from Jamaica, where he was born (like Dr Gully, an English colonial now settled in England) and where his partner and brother-in-law, a Mr Michael Solomon, had later worked closely with Mrs Cox's late husband. Mr Solomon and his wife had also been godparents to one of Mrs Cox's younger sons.

Joseph Bravo was glad to help the unfortunate woman who came to him that day, and advised her to invest her savings in the purchase of a house, pointing out that with an outlay of £200 she might rely on the rents from it as an insurance against penury and the work-house. Mrs Cox followed his advice, and after securing a house suggested by him – number 150 Lancaster Road – she furnished it and let it, and then borrowed from him the sum of £60 to enable her to enter her two eldest boys into a boarding school for 'distressed gentlefolk' in Streatham Hill, the Royal Asylum of St Anne's Society. This done, and with her youngest son being cared for elsewhere, she rented a single room for herself in a lodging house in Streatham while she took a post as a daily governess, from her wages paying back her debt to Mr Joseph Bravo.

The support of herself and her three children remained a struggle, however, and in May 1871 she advertised for more pupils. As a result she took an additional post as daily governess to the elder daughter of Mr Henry Brooks, at whose house she met Mrs Florence Ricardo. And so it was that the whole dreary routine of her life was changed.

In August 1872, when Mrs Cox moved into Stokefield in Leigham Court Road as Florence's companion, her starting salary was £80 a year, an extremely generous sum considering that the usual salary for a companion was about £30 a year, and that a kitchen maid could not hope for more than about £12 or £13 a year for her labours.

Along with Mrs Cox's duties as resident companion there must have been a tacit demand for her discretion. She was not naïve, and she must have been well aware of the nature of the relationship between her mistress and Dr Gully – to which the frosty looks and whispered asides that greeted her locally would also have testified. For the sake of her three boys, however, storing up the advantages of their education (her third son went to St Anne's in 1873, for which purpose she borrowed a further £81 10s. from Mr Joseph Bravo), Jane Cox was prepared to compromise. And not surprisingly, for fortune seemed to be rewarding her industry and single-mindedness at last.

Late in the summer of 1873 Florence and Dr Gully travelled abroad once more, this time to Kissingen, a picturesque spa in Germany which was reminiscent in many ways of Malvern. Dr Gully had chosen the resort, where he had many friends, and where he had persuaded Florence to undergo further water-treatments.

For the sake of propriety while staying at the boarding house in the town, Florence and the doctor took separate rooms. There Florence was attended by her new maid, Humphries. (Humphries had recently replaced her maid Fanny Plascot on the latter's marriage to Griffiths, Florence's coachman. It had been necessary for Fanny and George Griffiths to leave after their marriage as Florence could not provide accommodation for a married couple.)

During the trip to Kissingen Mrs Cox was left in charge of the household, though it appears that she had some trouble controlling the servants. Whatever the cause, she wrote to Florence of instances of insubordination while at the same time keeping her up to date with the news. Florence's reply, written in Kissingen on 23 August, gives a picture of the situation, and of Florence's evident efficiency in running her house:

My dearest Mrs Cox,

Many thanks for your kind letter . . . will you tell Rance [gardener] that I have no intention of building a greenhouse and will have nothing ordered from Mould or elsewhere without my order . . . I told MacGrath [footman] that he was not to sleep in the house and my order is to be obeyed. Will you write to Mrs . . . for me and demand my book back and tell her that unless she returns it, I will write to her mistress. Will you find out if she comes to Stokefield as I gave strict orders that she was not to come at all, and you can tell Barton [butler] it is as much as his place is worth if she comes to my house. I never gave Anna [housemaid] permission to have her sister and am writing to her about it. If all is well I shall be home on 24th or 25th September. Will you kindly get me eight laying hens by that time from the Exchange & Mart – hens that will lay through the autumn and winter.

I have such horrid baths now – peat soil containing iron is mixed with mineral water just like liquid manure. It is for soothing the nerves but it is horrible, and one has to take a hot bath afterwards to get clean.

Then I have three glasses of cold mineral water from seven to eight in the morning and another glass at 6 p.m. I feel quite wearied out by eight-thirty and I'm glad to get to bed. If it does me good I shall not mind but it is not agreeable.

Will you in the course of next week compare Pegg's prices for coal with Piggott's as I should like the cellar filled before I return.

I am glad all the dogs and horses are well. I often wish Bruce [dog] was here. Humphries is very well and going on alright. Rance must manage as well as he can about the cuttings for next year; he has more shelves than he had last winter.

I am getting on well with the lace for the mantelpiece.

With kindest love,
Yours affectionately,
Florence Ricardo

The interlude at Kissingen was pleasant for Florence, despite the rigours of the water-cure. The result of the stay, however, banished any taste of pleasure she might have known, for it was not long before she discovered that she was pregnant.

As a result, at the beginning of November 1873, Dr Gully performed an abortion on her. Becoming seriously ill afterwards she had no choice – in the absence of a nurse – but to rely on Mrs Cox. And it must have been a remarkable test of the latter's discretion, for she managed to conceal completely from the other servants the nature of their mistress's indisposition. Later she would claim that Florence's illness had resulted from a completely different cause, denying that there had been an abortion, which, there can be no doubt, there had been.

As for Florence, she found Mrs Cox a great comfort at this difficult time; indeed she claimed later that she owed her life to her companion. There can be no doubt that the selfless care that Mrs Cox gave to Florence during the delicate period of her illness greatly increased the affection between the two women. As a result of Florence's growing trust and gratitude the two dispensed with formalities and began to call one another by their first names.

However, whereas the relationship between the women blossomed, where Florence and her lover were concerned the crisis had the opposite effect.

The pain of the abortion, and her resulting illness and depression, brought about a change in Florence's feelings towards Dr Gully, and after her recovery the two of them were no longer lovers.

She made it quite clear to him that although she still felt great affection for him and did not wish to end their friendship, from that time onwards the physical side of their relationship was over.

3

Brighton Romance

In March 1874 Florence and her household moved into The Priory, a splendidly fanciful pseudo-Gothic house at the top of Bedford Hill – then known as Bedford Hill Road – in Balham, at that time little more than a village just a stone's throw from Streatham.

Though not the largest of the houses in the area, The Priory was by far the most unusual, and Florence was much attracted to its romanticism. Furthermore, its ten acres of gardens and paddocks, though not to be compared with the grandeur of Buscot Park, nevertheless had great charm and she took enormous pride in them. Able to indulge her love of gardens she employed three gardeners and, supervising much of the work herself, had a shrubbery made and a landscaped rose-garden with dozens of rose trees and ornamental shrubs. Adding a more rural touch to the scene were orchards prolific in various summer and autumn fruits, melon-pits and vineries and a well-stocked kitchen garden, while along the rose-walks and among the trees strutted ducks, geese and fantail doves.

Contemporary reports present The Priory's setting in idyllic terms as it appeared in 1876, two years after Florence had taken over its occupation. With the paddock hiding from view the railway – 'that dreadful innovation by occupiers of eligible suburban residences' – the road next to the Lodge is described as being like a country lane where 'climbing rose trees . . . present their blossoms to every passer-by, without even the protection of the simplest fence . . . whilst the nature of the ground renders it a favourite "spin" for the bicyclist'.

In addition to its own special attractions, the grounds were granted a greater sense of spaciousness by virtue of their bordering the wide acres of Tooting Bec Common, whose open reaches enabled Florence to indulge her passion for horses.

As to the house itself, its interior was every bit as attractive as its exterior would lead one to suspect. To the right of the arched entrance was the dining room, in its centre a large dining table of Spanish mahogany, the windows overlooking the front lawn with its beautiful oak tree, beyond which lay the common, laced with carriage-ways and tree-lined walks.

To the left of the entrance hall was the morning room and it was here that Florence came to enjoy relaxing in the afternoons. The room held a Broadwood cottage piano and a fine collection of Venetian glass, its beauty embellished by the polished mahogany and gleaming mirrors. Like the rest of the house Florence had furnished it lavishly, but with care. By present-day standards the room was grossly overdone with its whatnots, elaborate jardinières, and a chaise longue that seemed to be sinking under a sea of tasselled cushions, but by contemporary tastes it was the height of fashionable elegance.

At the rear of the house was the drawing room, furnished in blue, its delicate french windows overlooking the shrubbery. It was here that Florence kept her Sèvres and Dresden ornaments, elegantly displayed in an ebonized cabinet inlaid with ivory. Leading from the drawing room was the conservatory containing a fernery in which she cultivated many rare plants – an expensive hobby at twenty guineas apiece.

Next door was the library – 'sufficiently large for the reception of unexpected visitors, and also for the delectation of studious occupants of The Priory'. To the right of the morning room was the staircase leading to the four bedrooms on the first floor. More bedrooms were on the second floor, which was occupied by Mrs Cox and the other servants.

After taking up residence at The Priory, one of the first things Florence did was to commission the building of a new Entrance Lodge and gates, after which she set about having alterations carried out to the Lower Lodge. When the latter was complete she was able to offer it to the coachman George Griffiths and his wife Fanny, her former employees, so persuading them to leave their new employment at Warwick Square and return to her service.

While Florence and her servants were settling into their new home Dr Gully was settling into his. Shortly before Florence had taken a lease on The Priory, the doctor had taken one on a red-brick villa, also situated on Bedford Hill. After the house where Florence had stayed in Malvern he named it Orwell Lodge. Following her move to Balham, Florence, with Griffiths driving, would pick up the doctor at some point between The Priory and his new home and go for a drive across the common in her smart new phaeton. More often than not at such times Mrs Cox would accompany the young widow and her erstwhile lover.

If Florence was happier at The Priory, Mrs Cox had good reason to be happy also during that spring of 1874. Apart from her content-ment in her well-paid post as Florence's companion she had received some good news from her aunt (by marriage), Mrs Margaret Cox, living in Jamaica.

This gentlewoman had been the wife of Philip Cox's paternal uncle. They resided in St Ann's Bay, where they owned two houses, Content and Carlton, living in the former. In 1861, on arrival in Jamaica, Philip and Jane Cox and their infant son had gone to stay with Philip's aunt at Content, where Jane Cox's twins were born the following year. Now, widowed and in old age, and with no family of her own, Mrs Margaret Cox had become concerned as to what would become of her properties when she died. As a result she wrote from Content on 26 March 1874 to Jane Cox:

> My dear Jane,
>
> I think it right to let you know I have left in my will all I have to Leslie [Mrs Cox's eldest son] – Carlton, Content, cattle, horses, carriage, plate, books, furniture, &c, &c; and should I die before he comes of age that you will not allow these properties to be sold, but carried on for his benefit. Mr Sol-omon and Mr John Sinclair are my executors, and I have no doubt but they will see every justice done. All my trinkets I leave to you. Some years ago I wrote to the Rev. John Cox [father of Philip], when he was living at Walgrave, that I would leave these properties to his three sons by his first wife, M. A. Woodward, but have long since revoked this, and I do not

wish any of his family, except *Leslie*, to have anything belonging to me. I never got anything from them. My own money paid for these properties, and I can leave them to whom I please. You had better keep this to yourself; say nothing about it to anyone, not even to Leslie, while I am alive.

Margaret Cox

Mrs Cox must have been very pleased. She had worked hard all her life for her sons, and now at last, through Leslie's coming inheritance, there would be some reward.

In the autumn of that year, 1874, Florence and James Gully, with Mrs Cox as a chaperone, travelled abroad once more – this time to Italy. However, if the doctor hoped to rekindle Florence's passion during the trip he failed dismally, for having reached Paris on the return journey he was abruptly left to his own devices while Florence, with Mrs Cox in tow, resumed the journey home. Florence's resolve had not weakened, and James Gully was forced to content himself with no more than the affectionate esteem that his ex-mistress was prepared to give him.

Then, as the lives of the ill-matched couple began to settle into a routine of compromise there came on the scene another man, Charles Bravo.

The unforeseen appearance of the handsome young barrister was to change everything for Florence, Dr Gully and Mrs Cox, and for at least two of them to demolish the relative peace of their lives forever.

It was Mrs Cox who brought about the first meeting between Florence and Charles Bravo.

One day in December 1874 Florence had planned to lunch in town while Mrs Cox had promised to take her three sons on a traditional pre-Christmas visit to Mr and Mrs Joseph Bravo, who had recently gone to live at their splendid new residence at 2 Palace Green, Kensington.

As Florence would be going through Kensington on her way to town she insisted on taking Mrs Cox and the boys in her carriage, promising to collect them later on her way back to Balham. On calling at Palace Green later that day she was invited in. Then, as she exchanged pleasantries with Mr and Mrs Bravo in the drawing room, their son Charles appeared and was introduced to her.

The attraction between the two was not an immediate one, for ten months were to elapse before their next meeting. In the meantime Florence accompanied Dr Gully on a tour of the West Country and afterwards to Southsea. On these trips it appears that she and Mrs Cox shared a bedroom – further indication that all sexual intimacy between Florence and the doctor was at an end.

Florence was growing increasingly independent of James Gully and also showing a wish to live a little more freely – one sign of which was that by the summer of 1875 she was dyeing her hair a deeper shade of red and wearing a style of dress that was noticeably more flamboyant. Not only that, she had developed a liking for sherry, of which fact knowledge was soon transmitted from her own servants to those at Orwell Lodge.

To Dr Gully, aware of this growing weakness of Florence's, it was a further disappointment to add to that already engendered by her use of cosmetics and dyes. He also knew, however, that his opinion no longer carried much weight and that she was no longer susceptible to his influence. For the first time in their relationship he felt powerless to intervene.

During that summer of 1875 Florence heard that her mother was ill and, not having been reconciled to her family over the affair with Dr Gully, she was very distressed at the news. Plagued with doubt she finally made the decision to end completely her relationship with the doctor and so effect a reconciliation with her mother. So it was that, when Dr Gully stated his intentions of visiting Italy in August to renew old friendships, Florence voiced an inclination to spend the summer at Eastbourne. She later said she would have informed the doctor of her decision to end the relationship before his departure for Italy, but 'didn't want to spoil his holiday'.

In Eastbourne, Florence, becoming restless, decided to change the venue and after two weeks she and Mrs Cox moved on to Brighton. The move was also prompted by the wishes of Mrs Cox, whose eldest son Leslie was now a pupil in the town. So, following their arrival at their lodgings in Kings Road, the two women were able to visit him and watch him competing in a sports event at his school.

The time went by, and then, in mid-October, on the sea front, purely by chance, Florence Ricardo and Charles Bravo met for the second time. The meeting was clearly a pleasurable one, for when they parted a little later it was with the arrangement that Charles would call on Florence at her rooms next day. Said Florence later of the time immediately following that chance meeting, 'Wherever we went, he was there.' Clearly, Charles had been impressed.

Charles, baptized Charles Delauney Turner, was born on 30 May 1845. There is no record of his birth in the General Register Office at St Catherine's House, London, so one must assume that he was born abroad. Likewise there is no English record of his father's death, which occurred soon after Charles's birth, or of the remarriage of his mother, Mary (née Hougham), to Joseph Bravo, his stepfather – suggesting that these happenings also occurred abroad. With regard to Charles's father, almost nothing is known; the only information so far gained about him is that given on Charles's marriage certificate, where he appears as *Augustus Charles Turner, Gentleman*. A possible clue to Charles's birthplace comes through his stepfather, Joseph Bravo; as the latter had lived in Jamaica* for a considerable time before moving to England it is very possible that it was there that he met and married Charles's widowed mother.

At the time of Mrs Turner's remarriage she had three children, Charles, aged four, and his two younger sisters, Alice and Ellen. Alice was a deaf-mute, while Ellen was said to be a mental defective; she was later placed in a convent.

The marriage turned out to be a positive step, particularly where the children were concerned, for Joseph Bravo turned out to be a good and affectionate father, to the extent that when Charles came of age, he, reciprocating the great affection shown to him, took his stepfather's surname.

In that autumn of 1875 when Charles came into the focus of Florence Ricardo he was an up-and-coming young lawyer of thirty,

---

* The number of associations with Jamaica in the Charles Bravo story is surprising, though of course in the Victorian era, when Britain's empire was expanding so rapidly, Britons were colonizing in all parts of the globe, and the West Indies were a valued source of revenue. An interesting note with regard to the number of expatriates living in Jamaica in the 1870s is that there were sufficient numbers there to support several newspapers catering just to the British white population, without taking into account the island's black population.

Florence's senior by three months. And if there was an air about him that reflected an indulged childhood, nevertheless he also exhibited an attractive self-confidence. One of the photographs of him taken at Brighton later that year shows a self-assured, handsome young man sporting a rather sardonic smile for the camera. He had had an excellent education at Trinity College, Oxford, possessed a wry humour liberally peppered with cynicism and was a man of the world. Although he had committed himself to law as a career he had a great interest in medicine, on occasion going to King's College Hospital to watch the performance of surgical operations; he was also greatly interested in politics and had voiced a wish someday to make a career for himself at Westminster. His other interests included a passionate love of the works of Shakespeare.

Aware as he must have been of Florence's considerable fortune, there can be no doubt that it met with Charles's approval. Whether it was the main attraction, however, must remain a matter of speculation, one on which the reader must make up his own mind. Charles himself was not a wealthy man, though he stood to inherit most of his stepfather's money on the latter's death. In the meantime he earned the modest income of about £200 a year, an income supplemented by gifts from his stepfather. In an effort to improve his livelihood he sometimes, to the disapproval of Joseph Bravo, speculated on the stock market.

There are certain writers who believe that Charles was motivated solely by Florence's fortune, among them John Dickson Carr, who describes him in the foreword to John Williams's *Suddenly at The Priory* as 'as nasty a bit of work as ever lived' – and also Yseult Bridges who, clearly holding him in no higher esteem, speaks of him as a man suffering from 'money mania'. The present writers do not share such views. Florence Ricardo had other attractions for Charles Bravo apart from her money. She had looks, personality and breeding, and these must have played their part. Furthermore, the letters that later passed between the couple give evidence of a genuine affection, particularly on Charles's side.

Whatever was in Charles's mind that autumn of 1875, however, there can be no doubt that to Florence's slightly jaded *joie de vivre* his attentions must have been a tremendous lift. She received his attentions with pleasure; after spending four years on the arm of an elderly lover and with the resulting preoccupations it had brought she found herself enjoying the company of a handsome and vital young man.

Charles having come into her life, Florence had even more incentive to break off her association with Dr Gully; therefore, at the time of the doctor's return to London from his holiday abroad she wrote asking him to visit her in Brighton. When they met, however, her courage must have failed her, for although she referred with regret to the fact that she was still unable to visit her sick mother, she spoke of no wish to break off her relationship with him. As a result Dr Gully left Brighton none the wiser.

After returning to Balham Dr Gully wrote twice to Florence at her Brighton address. Then on the following Saturday he received from her a letter telling him that their friendship was over and that they must never meet again. With the shock of her words he succumbed to a turmoil of regret and despondency; according to his butler, Pritchard, he seemed stunned by this rejection.

While Gully was in the depths of despair, however, Florence, having executed the disagreeable task, could now give her attention to the new man in her life. Her affair with Charles was proceeding at a breathless pace; he had even spoken of marriage. Furthermore, in his growing affection he had confessed to a four-year affair with a certain lady in Maidenhead. This confession came as welcome news to Florence for it gave her in turn the opportunity to confess her attachment to Dr Gully – although she was careful to give the impression that the liaison, though imprudent, had been an innocent one, describing her ex-lover as 'an old family friend'.

Charles, on learning that the doctor was in his sixties, seemed more amused than concerned – and Florence was not prepared to risk telling him the true nature of the attachment, for, lacking his mother's approval, he had yet to make a formal proposal of marriage and Florence wanted nothing to jeopardize her chance of making a happy and respectable match.

On 21 October she sent Charles a letter of encouragement, writing from her rooms in Brighton:

My dear Charlie,

    After serious and deep consideration I have come to the conclusion that if you still hope to gain my love, we must see more of each other, and be quite sure that the solemn act of marriage will be for the happiness of both. This is what I think you ought to tell your mother. I would never enter any family where I was not welcome. I have no fear of not gaining her affection, but of course, she must know me and judge for herself. All I can say is that you have behaved in the noblest manner and that I have no doubt of being happy with you, but of course, before giving up my present freedom I must be quite convinced it would be for our mutual happiness.

Need I tell you that I have written to the doctor to say that I must never see his face again. It is the right thing to do in every respect, whatever happens, whether we marry or not. I shall ever have a regard for you and take an interest in your welfare for I think you are a very good man.

Write and tell me what you think of this letter, and with every kind wish,

> Ever your sincere friend,
> Florence Ricardo.

In the meantime, after Dr Gully's initial shock on receiving Florence's letter he telegraphed to say that he wished to see her and would travel to Brighton on the following Monday.

The news agitated Florence to such a degree that Mrs Cox, who was going to London on that day, offered to meet his train at Croydon and try to placate him before he arrived in Brighton. Florence agreed to the suggestion, and, when the Brighton train drew into Croydon station, Dr Gully found Mrs Cox waiting for him.

Meanwhile, in her Brighton rooms, Florence was becoming more and more nervous at the prospect of meeting the doctor, and she eventually sent for Dr Dill, her Brighton physician. Told of the awkward situation she was in, he wisely suggested that she meet Gully on neutral ground. Florence took this as sound advice and when the train from London arrived at Brighton, Florence – much to the surprise of Dr Gully and Mrs Cox – was waiting on the platform.

With Mrs Cox deposited in the ladies' waiting room, Florence, stricken with nerves and ill prepared for the interview, led the doctor to the Prince Regent Hotel. There she managed to convey to him the interest that Charles had shown in her, even admitting the possibility that he might propose. She then made it clear that, whether she married or not, the connection between herself and the doctor must end because she could no longer bear being estranged from her mother.

Despite the embittered atmosphere that ensued as a result of the revelations, Florence agreed to lunch with Gully at her lodgings, and they set off, on the way picking up Mrs Cox from the station. By a trick of chance as they made their way to Kings Road their carriage passed Charles Bravo. On seeing Florence the young barrister cheerfully raised his hat, whereupon Dr Gully asked Florence the identity of the gentleman and learned that it was none other than his rival.

The sight of Charles Bravo could only have added to Dr Gully's unhappiness and when luncheon was over and Mrs Cox had withdrawn a 'very painful interview' took place between the doctor and Florence, during which both became upset. Try as he might, however, Gully was unable to sway Florence from her intention to accept the advances of the young man and, faced with her decision, could only warn her 'not to be in a hurry, but to be acquainted with him, and especially with his family, for three or four months' before she committed herself. He then asked her whether she intended to tell Charles the truth about their attachment, to which she replied that she intended to tell him everything.

This reply probably pleased James Gully very much; surely, he must have thought, the young man's ardour would cool very quickly when he knew of the scandalous affair. For while there was no denying that a lovely woman with an indelicate past was quite acceptable in a mistress, it was quite a different matter when that woman was one's wife.

So confident was Gully that Charles would reject Florence once he was in possession of her secret, he called at her lodgings the following morning in a much calmer state of mind. His calm was not to last very long, however, for Florence proceeded to ask him to give up the lease on Orwell Lodge, 'in order to save her embarrassment', even offering to pay for the remainder of its duration. Indignantly Gully refused to entertain such a request and, leaving Florence's presence, caught a train back to Balham.

*

Despite Dr Gully's opposition and the barely concealed antagonism of Charles's mother, the couple became engaged in October 1875, just before Florence left Brighton. She had already informed her family of her decision to end her affair with Dr Gully and had received a letter of reconciliation from her father. On her return to The Priory she wrote to her father again – on 30 October – without mentioning her engagement to Charles:

> My dearest Father,
>
> Your kind and affectionate letter gave me great pleasure last night and I look forward with sincere and heartfelt joy to meeting you all again. My past has been a very sad one, but it will be ever blotted out and forgotten, and believe me when I say how much I regret ever having caused you pain with regard to the last sad years of separation.
>
> > With much love to yourself and all at Buscot,
> > > Ever your affectionate child,
> > > > Florence Ricardo.

Soon afterwards Florence informed her family of her engagement, a step which they heartily approved.

Dr Gully, however, was very disheartened when he received a note from Mrs Cox on 10 November telling him of the engagement of her mistress. Perhaps he had never believed it would happen. Impulsively he wrote Florence 'a very angry letter', the contents of which were so hurtful that she quickly burned it. Shortly afterwards Gully wrote to her again, this time apologizing for his previous words.

His remorse, however, was not entirely genuine. Florence had hurt him deeply and, unable to conceal his burning anger, he told his butler that Mrs Ricardo had treated him 'very badly', and that if she or Mrs Cox ever came to his house again they were 'not to be admitted'.

4

Mr and Mrs Charles Bravo

Dr James Gully was not the only one to view the engagement of Charles and Florence with displeasure. Charles's mother also had decidedly negative feelings on the subject. Extremely over-protective and jealous of her son, Mrs Bravo would probably have viewed any prospective daughter-in-law with a jaundiced eye, but the young, painted widow Mrs Ricardo she regarded with great distaste and, regardless of Florence's wealth, reacted to the news of Charles's engagement with horror.

Florence had problems apart from the evident dislike of her future mother-in-law, however. Through shame, and fear of losing Charles's interest, she was still reluctant to admit to him the truth about her attachment to Dr Gully. However, once back from Brighton and with Charles becoming a frequent visitor to The Priory she could conceal the truth from him no longer and told him that she and James Gully had been lovers – but on one occasion only, during the trip to Kissingen in 1873. Immediately after telling him – probably being overcome with embarrassment and fearing to see anger or disgust in his face – she left the morning room to allow him some minutes alone to review his proposal of marriage. After some twenty minutes she returned to discover his reaction to her confession. She had not lost him.

'I am quite satisfied to make you my wife,' he told her, 'but of course you must never see Dr Gully again.'

Greatly relieved, Florence at once agreed to abide by his terms and swore before God that her past indiscretion would remain a secret between them. Charles on his part promised to give up his mistress in Maidenhead. Said Florence later, 'We made a solemn compact that he would never mention Dr Gully's name nor I this woman's.'

Plans for the wedding were going ahead – even though Charles's mother made no secret of her feelings about the match. Florence's mother, on the other hand, was delighted at the engagement, and, much improved in health and overjoyed at the reconciliation with her daughter, wasted no time in making her first visit to The Priory. There she listened with relief as Florence told her that she had made a complete break with Dr Gully, and that they had returned one another's presents and burned all the letters that had passed between them.

On 10 November Florence introduced Charles to her parents and family at the home of her aunt, Mrs Thomas Campbell, in Kingston, Surrey. Following the meeting Florence's mother and aunt, supported by Mrs Cox, voiced their opinion that Charles should tell his mother of Florence's affair with Dr Gully. Charles, informed of their views, firmly rejected the advice. Mrs Cox, always willing to help in a crisis, volunteered to bear the news to Mrs Bravo in person. Charles declined her offer, however, and diplomatically she retreated. Consequently on a visit to the Bravos at Palace Green she assured Mrs Bravo that her mistress would make an excellent wife for her son.

While Mrs Bravo remained unconvinced, Mr Joseph Bravo saw his stepson's choice in a far more favourable and realistic light; after all, Mrs Ricardo was a beautiful and wealthy woman, and he considered that Charles had done well for himself. Where Charles himself was concerned there was no doubt at all, and he made clear his determination to marry Florence before the Christmas of that year, 1875.

With Charles earning about £200 a year at that time, his stepfather agreed to give him a first life interest on £20,000 as a wedding gift, the yearly income from which would amount to about £800. Taking into account a further £200 coming from investments, Charles would then bring to the marriage about £1200 a year. This was an excellent income by the standards of the day, but it was a small sum compared to the fortune in the purse of his future wife from which the interest alone brought her a yearly income of £3000.

It was later to be revealed that of the quarrels that arose between Florence and Charles the cause of many of them was money, one of the very first being over Florence's marriage settlement.

Up to 1870 the law entitled a husband on marriage to all of his wife's assets. The Married Woman's Property Act of 1870, however, changed all this, allowing the wife, by means of a legal settlement, to keep certain moneys or properties in her own name. Florence, in considering the terms of her marriage settlement, decided to retain in her name not only all her money, but also the lease of The Priory and all the contents of the house and stables. Very angry over the settlement concerning the latter items, Charles strongly objected, saying to her:

'I cannot contemplate a marriage which doesn't make me master in my own house. I cannot place myself in the position of having to sit at a table or upon a chair which doesn't belong to me. Unless things are so settled I cannot marry you.'

Henry Brooks, Florence's solicitor, also encountered Charles's anger over Florence's decision. When Charles called at Brooks's office that November to discuss the marriage settlement he dismissed the solicitor's congratulatory remarks with a curt: 'Damn your congratulations! I've come about the money.'

Yseult Bridges in *How Charles Bravo Died* uses this incident to illustrate her theory that Charles was subject to 'money mania' and heartless in his attitude towards Florence. She misses the psychology of it; apart from the anger and stung pride behind Charles's words they were obviously also coloured by his opinion of solicitors and lawyers – 'packs of ravenous sharks feasting on my goods'. And the year, it must be remembered, was 1875. One must not view such an incident in the climate of a society over a hundred years later. Frederick Veale, in his short volume *The Verdict in Doubt: The Bravo Case*, has a further explanation for Charles's dismissal of the solicitor's congratulations by pointing out that in Victorian England's caste system of class distinctions there was an enormous gulf between a solicitor and a barrister. Veale illustrates his point by citing Charles Dickens's *David Copperfield* in which the gulf is referred to by Mr Spenlow, who states that the profession of a barrister 'was the genteelest profession in the world and must on no account be confounded with the profession of a solicitor ...

[Solicitors were] an inferior race of men, universally looked down upon by all proctors of any pretensions'. It would appear, therefore, that Mr Brooks overstepped himself and was presumptuous in offering his congratulations. That Brooks himself was aware of his *faux pas* and recognized the justice of Charles's rebuke was made very clear, for he was later to state: 'It is not usual for persons in our branch of the profession to give congratulations.'

Even though Florence's father supported Charles in his view, Florence could not be swayed. Then, on 27 November, only ten days before the projected wedding, still undecided as to whether she should follow through her determination, she took the extraordinary step of seeking the advice of her former friend, lover and mentor, James Gully.

Florence sent Fanny Griffiths to ask the doctor to meet her in the parlour of the Lower Lodge and, somewhat surprisingly perhaps, the doctor obeyed her summons.

The meeting lasted only a few minutes, but in the course of it Gully told Florence not to quibble with Charles over such trivial matters, adding that it was a small price to pay for happiness. Then, before the pair took their leave of one another Florence told him that Charles knew about their former attachment, to which the doctor replied that he hoped they would 'both be very happy', and that things would 'turn out well for them'. He then kissed her hand in farewell and she left him to walk back through the gardens to the house.

They were never to meet again.

Florence, having taken Dr Gully's advice, acceded to Charles's wishes and the lease of The Priory and the contents of the house and stables were made over to him. They were married the following day, 7 December 1875, at All Saints Church, Ennismore Gardens, Kensington. They had originally planned to marry on the 14th, but as Charles's mother had stated that she could not attend on that day they had brought the wedding day forward. And still Mrs Joseph Bravo did not attend the ceremony. However, as her sister had died only two weeks previously, she had an excuse for being absent.

Charles and Florence had spent the week before the wedding at Palace Green, where it had become obvious that Mrs Joseph Bravo was unwilling to accept Florence as a suitable wife for her son; as a result their relationship remained one of strain and reserve.

Another who took a sour view of the marriage was Florence's coachman, George Griffiths. At Charles Bravo's instigation Florence had given Griffiths notice to quit her employ – he subsequently left on 3 January. According to Charles he was a careless driver and incapable of conveying Florence with safety through the London streets. Griffiths had once before been dismissed from Florence's service – at that time due to her lack of space for himself and his new wife, Fanny, at Stokefield, the house in Leigham Court Road. Now, a year and a half later he was not only losing his job again but he and his family would have to leave their pleasant home in the Lower Lodge. Understandably he was bitter, and he made no attempt to conceal his dislike of his mistress and her intended husband.

On the morning of the wedding Griffiths was drinking in the bar of the Bedford Hotel, at the foot of Bedford Hill. Seeing him looking very morose, the barman asked him why he wasn't celebrating with the rest of the household. In reply Griffiths said he had to go on an errand to Wandsworth. Then, moving to the door he added:

'Mrs Ricardo will be sure to have had a lot of brandy this morning before the wedding,' and then: 'Poor fellow – I wouldn't like to be in his shoes . . . He won't live more than four months.' With that the disgruntled coachman left the bar.

After the wedding Charles and Florence went to Brighton, during which time Charles took the opportunity to speak to Dr Dill, Florence's doctor, on the fact that she was drinking more sherry than was good for her. The doctor, already aware of the problem, agreed to speak to her about it. The Brighton trip was followed by a visit to Florence's parents at Buscot – an interlude which proved a very happy one. Unlike Florence and Mrs Bravo, Charles and Mrs Campbell had taken to one another and achieved a rapport – with the result that Charles, taking his mother-in-law into his confidence, also spoke to her of his concern over Florence's drinking. Mrs Campbell responded by saying that it was a habit that must be broken as soon as possible, and recommended kindness tempered with firmness as the best remedy.

During the same visit Florence spoke to her mother about

Charles, complaining that he sometimes upbraided her about Dr Gully, behaved like a spoilt child, and had evinced a grudging attitude to her personal expenditure. He had, she said, suggested that the cost of maintaining the gardens was too high and he was forcing her to reduce the number of gardeners to two. The influence behind his criticism and actions, she felt, was his mother, who was disposed 'to interfere with household arrangements'.

In spite of any disputes caused by money and outside interference, however, the young couple showed a warm affection for one another, and the interlude at Buscot was so enjoyable that it was with reluctance that they took their leave on 6 January and returned to Balham. Mrs Cox was not at the house on their return; she was spending Christmas in Brighton with her sons and was not due back until the end of January. Florence and Charles, however, managed without her, and the following letter from Charles to his mother-in-law, written on 9 January 1876, reflects the light-hearted atmosphere that prevailed:

Dear Mrs Campbell,

Had I not the excuse that I wished you to know how Florence is getting on, I should loathe to trouble you with a letter merely for the purpose of thanking you for your kindness to me when I was at Buscot ... I would just venture to tell you that I shall forever count myself a debtor to you and your family for your great kindness to me.

Florence sends her love to you all,
as does,
Yours affectionately,
Charles Bravo.

PS. Florence, who is looking over my shoulder says that she sends not her love, but her very best love. I, therefore, unwilling to be behind her in anything, send my very, very best love.
[Postscript by Florence] I do hope Augusta [wife of her brother, William] is better. Charles, as usual, writes tersely as all barristers do, but you must imagine twice the amount of affection as I had to do when he wrote me love letters ...

Compared to the carefree days at Buscot, the visit to Palace Green which took place soon afterwards was fraught with disharmony. It was later implied that at this time some anonymous letters had been received by Mrs Joseph Bravo, letters relating to her daughter-in-law's past. These letters will be referred to later, but for now it is sufficient to say that if she had indeed received such letters it might well account for the fact that as the young couple were leaving Palace Green she told Florence that she had ruined Charles's life.

An anonymous letter received by Charles at about the same time referred to the fact that Florence had been Dr Gully's mistress and insinuated that Charles had married her for her money. Naturally Charles was furious. He showed it first to his wife, and then later to Mrs Cox whom he asked whether it was Dr Gully's handwriting. Apparently Mrs Cox replied that she thought not as the writing was little more than an illiterate scrawl.

Florence, understandably, was surprised at his action, saying later, 'It was only then that I learned that my husband had spoken previously to Mrs Cox on the subject of my intimacy with Dr Gully.'

According to Mrs Cox, Charles had indeed discussed the matter with her, volunteering his feeling that 'a woman who has once gone wrong is likely to be all the more particular afterwards'. With which sentiment, apparently, Mrs Cox had agreed.

However, the storm created by the anonymous letter passed and Charles found himself once again concerned with other matters – in particular Florence's extravagant life-style.

In 1876 most men had little faith in a woman's ability to understand the subtleties of finance, and Charles was no exception. It is true that Florence had known independence, and experience of running her own financial affairs, but now she was a married woman, and for a Victorian husband such as Charles it was no less than his duty to curb what he saw as his wife's extravagance.

In spite of Charles's preoccupation with Florence's expenditure, however, there was a positive reason for happiness in that Florence discovered that she was pregnant. Writing to her mother-in-law on 20 January Florence touched on the subject and on other matters:

My dear Mother,
    I am obliged to be quiet this week or would have driven up

to see you. But I sincerely hope you are feeling better. Charlie
is better, but looks white. Charlie and I are as happy as we
possibly can be, and have never had an unkind word yet. I do
try, dear mother, to make his life bright, and it did hurt my
feelings very much when you told me on leaving Palace Green
that I had ruined him. But all is forgotten, and I do hope you
will love me some day, as I would do anything for you and
father Joseph.

With best love,
Ever your affectionate child,
Florence Bravo.

Meanwhile regular letters passed between Charles and Florence's
family at Buscot. These were penned in affectionate terms, for the
Campbells had accepted their son-in-law without reserve. Charles
wrote on 23 January:

My dear Mrs Campbell,

...Florence is going on finely and I bless the day I married
her. With her usual good nature she not only had my deaf sister
here today, but also a deaf friend of my sister. We look forward
to a visit from you and Mr Campbell. When you do come, we
will show you that the lesson in hospitality which we had at
Buscot was not lost. Trade has been dull with me and I see no
signs of revival. This, with a pack of ravenous lawyers feasting
on my goods, is distressing to me. However, I suppose it will
not make much difference to me at the Great Judgement. It will
to the lawyers, though, which is a great consolation to

Yours affectionately,
Charles Bravo.

PS. Florence must think you are a born idiot; she imagines that
unless I tell you so, you will not know that she holds you in her
most affectionate love.
[*Postscript by Florence*] Is not Charles a goose? So dreadfully
terse and laconic? I told him to send my very best love to
you...

At the end of January Florence suffered a miscarriage. Mr Harrison, a Streatham surgeon, was called in, and heeding his advice Florence went for a short convalescence to St Leonards-on-Sea, Sussex, where her sister-in-law Augusta was recuperating for similar reasons. Although professional demands prevented Charles from joining her there his regret is evident in a letter he sent to her on 15 February from Palace Green, where he was staying during her absence. He wrote:

> ... I miss you my darling wife dreadfully. When you come back I will so take care of you that you will never leave me again. May you have bright weather and come back well. Looking back at the ten weeks of our marriage, I feel that many of my words, although kindly meant, were unnecessarily harsh. In future, my rebukes, if it is necessary to say anything, which God forbid, shall be given with the utmost gentleness. I hold you to be the best of wives. We have had bitter troubles but I trust that in times to come the sweet peace of our lives will not be disturbed by memories like these ... I wish I could sleep my life away until your return. Come back as well as you can.
>
> Your devoted husband,
> Charles.

By the beginning of March they were quarrelling once more, the causes being Florence's extravagance and Mrs Bravo's continuing interference in their affairs; at one point Florence was so angry that she threatened to go to Palace Green and 'have it out' with her. When Charles persuaded her against such a course she went alone to Buscot, to sulk. In her absence Charles visited his parents at Palace Green, where he tried to heal the rift between his mother and his wife. On 8 March he wrote to Florence:

My dear old Florence,

> My poor mother is glad to have me back with her. I am sure if you heard the kind way she speaks of you, you would not mind my being with her. Without you I feel as if I was at Brighton, in lodgings by myself. I cannot be happy in the absence of my best of wives. My only object is to make you happy.

There can be no doubt that Florence missed Charles too, and with her parents on holiday in Rome she wrote and asked him to join her at Buscot. Unfortunately he was called to Brighton on a case. He continued, though, to write her affectionate letters. In one he wrote:

> I miss you dreadfully and would willingly give £100, if times were not so hard, to have you here now...

These lines have been quoted by Yseult Bridges to indicate, again, a callously mean streak in Charles's nature, but it must be remembered that Florence was quite familiar with his wry and cynical humour; she even refers to it with amusement in letters to her family. To those determined to view Charles as avaricious, however, the fact that his words were obviously written in jest seems to have passed unnoticed.

On Florence's return to The Priory soon afterwards she found Charles absent. Then there came a letter (dated 15 March) from him to the effect that, his work having detained him in Brighton, he had decided to stay on in the town for a little while with his parents who had arrived there before going on to St Leonards-on-Sea for their holiday. His letter went on:

> ...as you make sunshine wherever you go, your presence here is much needed for we have rain and sleet. Father Joseph has promised us the barouche on condition we put down the cobs. By giving up the cobs and Mrs Cox we could save £400 a year, and be as comfortable.

His words rekindled her annoyance; she was fond of her ponies and was attached to Mrs Cox, and she was hurt and angry that Charles should wish to deprive her of what she regarded as essentials; she was also angered by the fact that he had discussed the matter with his parents.

One of the subjects of the contention between Charles and Florence, namely Mrs Cox, had her own preoccupations that spring. The good news received two years earlier from her aunt, Mrs Margaret Cox, had turned out to be a mixed blessing, for early in that March of 1876 Jane Cox had heard from her again, and this time the letter was asking her to return to Jamaica as soon as possible. Mrs Margaret Cox was far from well, it appeared, and wished to see her niece with some urgency in connection with the property she planned to leave. It appears that she was afraid of the possibility that upon her death some of her property, including one of her houses, might be appropriated by persons not entitled to it. Consequently she wanted Jane Cox to visit her in order to get the matter settled and acquaint her thoroughly with what she and her son would inherit.

Mrs Cox, however, did not want to leave England at that time and as a result – unknown to Florence who was at Buscot – she went to see Mr Joseph Bravo at his City office prior to his departure with his wife and family for the holiday at Brighton and St Leonards-on-Sea. There she told Mr Bravo of her aunt's letter and asked his advice as to what she should do. He advised her strongly to go to Jamaica, telling her that she had no future where she was. Mrs Cox, however, said she could not leave the country at present; it was not convenient for her to go, and she did not know what to do with her sons. At this Mr Bravo pointed out that it was her duty to go – not only to her aunt but to herself and her children. He could not persuade her, however, and when she left she appeared to be totally set against the idea.

Later she went to visit an old friend in Norwood, a Mrs Ellen Harford, wife of a Lloyds underwriter. She had known the Harfords since 1857 when as Miss Jane Edouard she had been governess to the daughter of the Rev. John Papillon at Lexden Rectory in Colchester and at the same time had taught the two young daughters of the Harfords.

Now, at the Harfords' home at 4 Norwood Hill, Mrs Cox told her friend of her aunt's letter, adding that she did not know 'what to do for the best'. Mrs Harford was of the same mind as Joseph Bravo and, as she later told the inquiry, she advised Mrs Cox that it was her 'duty to go to Jamaica at the earliest possible moment', and that she would 'see that her boys were cared for while she was away'. Mrs Cox eventually agreed that she had no alternative and on a second visit she got Mrs Harford to draft for her a letter in which she told her aunt that if she could be provided with funds she would travel by the next available boat.

*

A short while after her visit to Mrs Harford, Mrs Cox saw Dr Gully at Balham railway station. This was their second chance meeting that year. On a previous day they had come across one another outside the Army and Navy Stores in Victoria, and Dr Gully had made use of the meeting to ask Mrs Cox to look for a book of press-cuttings which had not been returned to him with his other mementoes and which he wished to preserve for his grandchildren. Mrs Cox, ever obliging, had promised to send it to him as soon as possible.

On this second occasion Mrs Cox made some remark about the anonymous letter that Charles had received, responsibility for which Dr Gully strongly denied. She also mentioned her proposed visit to the West Indies and asked him for a prescription for Jamaica fever which he promised to send to her through the post.

The prescription duly arrived on 25 March. On that morning the companion was walking to Balham station when she was overtaken by Charles. He seemed very agitated about a letter that had arrived for her in the morning post. Having seen an example of Gully's handwriting, he was sure that the handwriting on the envelope was that of the doctor. Now, handing Mrs Cox the letter, Charles insisted that she open it in front of him.

Reluctantly Mrs Cox opened the letter and showed Charles three sheets of paper on which Dr Gully had written the treatment for Jamaica fever. Only then did Charles allow her to go on her way.

5

Prelude to Death

Soon after her miscarriage Florence had conceived again, but on 6 April she miscarried once more. Very concerned, Charles consulted his cousin and close friend, Royes Bell, a Harley Street surgeon, who prescribed a convalescence by the sea as soon as Florence was strong enough to travel.

On the day following Florence's miscarriage, Mrs Cox chanced to come upon Dr Gully yet again at Balham station where he was studying the train timetable. During their conversation she told him of Florence's condition, adding that Florence was suffering from sleeplessness and pain in her back. In response Dr Gully advised the use of sitz-baths and spinal washes for Florence's back pain, and said that he would send something to help her sleep. Rather than deliver it to The Priory, however, he added, he would leave it at Mrs Cox's house in Lancaster Road. On returning to The Priory, Mrs Cox told her mistress of her meeting with Dr Gully and of his advice.

When Mrs Cox went to her house the following Monday she found that Dr Gully had left there a small bottle of cherry laurel water.* By that time, however, Florence had no need of it. Over the weekend she had been using the spinal washes and sitz-baths and although her back still pained her she was able to sleep naturally once more. Mrs Cox therefore put the bottle in her medicine chest at The Priory in case it was needed at some later date.

Four days following her miscarriage, and while still confined to bed, Florence had dictated a letter to her mother which Charles, in

* A preparation taken from the cherry laurel plant; containing a small quantity of hydrocyanic acid, it is used for making up soothing solutions.

the absence of Mrs Cox, wrote for her. Having returned from his chambers earlier than usual he had spent the afternoon fussing over his wife. He was in a good humour as he wrote Florence's letter and found himself unable to resist adding comments of his own. The letter, written on 10 April (Charles's comments in italics), reads:

My dearest Mama,

Will you tell Augusta with my love that it was like her to write me such a kind letter, and that we are intending to take a small furnished house at Worthing; and take the servants and the carriages – it would be a wise plan if she came to us as she is going to the seaside . . . (Mrs Cox will cater so we'll have nothing to do but kick up our heels and get well). We think of starting tomorrow week. I am sorry Papa has been so ill. Charlie is well and equally happy. *He is not. The quality of the tobacco he is smoking has been impugned and his pipe ordered to be extinguished.* He has been so good and kind to me while I have been ill. Mrs Cox is pretty well and has been all kindness to me. I do not know what I should do without her. My back is very painful. I will not answer for any of Charlie's additions to this . . . he is a buffoon.

With our best love and plenty of kisses
Your loving child,
Florence Bravo.

It was in the same casual mood that Charles wrote to his own mother on the same day:

. . . Florence thanks you for your letter and sends her best love, and will answer it as soon as she can sit up. She lost Charles II on Thursday, a youth of great promise. Royes declares that he had the Hougham* cast of countenance. . . . Trade is very dull and I came home early to sit with my better half during Mrs Cox's absence in town to get some things. I am remarkably well, so well that I shocked Royes with the quantity I ate yesterday. I am sorry to think that Florence will have to go to

* Hougham was Mrs Joseph Bravo's maiden name.

Worthing when she is better. I am going to take a tiny house for her, and she will take her retainers to wait on her, and Augusta, who is ill and obliged to go back to the sea . . .

By the middle of April Florence had regained some of her strength and good spirits. Charles was at home for much of the time and in fine form. He took leisurely strolls about the grounds and wandered through the house reciting Shakespeare. His wry humour is illustrated by a letter he wrote to his mother on Good Friday, 14 April:

My dear old Grannie,

    My fowls lay as if they were Turks and their eggs the money due on coupons, and my spirits are nothing like they would be if the sun was visible. Florence is better, but very cross. I went to the library and brought her six volumes of books; three she had read, and three contain the uninspired preachings of an idiot. She has finished a pair of slippers for me in a rage, and is slanging me for not being able to tell a good book, as you tell good music, by the look . . .

    I rode the cobs the day before yesterday, and feel very much as if the muscles in my legs are ossifying. I have difficulty in dragging on my shooting-boots, which I am obliged *'par ordre supérieur'* to wear in addition to a red flannel garment which is a cross between a kilt and a sporran and a pair of bathing drawers, and has as many strings as a harp . . .

I am always, dear Grannie,
Your loving son,
Charles.

Mercifully unaware of the fate that was so soon to befall him, Charles wrote again to his mother two days later, his letter giving a glimpse of the happy atmosphere that prevailed between him and Florence over that Easter weekend:

My dear old Grannie,

    I passed the whole of yesterday most pleasantly. I rode Cremorne from nine-thirty to eleven and on Victor afterwards

by the side of Florence while she took an airing in the family
coach. We went to see if we could persuade the St Anne's
people to let Mrs Cox's babes pass the Holy Season with us.
We could not, but they are to come to us on Monday.

After lunch I put up the lawn-tennis net with the assistance
of Rowe, and under the superintendence of Florence, and after
that great work was completed I naturally had a game with
Rowe; and later on a vigorous one with Osman [gardener].
Mrs Campbell came over from Kingston and Mrs Fowkes
[former pupil of Mrs Cox, and daughter of Mrs Harford] with
her little girl (with whom I had another game) from Norwood.

Altogether I loafed vigorously and enjoyed myself. The east
wind made the day rather less enjoyable than yesterday and
lawn-tennis was avoided, partly from fear lest it might shock
the good people of Balham and Tooting, and partly because
Rowe was a-church and in his Sunday clothes – and Osman
was gone to tour the neighbouring gardens . . .

On that same tranquil Sunday Florence wrote to her mother:

. . . We hope Papa is gaining strength and will soon be quite
well. Auntie came over yesterday and is looking blooming.
Uncle and Peggy are coming tomorrow and Charlie is looking
forward to a game of lawn tennis. I never saw him looking so
well. The country is life to him and he walks about with a book
under his arm, as happy as a king. We leave on Thursday for
Worthing and hope to return to welcome you and Papa here. I
am getting stronger but it is a long business. It seems ages
before one feels really well, but by dint of sitz baths and spinal
washes I have wooed sleep back, one of the most important
steps to recovery. The flowers here are in such great profusion
and are so lovely . . .

Easter Monday proved to be a very enjoyable day at The Priory.
At some time during the day a carriage was sent to Streatham Hill to
bring Mrs Cox's two younger sons from their school to spend the
day, and Charles played tennis with them. He and Florence also
enjoyed the visit of James Orr (Florence's uncle) and his daughter,
and Charles arranged to lunch with him in London the next day.

After all the visitors had departed Florence retired to her room to rest, leaving Charles and Mrs Cox to dine alone, as they had done for the past eleven days of Florence's illness. When the meal was finished Charles went upstairs to wish Florence good night. Following doctor's orders he was sleeping in the spare room during Florence's recovery, and the fact that Mrs Cox was taking his place in Florence's bed during his absence indicates that Florence was intent on avoiding sexual relations for the time being.

The maid, Mary Ann Keeber, was busy in Florence's bedroom when Charles came in, and she later recalled that he sat on the chair beside his wife's bed complaining that he felt unwell. Turning to the housemaid he said, 'Mary Ann, I feel very cross!'

'Do you, sir?' the maid replied. 'What's the matter?'

'I have the toothache like you get sometimes.'

Later, when Charles left Florence's side to sleep in the spare room next door he was armed with her little bottles of chloroform and laudanum and some hot brandy provided by the maid.

At The Priory on the morning of Tuesday 18 April there were no outward signs of the impending tragedy. The staff at that time consisted of Mrs Hunt, the cook; Rowe, the butler; Smith, the footman; Parton, the coachman; Younger, the groom; the gardeners; two housemaids, Mary Ann Keeber and Elizabeth Evans; and Mrs Cox, the companion.

Early that Tuesday morning Mrs Cox left The Priory to travel to the small coastal town of Worthing to rent a house suitable for Florence's convalescence. Tucked into her handbag was a little comfort in the shape of a flask of sherry (provided by Rowe at her request) as the weather was cold and uncertain.

While Mrs Cox was off on her errand, Charles and Florence prepared to drive into London. Charles had his luncheon appointment at St James's Hall, Piccadilly, with Florence's uncle, and Florence, feeling a little stronger and wanting to do some shopping, had decided to drive into town with him. However, she suffered a fainting spell before she reached the front door and Charles urged her to remain at home. She was determined to accompany him, though, and soon after ten-thirty they set off, the carriage driven by Parton, and with Smith the footman in attendance.

The weather grew worse as their journey progressed, and as the now closed landau approached Clapham Common the rain and sleet became so bad that Charles ordered Parton to turn back. However, after about half a mile the weather became brighter and it was decided to turn and resume the journey.

In London they settled some bills at a bank in Stratford Street, visited Benson's, the jewellers in Bond Street, and from there went to Jermyn Street where Charles, having decided to take a Turkish bath before his luncheon appointment, parted from Florence, leaving Parton to drive her on to the Haymarket stores.

Florence did not spend long over her shopping, only buying two items, some tobacco and a bottle of hair-wash for Charles. Her purchases made, she told Parton to drive her back to Balham.

Charles, after his Turkish bath, enjoyed a pleasant luncheon with James Orr, in the course of which he consumed a large steak and half a bottle of burgundy. Afterwards the two men walked together down Piccadilly, where they chanced to meet one of Charles's colleagues, Frederick MacCalmont. The three of them then strolled the length of St James's Street, at the end of which James Orr took his leave of the company.

The two young barristers, both in fine spirits, made their way to Victoria Station. On the way Charles invited his friend to dine at The Priory, but MacCalmont was unable to accept. He did, however, agree to call the following day for a game of lawn tennis – weather permitting. With this pleasant prospect before them the two friends parted and Charles caught the 4.05 train to Balham.

Florence had got back to The Priory about one o'clock and following a light lunch prepared by Rowe had drunk a little champagne. When Charles reached home soon after four-thirty he found her resting on the sofa in the morning room. After launching into an account of his 'jolly' lunch with James Orr, he asked Florence about her shopping trip and was told to go into his room where he would find the presents she had brought him.

Charles was pleased with the gifts and after thanking Florence he got dressed for riding, saying that he intended to exercise the cobs. At the stables, however, after ordering the ponies to be saddled, he was advised by the groom, George Younger, not to ride them as, having been in the carriage harness a good deal the previous day, they were 'very skittish'. Charles, however, did not heed the advice and when Cremorne, the livelier of the cobs, was saddled he rode it through the stable yard, declaring that he would exercise the other one as well before dinner.

An hour and a half later, looking pale and shaken, Charles rode back into the stable yard. When the groom asked him what had happened he replied crossly:

'The animal bolted with me; took me nearly five miles, right over to Mitcham Common. He galloped so hard my hat blew off.' He added tersely that he had had to pay a lad a shilling to retrieve it from the grass.

Charles was still very shaken when he entered the morning room where Florence was still resting. She was alarmed to see how ill he looked, and called Rowe to arrange a warm bath for him. As Rowe helped Charles up the stairs to his room he said, 'I hope Cremorne didn't throw you, sir.' 'Oh, no,' Charles replied with a wry laugh, 'he didn't throw me.'

After Charles had taken his bath he told the maid, Mary Ann Keeber, to leave the water in the tub as he would use it again the next morning. (This action has been cited by Yseult Bridges as an example of Charles's 'uncouth habits'. In fact, there were problems with the water pipes at The Priory and Charles was trying to save the servants work.) Afterwards he was persuaded by Florence to allow her to dine downstairs that evening. He agreed, on condition that she retire again as soon as she had eaten. She promised she would.

On completing her errand in Worthing, Mrs Cox stopped in Brighton, where she met her eldest son. Afterwards she set off back to Balham, arriving at The Priory shortly before seven-thirty where she found Florence almost dressed for dinner. Deciding against changing, Mrs Cox washed her hands in her room and then joined Charles and Florence in the dining room where, as usual, Rowe and Smith were waiting at table.

Dinner consisted of whiting, roast lamb, eggs and anchovies. Charles, much out of humour, refused the first course and seemed in no mood for chatter. While the fish was being served to the ladies a letter arrived for Charles by the evening post. From his stepfather, it enclosed a letter from Charles's stockbroker which had been sent in error to Palace Green. The letter from the stockbroker announced that Charles had lost £20 in speculation on some shares.

Joseph Bravo, having read the letter, had forwarded it to his stepson with a note of his own voicing his disapproval of dealing in stocks and shares.

Charles, angry at the interference and at the loss of such a sum, was made even angrier by his stepfather's 'shirty letter'. Mrs Cox and Florence, who had been discussing the house at Worthing, tried to arouse his interest in it, but he impatiently dismissed the subject. A further cause for his anger was the apparent loss of a cheque which Mrs Cox had been given to post to a tradesman.

As the meal progressed the two women drank freely, between them consuming two bottles of sherry which, according to Rowe, was the usual amount he decanted at dinner. Charles drank more moderately, taking his usual three or four glasses of burgundy. Shortly after eight-thirty, with dinner finished, Charles, Florence and Mrs Cox went into the morning room. However, with Charles still out of humour the atmosphere was uncomfortable.

Just before nine o'clock Charles suggested to Florence that she retire as she had promised, and obediently she rose to leave the room, whereupon Mrs Cox offered to help her undress, as the maid was still having her supper in the kitchen. As the women reached the staircase Florence asked Mrs Cox to bring her a little Marsala and water from the dining room. Having poured the wine, the companion took it to Florence's dressing room where she found her mistress in her nightclothes.

Just before nine-thirty the maid, not waiting to be sent for, carried two cans of hot water upstairs, one for Florence, the other for Mrs Cox. Florence answered her knock on the dressing-room door and, giving the girl a small tumbler, asked her to go down to the dining room and fetch some more wine. Leaving Mrs Cox's can of hot water on the landing, Mary Ann went back downstairs to fetch the Marsala. As she carried the filled tumbler from the dining room Charles came from the morning room. She stood aside to let him precede her. He did so without speaking and as he climbed the stairs ahead of her he turned around twice to look at her – still saying nothing.

On the first landing, Charles entered Florence's dressing room while the maid went into the bedroom. There she set down the tumbler of wine and prepared her mistress's bed.

In the dressing room Charles remonstrated, in French, with

Florence over the amount of wine she was drinking and then left her
and crossed the landing to the spare room. Mary Ann, on hearing
the door of Charles's room close, came out of Florence's bedroom
and met Florence and Mrs Cox as they emerged from the dressing
room. After telling her mistress where she had left the wine she
went into the dressing room to put away Florence's clothes. When
this was done Mary Ann returned to the bedroom where she saw
that Florence was already in bed and, apparently, asleep. Mrs Cox
was still in her outdoor clothes and, 'as had been her habit recently',
was sitting on a small stool between the bed and the door.

The companion asked Mary Ann if she had seen to her mistress's
night-tray and, satisfied that it was all in order, told her to take Mrs
Bravo's two little dogs downstairs for the night. When only one of
the dogs could be found in the bedroom Mrs Cox suggested that the
other might be upstairs in her room. Mary Ann closed the bedroom
door behind her and went out onto the landing, where she crossed
to the foot of the stairs and called to the dog. A moment later, as she
stood there, the door of the spare room was flung open and Charles
appeared in the doorway in his nightshirt.

'Florence! Florence!' he screamed. 'Hot water! Hot water!'

With these words he staggered back into the room.

6

The Death of Charles Bravo

Shocked, Mary Ann turned and rushed back into her mistress's room where she told Mrs Cox that the master had been taken ill. At once Mrs Cox got up and hurried to Charles's room. Inside she found him standing at the open casement. As she moved towards him he was violently sick out of the window, the vomit landing on the leaded roof of the bay window below. Then, very loudly, he shouted again for hot water.

Turning, Mrs Cox ordered Mary Ann to fetch it. When the maid returned soon afterwards Charles was sitting unconscious on the floor near the window, propped up by Mrs Cox who was rubbing his chest. The companion sent the girl away again, this time for mustard. When Mary Ann got back with it she was told to mix some with water in a bowl. That done, she and Mrs Cox managed to put the man's feet into the bowl but suddenly he kicked out and lay rigid. Mrs Cox tried to bring him round, but could not.

Mrs Cox then told the maid to mix some mustard and water in a tumbler, but the girl was unsure how to do it and impatiently Mrs Cox mixed it herself, stirring it with her finger. Raising Charles's head, she tried to pour some of the solution into his mouth. Insensible, however, and with his jaws locked, he was unable to swallow, and most of the mixture spilled down the front of his nightshirt.

Mrs Cox then sent Mary Ann off to make some strong coffee, and when the maid returned with it they managed to get Charles to swallow some. In consequence he was sick into a basin. After being sent to wash the basin and bring it back, Mary Ann was sent hurrying off again, this time up to Mrs Cox's room for camphor from her medicine chest. While the maid was gone Mrs Cox hurried downstairs to the pantry where she shouted to Rowe to rouse the groom and send him to fetch Mr Harrison, the family physician in Streatham. Returning to Charles's side she began to massage his feet.

Mary Ann, unable to find the camphor in Mrs Cox's room, decided that her mistress should be told of the crisis, and going into Florence's room she woke her and told her what had happened. At the news Florence got up and dashed into the spare room. Mary Ann then went off to continue her search for the camphor.

At the sight of her husband's appearance Florence burst into tears. On learning that Mrs Cox had sent for Mr Harrison she became agitated and asked why a local doctor had not been summoned. Then, still in her nightclothes she ran from the room and downstairs, calling for Rowe.

'She was crying as she came,' recalled the butler, 'and she was crying out to me to fetch someone quickly. "I don't care who it is," she said, "get someone from Balham!" She screamed it at me.'

As Rowe ran off to fetch Dr Moore, who lived nearby, Florence, Mrs Cox and Mary Ann Keeber tried to lift Charles from the floor. Try as they might the manipulation of his dead weight was beyond them, and it was not until the other maid, Elizabeth Evans, was summoned that they managed to get him up and into a chair. That done, Florence and Mrs Cox changed his soiled nightshirt.

It was gone ten o'clock when Dr Moore appeared. On his arrival Mrs Cox gave him an account of what had happened, after which he went into the sickroom where he found Charles still unconscious. Fearing heart-failure, he had the patient placed on the bed and then administered an enema of brandy before applying a mustard poultice to his chest.

About half an hour later Mr Harrison arrived from Streatham. Mrs Cox met him in the hall. 'Mr Harrison,' she said at once, 'I am sure he has taken chloroform.'

Mr Harrison quickly joined Dr Moore at Charles's bedside. Charles was still unconscious, though his pulse had begun to improve slightly. Bearing in mind Mrs Cox's words, Harrison proceeded to examine the patient. He could detect no smell of chloroform, however, only mustard, and he informed Mrs Cox that chloroform was not the cause of the man's collapse. Suspecting that a 'large vessel near the heart had given way', he and Moore decided to administer brandy to stimulate the heart. As Charles was unconscious, however, and his jaws were locked, they were forced to inject it with a hypodermic syringe. Extremely puzzled by Charles's symptoms, the men expressed the need for another opinion – although they seemed doubtful of a recovery.

When Florence learned of the possible failure of Charles's heart she told the doctors how his horse had bolted with him. Then, appearing much alarmed at the pessimistic prognosis she suggested that they contact Charles's cousin, the surgeon Royes Bell, who had 'known Charles all his life and was familiar with his constitution'. A letter requesting his presence, and that he bring someone with him, was written by Harrison, and Parton was instructed to drive the carriage at once to Bell's residence in Harley Street. After Parton's departure, however, Florence discovered that the hired horses had been used and she became angry and upset, saying that the cobs should have been taken as they went much faster than the carriage horses.

It was past midnight now. Impatient for the arrival of Royes Bell, Florence returned to the sickroom. Finding Charles still unconscious she lay on the bed beside him, whispering endearments into his ear in an effort to waken him. However, exhausted by her recent illness, her anxiety and the effects of too much sherry, she fell asleep, her arms still entwined about Charles's neck. As tactfully as he could, Mr Harrison awakened her and suggested that she remove herself in case she interfered with her husband's breathing. She was then given a chair on one side of the bed while Mrs Cox sat on the other. And so their vigil began.

Royes Bell and a colleague, Dr Johnson, arrived at about two-thirty the following morning, Wednesday. Charles had just suffered a painful attack of vomiting and had passed a bloody mucus from the bowel. However, he was showing signs of consciousness. He managed to recognise Royes Bell, and also Dr Johnson whom he had met socially on a couple of occasions. Florence had earlier gone into another room to rest, but on being told that Charles was conscious she hurried into the sickroom whereupon he looked at her in a 'piteous manner' and asked her to kiss him.

Throughout this time Charles was in extreme abdominal pain, at one point his agony being so acute that he writhed on the bed and screamed out, 'Oh, Christ have mercy upon me!' At this Dr Johnson – who, it was agreed, should take charge of the case – administered a morphia suppository which gave Charles some temporary relief. By this time the medical men were convinced that he was the victim of a powerful poison. Royes Bell urged Charles to tell them what he had taken but Charles replied:

'I have taken nothing.' He repeated this twice, then added, 'I rubbed my gums with laudanum for neuralgia and I may have swallowed some.'

'Laudanum will not explain your symptoms, Mr Bravo,' said Dr Johnson.

'If it isn't laudanum,' Charles said, 'I don't know what it is.'

The doctors had noted bottles of chloroform, laudanum and Condy's Fluid in the room, and also a packet of Epsom Salts and some camphor liniment which Royes Bell had prescribed for Charles's rheumatism. They were satisfied, however, that none of these could account for his collapse – though, suspecting poison, they were remiss in not impounding the various bottles in the room. Then came a second bout of vomiting and bowel evacuation, both bloodied, and the doctors were swiftly confirmed in their opinion that the poison Charles was suffering from was an irritant one – not narcotic – and, furthermore, that he was unlikely to recover. As to what the particular poison was, however, they were in the dark. But then, not very long after Bell and Johnson's arrival it appeared that some light might be thrown on the mystery. Shortly before three o'clock in the morning, the butler entered the sickroom to say that Mrs Cox wished to speak to Royes Bell.

The companion was waiting in the dressing room, and after hearing what she had to say Bell quickly went to the sickroom and summoned Dr Johnson and Mr Harrison. All three then hastened to the dressing room where Mrs Cox repeated her statement. She told them that when she had gone to Mr Bravo on his first collapsing he had said to her:

'I've taken poison. Don't tell Florence.'

Hearing this, Mr Harrison angrily asked her why she had not told him so before. She replied that she had told him on his arrival at the house.

'You did nothing of the kind!' retorted Harrison. Mrs Cox, though, would not be swayed, and insisted that she had told him some four hours before.

On the doctors' returning to the sickroom, Dr Johnson spoke to Charles, saying:

'Mrs Cox tells us that you have spoken to her of taking poison. What is the meaning of that?'

'I don't remember having spoken of taking poison,' Charles said, and went on to repeat his earlier statement about having taken laudanum for his gums. At this Dr Johnson insisted again, most emphatically, that laudanum would not have caused his symptoms. Charles said wearily:

'If it isn't the laudanum I don't know what it is.'

Dr Johnson then asked him if there were any poisons in the house, to which Charles replied:

'Yes, several – chloroform, laudanum – and rat poison in the stables.'

Already the effort of speaking had exhausted him, added to which he suffered another severe attack of vomiting and abdominal pain. In view of this, no further questions were put to him for the present. However, as a result of Mrs Cox's 'poison' statement some of the vomit and bowel excreta from the last attack were set aside for analysis.

As the time wore on and there was no improvement in Charles's condition, Dr Johnson questioned Mrs Cox again as to her statement about Charles having taken poison. Florence, overhearing the conversation, turned at once to the companion.

'Did he say he's taken poison?' she asked.

Mrs Cox replied that he had, then, urging Florence to her room, persuaded her to lie down. Dr Johnson said later that he was surprised that Florence showed 'so little astonishment' on hearing Mrs Cox's words.

At five-thirty Dr Johnson left The Priory taking some of the evacuated matter for analysis. Mr Harrison and Dr Moore also left at this time, needing to rest after attending Charles for seven hours without a break.

Royes Bell remained with his cousin. The two men had been friends since childhood, were as close as brothers, and could speak quite freely to one another, but, although they were left alone on several occasions, Charles gave Bell no indication whatever as to the cause of his collapse.

At one point while Royes Bell, Florence and Mrs Cox were grouped around his bed Charles asked Royes if he thought he would recover. His cousin answered him:

'I hope so, Charlie, but you're very ill indeed.'

After Charles had reflected upon the gravity of this reply he asked Royes to read some prayers for him. His cousin agreed, but his voice shook so with emotion that he could not continue. Charles then said an extempore prayer himself in which he mentioned those at his bedside.

As the first light of that Wednesday morning warmed the walls of The Priory the gravity of Charles's condition seemed more harshly revealed. Florence was advised to send for his parents and at once she sent a telegram to Warrior Square, St Leonards-on-Sea, where they were staying: *Charlie is seriously ill. He wants to see you. Come at once. Florence.* That done, she sent a telegram to her parents: *Charles is dangerously ill. Internal inflammation. Have telegraphed his mother. Florence.*

In preparation for the arrival of Charles's parents the maid was instructed to tidy the sickroom. As she entered the room Charles, with Florence and Royes standing at his side, asked her how she was.

'Very well, sir, thank you,' Mary Ann replied. 'How are you feeling?'

'Not much better, Mary Ann. We shan't have our trip to Worthing now.'

Mary Ann expressed the hope that they would, but Charles said, 'No, my next trip will be to Streatham cemetery.'

At this Mary Ann burst into tears. Charles then looked up at Florence, saying: 'When you bury me, make no fuss and have no feathers...' to which Florence replied that she would do as he wished, and then she, too, began to cry bitterly. Charles turned then to Royes and said with great weariness:

'Oh, Royes, I'm dying. Shall I linger long in such pain?'

Later on Charles urged Florence to marry again after his death. He also asked her to give his watch to Royes, and to be kind to Rowe. He then told Royes that he wished to make a will, and Mrs Cox was sent to fetch writing materials. When they were brought he dictated to Royes Bell the simple words that constituted his last will and testament: *I give all that I possess to my wife Florence whom I appoint my executrix.*

Afterwards the document was witnessed by Royes and Rowe.

The violent purging continued throughout the day and Charles suffered greatly, while his family and friends tried their best to minimise his discomfort. Rowe was frequently called upon to help with the lifting of the patient, and Mary Ann fetched and carried tirelessly. About three o'clock that afternoon Mr Harrison, Dr Johnson and Dr Moore returned to The Priory, but there was little they could do. Questioning Charles yet again as to what might be the cause of his sickness they simply drew from him the weary, impatient response: 'If I knew what I was suffering from, why the devil should I send for you?'

Soon after four o'clock Mr and Mrs Joseph Bravo arrived from St Leonards-on-Sea, bringing with them an elderly trusted servant, Amelia Bushell, who had known Charles from his boyhood. Anxiety must have softened some of the usual reserve between Charles's mother and his wife for they greeted one another kindly.

While Joseph Bravo lingered briefly to speak to Dr Johnson in the drawing room Florence turned to lead the two women to Charles's side. As they climbed the stairs Florence said to Amelia Bushell:

'What a dreadful thing, Amelia. The only thing by which I can account for it is that Mr Charles took lunch at St James's Hall and had something cooked in a coppery pan.' (Florence's mother was apparently conscious of a danger of poisoning by copper pans and had told her daughter about deaths caused in this way.)

Charles's parents were shocked by his pitiful appearance and were dismayed to learn that the doctors still had not identified the poison responsible for his condition.

A little later Mrs Bravo made it known that she, with the assistance of Amelia, wished to undertake the nursing of her son. Under the circumstances Florence felt she could do nothing but agree, and if she felt any rancour or resentment she kept it to herself. Furthermore, deciding that Mr and Mrs Bravo ought to sleep as near to Charles as possible, she gave them her own bedroom, opting to share Jane Cox's room on the floor above.

Not long after the arrival of Charles's parents Florence received a telegram from her brother William: *Very grieved to hear about Charlie. Telegraph how he is and whether you would like mother, Augusta or myself to come to you. William.*

It must have appeared about this time, however, that Charles's condition had somewhat improved, for Florence sent back a wire to William: *Charlie rather better. Still very ill. Will telegraph you again should I wish you to come up. Florence.*

Any slight hopes that were entertained for Charles's recovery, however, were soon to fade. As the night wore on he became worse, and the next morning, Thursday 20 April, Florence sent another telegram to her family:

If you wish to see Charles alive you must come at once. I fear the worst. Florence.

Later, at Buscot, as Mrs Campbell and William (Robert Campbell was still unwell and was staying at home) were hurriedly preparing to leave to catch the 11.55 train from Faringdon to Paddington, there came yet another telegram:

No hope for my darling. He cannot live long. Florence.

Dr Johnson, having tested the vomit *for arsenic only* and found none, remained mystified. Discussing the grave situation with Joseph Bravo, however, he made it clear that Charles could not recover. At this time Joseph Bravo decided that he must try to prepare Charles for death, which he proceeded to do. Charles, exhausted by his suffering and racked with pain, met his stepfather's words with remarkable stoicism.

Florence reacted differently. When Joseph Bravo repeated the doctor's prognosis to her she seemed unable to accept it, and made it clear that she still hoped for a recovery. Minutes later she was translating her hopes into deeds. Her actions may seem extraordinarily imprudent in the circumstances, but it does indicate that although the doctors had given up hope she herself was determined to try anything that might save her husband's life. In the event she sent Mrs Cox hurrying off to Dr Gully's house with an urgent plea for him to prescribe something for Charles. The companion duly returned with Gully's advice, and as a result Florence asked Dr Johnson if Charles could be treated with cold water applications to the stomach, a mustard plaster on the spine and doses of arsenicum. Forbidding the use of the cold water and mustard plaster on the grounds that they would only increase Charles's pain, Dr Johnson nevertheless allowed Florence to administer very small doses of the arsenicum, though he was sceptical of its possible benefit at this late stage.

Dr Johnson left The Priory later that morning, promising to return later and, if possible, to bring with him the surgeon Henry Smith, Mrs Joseph Bravo's brother-in-law, who, he hoped, might be able to assist in the grave situation.

Following the doctor's departure Charles's deaf-mute sister Alice arrived. She was brought to The Priory by Royes Bell's sister Anna Maria, who had been looking after the girl at St Leonards-on-Sea. Charles was pleased to see Alice but the situation was too distressing for her to bear, and after she had kissed her brother she was led from the room.

A little later Anna Maria joined Florence for a walk in the garden. There they wandered into the conservatory where Florence sat weeping as she told Anna Maria how happy her marriage to Charles had been, and how only a few days before being taken ill he had said that he had never been so happy.

Dr Johnson returned early that afternoon in the company of Henry Smith – to whom he had confided his opinion that Charles had voluntarily taken the poison. Regardless of his own views, Mr Smith was unable to do anything to help the patient. Florence, however, still did not give up hope, and tried to think of other measures that might help. After some thought she determined to seek the opinion of Sir William Gull, a man recognised as the finest diagnostician of the day and the 'first opinion in London'. Florence's father was known to Sir William and it was almost certainly on the strength of this connection that, after a discussion with Royes Bell, Florence sent Mrs Cox hurrying off to Sir William's residence at 74 Brook Street, Mayfair. The tireless companion carried a note which read:

Dear Sir,

My husband is dangerously ill; could you come as soon as possible to see him? My father, Mr Campbell of Buscot Park, will feel very grateful to you if you could come at once. I need not say how grateful I shall be to you.

Yours truly,
Florence Bravo

PS. Dr George Johnson is coming in the course of the afternoon. Mr Royes Bell of Kings College, who is the cousin of
Mr Charles Bravo, acquiesces in the wish for you to come.

In writing the note, Florence made no mention of the nature of
Charles's illness or that the doctors believed him to be suffering
from an irritant poison. As Sir William was famed for his ability to
diagnose *disease* one wonders why Florence sent for him. She
testified later that she did not know at that stage that her husband
had been poisoned. If she *did* know then she may intentionally have
omitted any mention of poison for fear that he would not respond to
her plea. After all, Royes Bell would have known that Sir William's
speciality was disease.

Just as Florence's note gave no information concerning Charles's
illness, neither did Mrs Cox herself volunteer any when she arrived
at Sir William's house. Nevertheless, the eminent man agreed to
consult Dr Johnson on the matter and do his best to attend.

On her return to The Priory, Mrs Cox was dispatched to Balham
station to meet Mrs Campbell and William after their five-hour
train journey from Faringdon. Arriving at the house Mrs Campbell
hurried to the sickroom where Charles greeted her warmly. Then,
turning to his mother, he said, 'Mother, will you be kind to Florence? She's been the best of wives to me.'

Replied Mrs Bravo: 'I'm never unkind to anyone, Charlie, and I
assure you I'll be kind to her.'

At six-thirty that evening Sir William Gull arrived at The Priory
in the company of Dr Johnson. Sir William was a large, impressive
man of sixty with a powerful and authoritative bearing, said to be
kind-hearted and benevolent, yet at times brutally honest. Highly
regarded in the medical profession, his career had reached a pinnacle
in 1871 when he had been awarded a baronetcy for aiding the
recovery of the Prince of Wales who had been gravely ill with
typhoid.

Having acquainted himself with the other medical men he went
upstairs and, in the company of Bell and Johnson, made a swift
examination of the patient's pulse and abdomen. Then he said to
Charles:

'This isn't disease. You are poisoned. Pray tell us how you came
by it.'

'Laudanum,' came the weary reply. 'I took it myself.'

'You've taken more than laudanum,' observed Sir William, to which Dr Johnson added:

'If you die without telling us more than we know at present someone may be accused or suspected of having poisoned you.'

'I am aware of that,' Charles said, 'but I can tell you nothing more.'

Sir William asked him yet again to reveal the name of the poison so that an antidote might be found, but then added gravely, in case he had raised the patient's hopes: 'But I fear that would not be quite fair, as I fear no antidote would do you good.' Charles responded by closing his eyes and turning away.

There remains some doubt as to when and by whom Sir William was first told that Charles had been sick, but on learning that the vomit lay on the leads outside the window he ordered Joseph Bravo's footman to climb out and scoop it up with a silver spoon. (A silver spoon was necessary; being a pure metal it could not affect the constituents of the vomit.) This the footman did, and the vomit was put into a glass jar, which Dr Johnson sealed.

When the medical men had left the sickroom permission was given for Charles's family and friends to go to his side once more, and quietly they went in. At the same time Sir William, Royes Bell and Dr Johnson gathered in Florence's dressing room to discuss the case.

Surprisingly, it appears that Sir William had not been informed that tests for arsenic poisoning had already been carried out, for he gave his opinion that the poison involved was arsenic, and possibly laudanum as well. The other two doctors, however, at once informed him of the test and its negative result.

The discussion of the three men was interrupted at this point by Anna Maria who, at Charles's loud-voiced request, came knocking at the door to summon Sir William back to the sickroom. On Sir William returning to the bedside, Charles, appearing very agitated and anxious, said earnestly:

'Sir William, I wish to tell you now that I've told you the truth and nothing but the truth.'

In reply, Sir William repeated that laudanum would not account for his symptoms, adding, 'There must be something else. You must consider the gravity of your situation and of all you say and do.' He then told Charles that he would not live much longer.

'I know that,' Charles said. 'I know that I'm going to appear before my Maker. I can't tell you anything more. I took nothing but laudanum to rub on my lower jaw for toothache – like this . . .' With his words he lifted his hand and feebly touched his mouth with his fingers.

At this Florence said, 'Charles, dearest, tell us where you got it.'

'Out of your bottle, Florence,' Charles said. 'If there was anything else in it I don't know what it was.'

Again Sir William asked him what he had taken, and again Charles answered:

'I've taken laudanum. Before God I've taken only laudanum. If it wasn't laudanum, so help me, God, I don't know what it was.'

In excruciating pain, and weary beyond endurance, he then asked whether there was any hope for him. Sir William replied:

'Looking at your condition, Mr Bravo, it wouldn't be right to give you any hope.' And feeling the pulse of the stricken man he added: 'There's very little life left in you. In fact, you're half dead now.'

While Florence and Anna Maria wept, Mrs Campbell asked Charles if she should send for Mr Nichols, the rector of Streatham. Charles declined the offer, preferring to lead the assembly in the Lord's Prayer, which he delivered falteringly while the others knelt and bowed their heads.

Sir William Gull, realising that he could do nothing further, prepared to take his leave. After wishing Charles goodbye he handed to Mrs Joseph Bravo a prescription for a preparation that might ease her son's pain during the night, though he quietly gave his considered opinion that he would not live another day.

After Sir William's departure Charles summoned all the members of his family, his friends and his servants, and asked them to join him in prayers. When they had finished he took his farewell of them. Afterwards all left but Florence, his mother, Royes Bell and Anna Maria. Sharing the night's vigil and taking short rests in turn, the four watched helplessly as Charles bore the agony of his last hours.

At about four-thirty in the morning of Friday 21 April Amelia Bushell was sent to Mrs Cox's room where she found Florence asleep, Mrs Cox sitting on the bed beside her. The old servant softly said:

'Will you come down, please? – Mr Bravo is worse.'

When Amelia had gone, Mrs Cox woke Florence and they went downstairs together. They found Charles unconscious and near to death, his mother and Royes at his bedside.

Not long after five o'clock Florence, weeping, woke Mary Ann and asked her to make some tea. Shortly afterwards the maid was coming upstairs with the tea things when she was met by Mrs Cox, who told her that Florence wished to speak to her in the dressing room. When the maid entered the room Florence said to her:

'Mary Ann, Mr Bravo is dead.'

'Oh, madam, when did he die?' the maid cried, very upset.

'A few minutes ago.'

Charles had died at five-thirty that morning. His last words had been to his mother when, before lapsing into unconsciousness for the last time, he turned to her and breathed softly, 'Ah, Granny...'

It was a ghastly end to a young life and too pitiful to dwell upon but for the mystery that surrounded it – a mystery which made it no ordinary death, but one which guaranteed Charles Bravo a degree of immortality that, with his love of life, he would have enjoyed tremendously.

PART TWO

'Public feeling has been
revolted by the manner in
which this investigation has been conducted.'

The Times, August 1876

7

The First Inquest

Soon after Charles's death Mrs Joseph Bravo, leaving her husband
to assume responsibility for matters at The Priory, left with Alice,
Anna Maria and Amelia Bushell for Palace Green. There, in a
wretched state, she took to her bed, never to recover from her son's
death. In poor health before her loss, she was to decline and die
within fifteen months, physically and emotionally broken at forty-
eight years of age.

Meanwhile, informing her father of Charles's death, Florence
sent him a telegram saying that Charles 'had passed away peace-
fully'. Mr Campbell immediately offered to come to The Priory and
take charge of things, but Florence hastily telegraphed him again,
saying: 'Mr Bravo is here and will do all that is necessary. Keep
where you are and take care of yourself.'

Later that morning of Friday 21 April Charles's friend and fellow
barrister Frederick MacCalmont, ignorant of Charles's fate, called
at The Priory to see how he was. He and Charles had planned to play
tennis the previous Wednesday but bad weather had made it necessary to postpone the game. Arriving on Thursday he had been told
that Charles was ill. Now, however, he was met with the devastat-
ing news that his friend was dead. He left The Priory shocked and
bewildered.

Royes Bell, in the meantime, suffering from grief and lack of
sleep, had gone to inform the coroner for East Surrey of his cousin's
untimely death. As none of the doctors would issue a death
certificate an inquest was necessary. With the agreement of the
bereaved family, Bell then enlisted Mr Joseph Payne of St Thomas's
Hospital to perform a post-mortem.

The post-mortem was conducted the following day in the presence of Dr Johnson, Dr Moore, Mr Harrison and Royes Bell. At the end of the examination certain organs were removed and taken away in sealed jars by Royes Bell to be delivered to Mr Theophilus Redwood, Professor of Chemistry to the Pharmaceutical Society of Great Britain. The contents of these organs, along with the vomit that had been taken from the leads below Charles's bedroom window, were to be thoroughly analysed.

On Sunday 23 April Florence, having learned that the inquest was set for the following Tuesday, got Mrs Cox to write to the coroner's officer: 'Mrs Charles Bravo writes to say that she wishes the inquest to be held at The Priory where she will have refreshments prepared for the jury.'

Inquests (and post-mortems) were commonly held in the homes of the deceased when space allowed, and the coroner, Mr William Carter, readily complied with Florence Bravo's request. It is probable that he assumed, or had been led to believe, that he was dealing with a case of suicide, and therefore he wished to shield the dead man's widow and other relatives from the strain of a more public inquiry.

Certainly Sir William Gull supported belief in a theory of suicide, and he wasted no time in writing to Robert Campbell with his opinion that Charles had killed himself, or, more to the point, with the view that it would be expedient to assume that this was the case. Although suicide was a shameful disgrace it was nevertheless straightforward and would, in the long run, save Charles's widow and family a great deal of anguish.

The inquest jury was selected from local tradesmen, seventeen in number, a saddler, a couple of gardeners, a groom and several shopkeepers. Their instructions were to present themselves at The Priory on Tuesday 25 April at eleven o'clock sharp. The coroner had not informed the press of the impending inquest, but in compliance with the law that the proceedings be seen as public the doors of The Priory were left open – so allowing access to any persons who wished to attend.

The inquest was to be held in the dining room, the largest room in the house, and there the coroner, the jury and the spectators began to assemble. Those who were hoping for a sight of the widow, however, were to be disappointed, for Florence remained in her room throughout the inquiry.

Among those who were present that morning was one of Charles's barrister friends, John Reid. And it was to prove most fortunate that he was there, for he took notes during the proceedings, without which only the barest outline of the evidence would have been recorded.

As soon as the inquiry had been opened the jurors were conducted to a room upstairs to view the mortal remains of Charles Bravo as he lay in a coffin lined with white satin. His hands had been laid across his chest and white lilies placed between his fingers. The room was peaceful and filled with flowers, carefully arranged by Mrs Cox and the two maids.

On the jurors' return to the dining room the first witness was called. This was Mr Joseph Bravo, who stated that he had been summoned to The Priory on Wednesday 19 April and that his stepson had been conscious but did not complain to him of any pain.

Mrs Cox was questioned next and described Charles's collapse, stating that as soon as she had reached his side he told her that he had taken poison. She added that he had no reason to commit suicide and lived on 'good and affectionate' terms with his wife.

Amelia Bushell, next called, said that she had attended Charles from the time of her arrival at The Priory until his death. He had appeared to be in great pain, she said, but at no time did he account for his condition, nor was there any written note or letter to account for it.

The next witness was Mr Harrison, who told the coroner that when he reached The Priory on the Tuesday he found Dr Moore already there and Charles 'unconscious and unable to swallow'. After describing Charles's condition prior to regaining consciousness he said that he was aware at an early stage that the patient was suffering from an irritant poison. However, he added, 'I had not been informed that he had taken any ingredient. We all repeatedly asked him. He denied having taken anything.'

At this point the inquest was adjourned until Friday 28 April, at which time, it was assumed, evidence would be heard from Professor Redwood following his analysis of the vomit that had been collected from the leads.

Professor Redwood had in fact already completed his work over the weekend, and even before the inquest was opened certain parties had been unofficially informed of the results of his analysis. It could not be broadcast yet, but the professor had determined that Charles had been poisoned with antimony.

Joseph Bravo was already aware of the professor's findings when, following the inquest's adjournment, Robert Campbell came to him at Palace Green in the hope of promoting the belief that Charles had killed himself. Campbell was armed with a letter from Sir William Gull stating his opinion to that effect. Joseph Bravo was not impressed, however. His stepson had been killed with antimony, he said, and antimony was not a poison one would use to take one's own life.

Not giving up, Robert Campbell then sought the support of Dr Johnson, who was himself of the opinion that Charles had wittingly taken the poison. Johnson said, however, that regardless of one's belief there was no *evidence* to show suicide, and the only possible verdict would be an open one, that death was by antimony. But Campbell would not be deterred; he could 'get a verdict of suicide in five minutes', he said; all he needed to do was to produce Sir William Gull's letter. He did not even think it would be necessary for Dr Johnson to attend the resumed inquest.

(Sir William Gull's support for Robert Campbell is somewhat surprising. Firstly he had gone to Charles's bedside when Florence had sent for him with mention of her father's name, and then he had unhesitatingly given support to the notion that Charles had committed suicide. His unquestioning assistance suggests either a very strong friendship with Robert Campbell, or some other connection – perhaps an allegiance through the brotherhood of Freemasonry.*)

Notwithstanding Robert Campbell's advice, Dr Johnson was at the inquiry when it was resumed on the Friday morning. There also were Charles's friends MacCalmont and Reid – joined by another friend and colleague of Charles, Carlyle Willoughby. He, like his two companions, was finding Charles's death increasingly disturbing.

Mary Ann Keeber was the first witness and she described the events after Charles had collapsed, and detailed the treatment that she and Mrs Cox had applied, stating that 'at no time did he speak of

---

* Stephen Knight, in his book *Jack the Ripper – the Final Solution*, states that Sir William Gull was a high-ranking Freemason.

his illness'. She added, 'He did not make use of the word *poison* in my hearing, nor was it made use of by Mrs Cox on Tuesday night.'

At this point Mr Harrison said he wished to add to his previous evidence and stated: 'I was not told that the deceased had said he had taken poison. Mrs Cox said she was sure he had taken chloroform.'

The next witness was Mr Joseph Payne, who had carried out the post-mortem examination. After describing the various organs as 'natural' he concluded by saying that he 'did not find any disease of the body or head as accounting for death'.

Royes Bell was called next and he gave an account of the doctors' interrogation of the patient, saying that at no time did Charles admit to taking anything but laudanum.

Next came Professor Redwood, whose evidence was eagerly awaited. He stated that he had analysed the vomit from the leads and found that it contained about ten grains of antimony, which, he added, was probably taken into the body in the form of tartar emetic. 'Antimony,' said the professor, 'is a metal, and the oxide of this, combined with tartaric acid, produces the tartar emetic.'

It might be noted that tartar emetic, in the form of a white powder which will dissolve easily in water, is the most easily assimilated form of antimony. With regard to its general effects, it should be pointed out that its various preparations are all irritants, and while in certain preparations *small* doses can be beneficial,* in large doses they are poisons, producing vomiting, purging, and also paralysis of the heart and nervous system. Nowadays it would be relatively difficult to purchase the product, but, as will be shown, in mid-Victorian times it was quite freely available, and was a fairly common constituent of certain patent remedies.

After the professor had stepped down Joseph Bravo rose to suggest that the poison might have been in the food taken at dinner. Mrs Cox was then recalled to give details of the food eaten. However, she stated, both she and Mrs Bravo had sampled the same dishes and neither of them had suffered any ill effects. This seemed to satisfy the coroner and, surprisingly, he began to sum up – but then it was pointed out that there was no evidence before him 'as to the

---

* In certain of its forms antimony later became a popular constituent in preparations for the treatment of fever and bronchitis; it is now used only in the treatment of certain tropical diseases.

deceased's state of mind on the day of his seizure'. Frederick Mac-Calmont volunteered to give evidence of this and proceeded to tell the coroner of his meeting with Charles in Piccadilly. After saying that Charles was 'in his usual health and spirits' he added that in his opinion he was a most unlikely person to commit suicide.

Mr Carter was once again preparing to sum up the evidence when Dr Johnson rose to say that he wished to give evidence. To the doctor's great surprise and embarrassment, however, the coroner dismissed his offer, saying crisply that the jury did not require any further medical evidence, and that it was unnecessary to examine him.

The coroner's refusal to hear him was, to say the least, surprising – particularly as Dr Johnson had been in charge of the case. In the light of the coroner's action, and his precipitate attempts to sum up, it might be inferred that he was anxious to bring the proceedings to an end. Such an inference is bolstered by an incident that followed Dr Johnson's dismissal, when a juror asked if Mrs Bravo might be called to give evidence. Mr Carter declined, 'on compassionate grounds', to call her. Then once more he began his summing-up – of which he made no record; only John Reid's brief notes telling that the coroner stated that, '. . . the jury would have to say whether the poison was taken by Mr Bravo himself, or administered to him, or taken by accident. If they believed Mrs Cox, he had taken the poison himself; if that were so it was a case of *felo-de-se* [suicide], unless he was insane, of which there was no evidence.'

With further regard to the notes taken during the proceedings, only Reid's bore a record of Mrs Cox's testimony that Charles had said to her, 'Don't tell Florence', after telling her that he had taken poison. Also, and very importantly, it was only Reid who made a note of Mr Harrison's categorical denial that Mrs Cox had ever told him that Charles had taken poison. In the circumstances it might be assumed that the coroner preferred not to have to deal with Mr Harrison's refutation; certainly without it the theory of suicide was much more tenable.

At that stage the idea that Charles might indeed have been murdered had not yet been fully comprehended to any great extent; many of those opposed to the idea of his having killed himself were of the opinion that he might have died as the result of some kind of misdeed, but one which had not necessarily been meant to be fatal;

in effect an accident – which was now being covered up. This was originally Joseph Bravo's view and naturally, therefore, he refused to give any support to the notion that Charles had taken his own life.

For Robert Campbell, however, the theory of suicide was the only one he would entertain. Granted, there was not much evidence to support such a theory, but on the other hand there was even less to support the idea that Charles had died as the result of some sinister accident – and the belief that he had done so would lead to much unwelcome probing and publicity. The only alternative was murder, and that was not to be even considered. A suicide verdict was the only one that could be borne, and it was to achieve such an end that Robert Campbell had done all in his power.

So, while the jury was out considering its verdict the Bravos and the Campbells waited anxiously. And then at last came the jury's verdict. Said the foreman:

'We find that the deceased died from the effects of poison, anti-mony – but we have not sufficient evidence to show under which circumstances it came into his body.'

And that was it. Mrs Cox had offered testimony to support a theory of suicide and the jury had not accepted it. Perhaps Robert Campbell should have produced Sir William Gull's letter or, better still, presented the great man in person.

At any event, the inquest was over. And as it turned out no one was satisfied, neither the Bravos, the Campbells, nor the jury itself.

However, in spite of the unsatisfactory outcome, Robert Campbell might well have consoled himself with the thought that it could have been much worse. There had been no suicide verdict, but even with an open verdict the matter was over and done with, the case was closed.

Or was it?

Joseph Bravo was most dissatisfied with the outcome of the inquest and made it clear that he was not going to let the matter rest. And his suspicions were growing – as they were in the minds of many others.

If there had been a gulf between the Campbells and the Bravos before the jury's verdict it was even wider once that verdict had been delivered. Sadly, the one person who might have united them and helped to smooth the edges of their discontent with his hearty bonhomie was Charles – and he was to be buried the next day.

8

Suspicion and Dissent

On the morning of Saturday 29 April, the day of Charles's funeral, an announcement of his death appeared in *The Daily Telegraph*:

> BRAVO: on 21st inst. at The Priory, Balham.
> Charles D. T. Bravo

The simple words gave no hint of the tense and suspicious atmosphere that surrounded the young man's death, one indication of which was that, at the start of the funeral, his friend Carlyle Willoughby refused to enter The Priory, electing instead to wait at the open front door. As he waited there for the coffin to be brought out he saw Florence as, unaware of his presence, she carried a wreath of white blossoms through the hall. It was not customary for women to attend funerals at this time, so Florence was not among the mourners who followed the coffin to the cemetery. Remaining at home, she watched from an upstairs window as the procession left the gates of The Priory and turned on to Bedford Hill.

Borne on an open hearse fringed with violet trappings, Charles's coffin, covered with white flowers and exposed to view, was taken to Norwood (now West Norwood) Cemetery.

As Charles's body was laid in the earth on the higher slopes of the tree-lined cemetery his family and friends were far from tranquil in their thoughts. Joseph Bravo was so troubled, in fact, that as soon as the ceremony was over he voiced his growing disquiet to his physician brother-in-law, Henry Smith, remarking that there were 'poisons in every room' of The Priory (he was, in fact, referring to

Florence's homeopathic remedies). He had already hurled this comment at Robert Campbell in retaliation for a remark made by the latter to the effect that antimony was used in the stables at Joseph Bravo's house at Palace Green – a remark which insinuated that Charles had killed himself with poison belonging to his stepfather. Joseph Bravo also showed to Henry Smith the carefree letters that Charles had written to his mother shortly before he died, letters which seemed to deny any likelihood of suicide.

Having listened, Henry Smith advised him to inform Scotland Yard of his suspicions. Forthwith Joseph Bravo retained the services of a rising young lawyer, George Lewis, then went to Scotland Yard and put the matter before Chief Inspector Clarke, who undertook to inform the Home Office of the disquiet.

Carlyle Willoughby, who also entertained strong suspicions over Charles's death, was another visitor to Scotland Yard. There on Monday 1 May he informed the authorities of 'several circumstances which were worrying him' in connection with his friend's death.

On the day of the funeral Mrs Cox had been in Brighton arranging to rent a house, a place where Florence could stay and for a while get away from the scene of so much unhappiness. A temporary rental was taken on 38 Brunswick Terrace – a short distance from number 21 which was occupied by Florence's parents. Subsequently on 3 May Florence and Mrs Cox and other members of the staff travelled to Brighton. On arrival at Brunswick Terrace, Florence was visited by members of her family, and together they discussed the theory of Charles's suicide, no doubt finding comfort and support in the formidable weight of Sir William Gull's opinion.

However, if the change of scene brought Florence any sense of peace it was not to last for long, for two days after her arrival in Brighton she learned of Joseph Bravo's visit to Scotland Yard. And there were further disturbing developments, so much so that on 5 May Florence was sufficiently moved to write to her father-in-law:

My dear Father Joseph,–

    I am astonished to hear from my solicitor, Mr Brooks, that you had dear Charles's drawers* sealed, as legally, nobody but

* At his chambers.

myself has the power to touch one single thing belonging to him, he having left all he possessed to me – I must ask you to see that nothing he possessed is touched by anyone. With regard to what he died possessed of, I must leave to you, but he told me he had £200 a year of his coming from investments and of course his books, pictures and private property at Palace Green are now mine. His watch was left at your house, and by his own wish I give it to Royes Bell. Please see that it is delivered to him. My father will take care that I have all my dear husband left me, poor fellow! How he would have grieved at all the unkind feelings shown me.

> Hoping you and Mrs Bravo are better,
>   believe yours sincerely,
>   Florence Bravo

PS. Poor Charles also told me that you promised to allow him £800.

There is no doubt that this is a letter of retaliation. For one thing it reveals the bitterness that Florence must have felt on having learnt that Joseph Bravo 'had had the detectives put on'. Also, and understandably, she was stung by what she saw as her father-in-law's presumptuous actions. Clearly she felt compelled to make clear the sovereignty of her own position. Her apparently grasping attitude towards Charles's worldly goods when her own purse was overflowing further reflects her sense of injury.

The day after writing the above Florence received a letter from Royes Bell. As a result she wrote again (6 May) to her father-in-law:

Dear Father Joseph,

A letter received this morning from Royes Bell fully confirms my suspicions as to poor Charlie's suicide. Hence his motive for reducing our expenditure as he did not tell me how hard he had been pressed by that dreadful woman. I wish he had, poor fellow, for I should not have been hard upon him, but it is a most sad reflection upon his memory and I intend to

sift the matter. We have Sir William Gull's evidence and shall
not allow the living to be under imputation such as is cast upon
them by such a wicked verdict. I leave it all in my father's
hands and shall abide by his decision.

> Yours sincerely,
> Florence Bravo

Florence was clutching at straws. At no time was there any
evidence that the woman in Maidenhead was demanding money or
anything else from Charles. The fact is more to the contrary, for it
appears from letters found in Charles's rooms at the Temple that the
lady's sister had lent Charles £500 on which he had been paying her
interest. Florence, though, having learned of the continuing suspicions and the alarming fact that her father-in-law had consulted
Scotland Yard, was desperate to push the theory of suicide to the
limits of plausibility. The open verdict which allowed a possible
assumption of murder was, with its implications, unbearable. So,
although the matter was officially closed she felt compelled, in the
light of the burgeoning ripples of disquiet, to protect herself. The
only way to do this, she felt, was to promote belief in the theory that
Charles had taken his own life, even though her suggested reason
for his suicide – financial pressure from an ex-mistress – was sordid
and unpleasant.

On 8 May Florence wrote yet again to Joseph Bravo, and in this
letter her attitude towards him appears, on the surface, to have
softened considerably. Clearly, feeling strongly his opprobrium,
she was trying to mend fences and enlist his sympathy. She wrote:

My dear Father Joseph,

The letter I wrote to you on Friday was written under the
impression that you had forced Charlie's drawers at the Temple, and I regret having been so impressed, as ever since I knew
you I have only experienced kindness and consideration.
Please try to think of me as your loving daughter and do not
address me as Mrs Florence Bravo – it pains me more than I can
tell you, and it is only in legal documents that I must be so
addressed. I hope you are all recovered from the dreadful and

sad last fortnight. My life is a complete blank and I am very ill.

> With love to you and yours,
> ever your affectionate daughter,
> Florence Bravo

PS. Have dear Charlie's photos been sent by mistake to you?

However, the attempt to enlist Joseph Bravo's sympathy failed, and the gulf between Florence and her in-laws grew wider. Furthermore, the disquieting reports and comments received by the authorities had borne fruit, and even while Florence was writing her letter of 8 May, Chief Inspector Clarke of Scotland Yard was travelling to Brighton to interview her and Mrs Cox and the other servants. It had happened – the Home Office had instructed the Yard to carry out investigations to see whether there was any truth in the rumours.

Afterwards Clarke had questionnaires distributed to the chemists of Balham and Streatham, and even followed a suggestion from a member of the public that the Sale of Poison registers in Worthing should be checked – just in case Mrs Cox had popped in for some antimony during her visit on 18 April. These inquiries, however, like those involving the local chemists, drew negative results.

In the meantime the rumblings of disquiet over Charles's death and the inquest continued from his friends and colleagues, growing in volume to such a degree that eventually there was a veritable avalanche of press coverage.

The article that nudged the first stone in this avalanche appeared in the weekly newspaper *The World* of 10 May under the title 'A Tragedy?'. In it the anonymous author gave an account of the death by poison of 'a young barrister rapidly gaining a position at Westminster Hall, who had recently married'. No names of those involved were mentioned but as a result there was a deluge of letters to the press voicing opinions and offering suggestions as to the mode of death, and the identity of the poisoner.

The Daily Telegraph dedicated several columns each day to 'The Death of Charles Bravo', starting their campaign with an article suggesting, incorrectly, that Sir William Gull was the only medical man able to diagnose the symptoms as being those of an irritant poison. This prompted both Henry Smith and George Harrison to

reach for their pens in protest, and on the following day their letters
duly appeared in *The Daily Telegraph*. Mr Harrison wrote:

> . . . Dr Moore and I were convinced that he was suffering from
> the effects of some irritant poison some time before he was
> seen by any other medical man. . . . Sir William Gull only saw
> him once, on the evening before his death, and was not present
> at the post-mortem examination or the inquest.
>
> Dr Johnson offered to give evidence at the inquest but it was
> declined by the Coroner.

And from Henry Smith:

> . . . a statement is made to the effect that it was not recognised
> as one of poisoning until Sir William Gull had been called in.
>
> I should feel obliged if you will allow me to state that I was
> requested by the family to see the unfortunate patient with my
> colleague, Dr George Johnson, some hours before Sir William
> Gull arrived, and not only was it clear then that the symptoms
> were incompatible with anything else but those produced by
> poison, but Dr Johnson, who had seen the patient thirty-six
> hours prior to this visit, had at once given his opinion that the
> cause was one of an irritant and not narcotic poisoning, such as
> chloroform or laudanum, and had acted upon that opinion in
> conjunction with Royes Bell, who was already in attendance.

The Daily Telegraph also printed a letter, signed simply 'A
Friend', which thanked the newspaper for the publicity given to the
circumstances attending Charles's death, saying of him: 'A more
honourable, straight-forward, intelligent and agreeable man rarely,
if ever, existed. I cannot imagine that he could have had an enemy in
the world.' The writer said that on 8 April he had been at the
Brighton Quarter Sessions with Charles, who had been in his usual
good spirits. Charles Bravo, he added, was the 'last man on earth' to
commit suicide.

Another letter published by *The Daily Telegraph* was from one
Joseph Newton, of Balham, who wrote:

> As one who attended the inquest on the late Mr Bravo, held in

the dining room of his residence in Balham, I should like to
make a few remarks. . . . To my thinking both the Coroner
and the Jury were very much to blame for the imperfect way in
which the inquiry into this melancholy case was conducted.
The Coroner himself was evidently disposed to rule that Mr
Bravo had destroyed himself. Fortunately the jury returned an
'open verdict' and the questions omitted at the inquest may
now be put by others more determined than Mr Carter or the
Jury appeared to be to elicit the truth.

While from a gentleman in Wood Green came the suggestion that
Charles had died after drinking from a badly rinsed wine bottle, and
quoting the tale of a hapless Scottish minister who had drunk the
dregs from a bottle of stout and subsequently died from the poisonous cleaning-shot in the bottom of the bottle. The moral of the
frugal churchman brought several letters from wine-bottlers with
similar stories.

Day after day the press continued to devote space to 'The Balham
Mystery', and such was the growing strength of opinion from both
professional and lay people alike that it seemed inevitable that
eventually an attempt must be made to instigate a second inquest to
elicit the truth in the mystifying affair.

On 15 May, in Brighton, Chief Inspector Clarke interviewed
Florence again – this time at the police office, where he warned her
that as part of the inquiry the Treasury Solicitor would need to
question her servants formally. At the same time, acting on behalf
of the Treasury, he requested and received permission to make a
search of The Priory and its grounds.

Sitting there facing the police officer Florence must have been
greatly distressed. It was now abundantly clear that no matter what
belief she wanted to promote the authorities suspected murder.

It may have been as a result of her fear at that second meeting with
Mr Clarke that she spoke to him of a certain matter concerning her
late husband, a matter which has been the subject of speculation and
debate ever since. She had, she told the chief inspector, spoken to Dr
Dill, her Brighton physician, concerning certain aspects of her
husband's behaviour – behaviour which, she had learned, constituted 'a grave charge'. This 'grave charge' will be dealt with more
fully at a later stage, but for the present it is enough to give an

account of her statement to Mr Clarke who, not knowing the nature of the subject, was puzzled and asked her to elaborate. This she steadfastly refused to do. However, she suggested that if he wished to know more he should consult Dr Dill, who would be able to furnish him with further information.

After Mr Clarke's departure, Florence, clearly feeling besieged by the publicity and unrest, was persuaded by her father to take the initiative in the drama, and consequently she instructed her solicitor to insert an announcement in the press. It appeared in a dozen newspapers on Tuesday 16 May, the day after the interview:

FIVE HUNDRED POUNDS REWARD

Whereas, up to the present time it is not known where or by whom the antimony or tartar emetic which caused the death of the late Charles Delauney Turner Bravo, of The Priory, Balham, Surrey, was procured on or before 18th April last, the above named reward will be paid on behalf of his widow by the undersigned to any one who will prove the sale of the said antimony or tartar emetic in such a manner as will throw satisfactory light on the mode by which Mr Bravo came by his death on 21st April last. Any information will be given to Superintendent Williamson, Scotland Yard, London.

Brooke, Jenkins and Co., Solicitors for Mrs C. Bravo, 7, Godliman Street, Doctors' Commons, London.

In the same issue there appeared a statement to the effect that Scotland Yard was reviewing the results of its investigations for the purpose of helping the authorities to decide what course they might legitimately take. The statement continued: 'A memorial to the Home Secretary is in the course of preparation praying him to cause a fresh inquiry into the cause of the late Mr Bravo's death – to be held by a Commissioner appointed by the Secretary of State.'

There is no doubt that at such news Florence's heart must have sunk. She must have been praying that in spite of everything she could still ride out the storm. Now it seemed almost inevitable that a second inquiry would be held. In the circumstances she might well have felt that it was expedient that her reward notice had been published.

In addition to the activity in the police department over the days that followed, more and more letters appeared in the newspapers. There were suggestions, insinuations, hypotheses and wild guesses centring on the mystery surrounding Charles Bravo's death. The case had acquired prime news value, in editions of some papers even eclipsing news of the Prince of Wales himself.

From Temple Bar came a letter bearing one of the first hints of Dr Gully's possible involvement in the strange affair, in the shape of a suggestion that all doctors, especially those residing in *Balham*, should be asked if they had purchased a large amount of antimony recently. If the newspaper's readers were puzzled by the nature of the insinuation they would be made wise in time, and it would not be long before Dr Gully's name was being bandied about in connection with the mystery.

By far the most comprehensive and expertly delivered support for a second inquest came in a letter published in *The Daily Telegraph* on 16 May, in which the writer, signing himself 'A Barrister', and seemingly an acquaintance and colleague of Charles, stated:

There can be no doubt that Mr Bravo died from the effects of a poisonous dose of antimony. Three hypotheses are possible:

a) Mr Bravo may have committed suicide.

b) That antimony may have found its way into what he took, by accident.

c) He may have been poisoned by malice.

I will deal with the hypothesis of suicide first. Mr Bravo was a young and rising man, full of life and strength, fond of society, attached to his wife to whom he had been married only four months – and, above all, entirely free from pecuniary embarrassment. It is a fact within my knowledge that up to the moment of his death, no trouble or anxiety of any kind was weighing upon him.

Although his practice was not large, he had considerable knowledge of law, and if he had wished to commit suicide he could have found in the library in his Inn all the best known treatises on forensic medicine; a glance at any of these is sufficient to negative the assumption that he deliberately poisoned himself with antimony. An intelligent man who wished to commit suicide chooses some painless drug such as chloral or opium . . .

Dismissing suicide, let me turn to the hypothesis of accident. It is certain that Mr Bravo took the poisonous dose either during his dinner or after it . . . We are consequently, if we accept the hypothesis of casualty, obliged to assume either the tartar emetic found its way into some dishes or wines during dinner, or that it was accidentally taken by Mr Bravo after dinner and before he went to bed.

Now in the first place, a large dose of tartar emetic is not the kind of thing that goes straying about a house casually. Ladies paint their eyebrows with antimony and I believe they dye their hair with it, but it is by a very unusual mischance indeed that a poisonous dose of the wife's hair dye should find its way into her husband's soup! . . . The hypothesis of accident is as absurd as that of suicide. The latter is possible but a man does not commit suicide with thirty grains of tartar emetic. Similarly, thirty grains of tartar emetic do not go straying about at random in an ordinary and well-regulated household.

But it was not only the newspaper editors who received letters on the Bravo case. So too did the principal participants in the affair. Within days of the inquest the first anonymous letters were sliding through the letter-boxes of The Priory and Florence's house in Brighton. And the police too had their own swiftly growing collection – some of which were quite bizarre. One writer, calling himself 'Justice', suggested that 'the woman calling herself Mrs Cox and companion to Mrs Bravo should be subjected to a medical examination and the *real* sex ascertained'. The writer added, 'It may be, and the idea is quite feasible, that she is a male in female disguise, for obvious reasons.'

Another letter informed Chief Inspector Clarke that Florence had been seen out driving with Dr Gully in Brighton on the day after Charles's funeral. (This could not have been, as Florence was in Balham on the day after the funeral. She went to Brighton on 3 May.)

The name of Dr James Gully having swiftly become a part of the gossip that circulated in connection with the mystery, one particular anonymous letter received by the police early in their investigations had the doctor as one of the main subjects. Written on 15 May, the letter would have been received by Chief Inspector Clarke just after his second interview of Florence in Brighton. If Florence had known of the letter and its contents there is no doubt that she would have been even more distressed than she was. The letter stated:

> I beg to report that I am told that Mrs Bravo had some intrigue with a Dr Gully before her marriage with her previous husband – Mr Ricardo – that the death of Mr Ricardo caused considerable comment at the time – that the intimacy with Gully continued throughout – that she became pregnant by him – that Gully had some hand in the death of Ricardo, who should be exhumed, and that he probably supplied the dose, if Mr Bravo has been poisoned.

The anonymous writer had been misinformed regarding certain facts, but even so there were elements of the truth in the letter – and with regard to the call for the exhumation of Alexander Ricardo, this letter was not the only one suggesting such a course.

Rumour, dissent, fact and fiction were forging the way towards more decisive action on the part of the authorities. It was clear that the law would have to act in instigating a fresh inquiry into the mysterious death of Charles Bravo, and in so doing try to establish the truth.

9

Questions and Statements

On Wednesday 17 May the jurors from the inquest, prompted by the publicity, met at the Bedford Hotel in Balham to consider whether they could further the cause of justice in the Bravo case by rectifying important omissions in the evidence. They discussed the situation at length, and a report of their meeting appeared the next day in *The Daily Telegraph*.

In the same edition space was also given to Dr Moore to enable him to refute any suggestion that he might have erred in his treatment of Charles. He wrote:

> On the night of April 18th I sent to my house for nothing save a syringe for the injection of brandy. At that time Mr Bravo was totally incapable of swallowing. I tried to administer brandy by the mouth, but finding it was running the risk of choking him, I desisted and resorted to the injection of brandy. To my knowledge he never swallowed a drug – the man could not swallow a drop of any fluid.

As to when Charles Bravo had swallowed the poison, Dr Moore stated his firm belief that it was in neither the wine nor the food, but that it was his impression that it had been drunk 'in one draught immediately before leaving the dining room, or as soon as he entered his bedroom'.

The Daily Telegraph also printed a letter from a barrister named Charles Baker, who introduced yet another disturbing element into the mystery – and one which would resurface at a later time. Said the barrister:

. . . the relatives of the deceased have reason for grave suspicion that the antimony administered to Mr Charles Bravo was not the first dose which he had swallowed. Quite recently, since his marriage, Mr Bravo arrived at his mother's house in Kensington and immediately asked for something to stay retching, adding that, coming up in the train from Balham he was quite ashamed of an attack of sickness to which all his life he was unaccustomed, and feared that his fellow passengers would think he had been drinking. This tends to show that mild doses had previously been given him, but, owing to his sound constitution he had thrown them off – until the extra dose, enough 'to kill a horse' as your correspondent so accurately points out, finally disposed of the poor fellow.

The campaign, which was gathering momentum, took a further important step on 18 May, the day following the jurors' meeting, when Mr Serjeant Simon, Liberal Member of Parliament for Dewsbury, asked the Home Secretary, Richard Cross, whether his attention had been called to 'the unsatisfactory character of the coroner's inquest on the late Charles Bravo'.

The Home Secretary, by now well acquainted with the basic facts, admitted that he was 'entirely dissatisfied with the way the inquiry had been conducted' and then informed the house that the papers in the case were being studied by the law officers of the Crown with a view to its being thoroughly investigated.

The developments as reported in the press were all going the way of the Bravo family and their fellow campaigners. While that faction heard the news with relief, however, Florence and Mrs Cox must have reacted with despair. Mrs Cox in particular was worried by the content of some of the reports and letters appearing in the press and was also very much aware that the open verdict at the inquest was proof that the jury had not accepted her word regarding Charles's admission of having taken poison. Consequently, after reading of the Home Secretary's involvement in the case, she wrote to Mr Harrison:

My dear Mr Harrison,

    The reports and comments in the papers make me most unhappy. I do wish that you would try to remember what I said to you about the poison. It is so dreadful for it to be said that I never mentioned anything about the poison until Mr Bell came. I told you I felt sure he had taken chloroform, for I smelt it when he was sick – when afterwards you said it could not be chloroform, I said, 'I feel sure he took chloroform and the bottle is empty,' and, 'he said he had taken either "some poison" or "poison"' – I forget which, and I also told you that I had given him mustard and water to make him sick, and that I had put his feet and hands in mustard and hot water, and mustard plasters on his feet. All this I did to keep him awake, as I thought, and you know you told me afterwards I could not have done better.

Do try to remember and say all you can for me. It is dreadful to have such things said as they are now doing. I know you will, with your usual kindness, forgive me troubling you, and will you kindly reply to me per return post?

> With kind regards, believe me, yours truly,
> Jane C. Cox

PS. I did not tell Dr Moore because I was expecting you every moment, and I quite thought he would recover from the effects of the chloroform, and he would be so angry at my having told he had taken poison.

Two days later she received Mr Harrison's reply.

Dear Mrs Cox,

I am willing to do my best to relieve your mind, but you did not use the word poison to me, nor did you tell me that he had told you he had taken it; but you did tell me that he had taken chloroform, and you told me so in such a manner as to imply that he was poisoned by it – but Dr Moore and I hunted for poison all over the room before Royes Bell arrived.

As you may remember we examined the liniment bottle, etc., and directly the vomiting commenced we became certain that it was an irritant poison, so that no difference could have been made in the treatment.

> Believe me, yours truly,
> George Harrison

Mr Harrison's response can have been little comfort to Mrs Cox.

To add to the anxiety of Jane Cox and Florence Bravo the small groups of sightseers that had been gathering on the steps of 38 Brunswick Terrace began to grow into considerable crowds. At the same time, in London, Mr A. K. Stephenson, Solicitor to the Treasury, had taken charge of the investigation into the case and was receiving the results of the search of The Priory and its grounds. It had lasted two days, 22 and 23 May, during which time the medicine chests belonging to Florence and Mrs Cox had been carefully examined and found to contain a great many homeopathic remedies, which, on analysis, proved to be harmless. The result of the search, in which even the drains were lifted, was that nothing of any significance was found anywhere in or near The Priory. Not surprising, perhaps, as some thirty days had elapsed since Charles's death.

But the investigation continued and by 27 May more than thirty individuals – maids, doctors, grooms, bottlers and chemists – had been formally questioned.

The two persons most closely connected with the death, however, Florence and Mrs Cox, had not been asked to make statements, which factor must have made it patently clear that they were the two prime suspects in the case. As a consequence Robert Campbell, realising that Florence's innocence would appear more convincing if she stepped forward with her own account of the tragedy, advised her to offer a voluntary statement to the police. Also aware that complicity between Florence and Mrs Cox in the commission of the dreadful crime was already proven in the minds of many, he considered it imperative that Mrs Cox approach the police with a voluntary statement at the same time.

So with this intention the two women left Brighton on 1 June and made their way to London and Henry Brooks's office in Godliman Street, near St Paul's Cathedral. From there they were escorted to the Treasury by Florence's brother William. On arrival they were introduced to Mr Stephenson who said that as their decisions to make statements were voluntary their examinations would be unofficial and therefore he would ask no questions. That said, the women, Florence preceding Mrs Cox, were conducted into his inner office to make their statements.

The statements given by them are fascinating documents, and, with study, may reveal as much – if not more – about the women themselves as about the subject, Charles.

As portrayed by Florence and Mrs Cox he is rather different from the public image presented by the newspaper accounts. His friends and colleagues had described him as a cheerful young fellow, with a lively and endearing personality, and happily married; the description of him given in the women's Treasury statements is far less appealing.

As there are similarities in various points of the two statements it has been suggested that Florence and Jane Cox collaborated over the general nature of what they would say. This does not follow, of course, for if the various events actually happened then it is *likely* that the women would remark upon them. And it is reasonable to assume that the events *referred to by both women* actually *did* take place – after all they were not that dramatic or extraordinary. However, one thing that is very interesting is that while the statements are similar in that they each present a picture of a passionately jealous man, at the same time in certain respects they differ remarkably from one another.

Florence began by giving details of her marriage to Alexander Ricardo. These were followed by an account of her meeting with Dr Gully in Malvern in 1870, her husband's addiction and their eventual separation.

Of Charles she said:

In the autumn of 1875 I met Mr C. Bravo, having been introduced to him some months before by Mrs Cox. We were married on 7th December 1875.

He was always pressing me to put down my garden and my cobs, my two great hobbies, and turn away Mrs Cox. I was paying her a salary of only £100 but he thus hoped, from all these sources, to save £400 a year. He was a very passionate man and short-tempered to the last degree. He once struck me because his mother was interfering in my household arrangements, requiring me to put down my maid. This was three or four weeks before the fatal Tuesday.

Mr Royes Bell, who attended me in my miscarriage, had recommended a change of air. Charles thought it was a useless expense. When we got to bed that night he continued very angry and at last he jumped out of bed and threatened to cut his throat. He rushed into the dressing room and I went after him and got him back.

On Good Friday last I had recovered from my second miscarriage. He was very restless. He got in an awful passion because I was very weak and had not left my bed for ten days, and he did not like my asking to be left alone to rest, as was my habit after luncheon.

He was always reading Shakespeare and we had a happy three weeks before then, and I got quite to like him and forget his meanness, which had previously disgusted me.

A compact between us before marriage was that Dr Gully's name should never be mentioned. This attachment was quite innocent and nothing improper ever passed between us. But although I never saw, heard of, or from, or spoke of Dr Gully after our marriage, he was continually, morning, noon and night speaking of him, always abusing him, calling him 'that wretch' and upbraiding me.

Her statement continued with an account of the journey to London on Tuesday 18 April. She said that as they passed Dr Gully's house a quarrel began between them and she had said she thought it 'a very cruel thing his always bringing up that name'. He admitted his error and asked her to kiss him. When she refused, he said: 'You will see what I will do when you get home.' 'He looked at me in a very determined way,' said Florence, 'and I became frightened and then I kissed him and he said I was always right.'

The statement continued with Florence's account of the bolting cob and the arrival of Joseph Bravo's letter during dinner. Said Florence:

His face worked the whole dinner, such a strange, yellow look. I thought he would go mad every minute, and if I tried to turn the subject he always returned to it.

And this was Florence's version of the night Charles was poisoned:

He came in and wished me goodnight – being so exhausted

with my first day in town I fell asleep almost directly. The next
thing I remember was being awoke by the housemaid. She said
he was ill. I got up immediately and went to my husband. He
was lying by the window, unconscious ... Not a word was
said of poison by anyone until Sir William Gull came ... When
we first married he thought I took too much sherry and I gave
it up to please him.

On Wednesday he said, 'You will take care of Katie', meaning the child of his former mistress.* He made no inquiry as to
what caused his illness.

So ended Florence's statement.

Leaving aside the two obvious lies – that her relationship with Dr
Gully had been 'innocent' and that she had given up drinking sherry
to please Charles – lies told for obvious reasons – Florence's statement effectively casts doubt on the idea that all was well with
Charles before his death; even so, nothing of his behaviour, as
revealed in her statement, could be construed as likely to lead to
suicide.

Mrs Cox's statement, however, which she gave immediately
after Florence, did more than merely corroborate this negative side
of Charles's nature; it presented a far more extreme picture.

Before she did anything else, though, Mrs Cox felt compelled to
say that she had not told the whole truth at the inquest. Now she
stated:

I was examined as a witness on the late Mr Bravo, but from
confusion and from a mistaken idea of shielding the character
of Mrs Bravo, I did not tell the full particulars, which I am now
anxious to state.

She then went on to say that whereas she originally attributed to
Charles on the night of his collapse the words, 'I have taken poison.
Don't tell Florence,' she now stated that in fact 'he said he had taken
poison *for Dr Gully*'.

Then to this the companion quickly added:

There was no cause whatever for the slightest reason for his

* Apparently Charles was not the father of the child.

committing suicide for Dr Gully and there was not the slightest
reason why I should not have stated it before. He had no reason
to take poison and she had not any communication from Dr
Gully since her marriage, and their acquaintance before marriage was, though very imprudent, I conscientiously believed,
entirely of an innocent nature.

This said, Mrs Cox went on:

On Good Friday, the first day she had come down after her
illness, he was annoyed with her for lying down after luncheon
and not wishing him to remain in the room. He was so restless,
she could not rest. He got very angry and went out of the room
and I put a match to the library fire, and he went and sat in
there. In the evening he said he despised himself for marrying
her and said she was 'a selfish pig' and that he had quite made
up his mind not to live with her, and that he was going away
and that he wished he was dead. He was in a temper. I
remained with him for some time and I said, 'What do you
think will become of Florence if you go away?' and he said,
'Let her go back to Gully!' I told him it was very wrong of him:
'You know her every thought is for you. You know she does
everything she possibly can to make you happy.'
He was quite determined, however, [that] he would go, and
when he said that he wished he was dead I said, 'It is wrong of
you to say such wicked things, as God has given you life to do
some good in.' He said goodnight but would not promise that
he would not go away. He seemed so determined that I followed him upstairs. He went up and locked his bedroom door.
I was so unhappy at thinking of his leaving the house I knocked
and told him I wanted to speak to him. He would not open it
for some time. I knocked again two or three times. He then
opened it and I begged him not to leave the house. He said he
had quite made up his mind to go and that he would not live
with her any longer. I again reasoned with him for a long time
but he seemed quite determined and shook hands, saying,
'You are a good little woman. I will always do what I can for
you.' He turned and kissed me on the cheek and said, 'Goodnight.' He thanked me again saying, 'You love Florence and
you do the best you can for me. I thank you for it.'

In the words of Mrs Cox, too, Charles was appearing as a passionately jealous man, given to sullen moods. She continued:

> I then went down and told his wife she had better go to him as he was going to leave the house. She went and I understood that he was still very angry. He was determined to go. I could not rest all night; I thought he would go.
>
> The next morning he came up to my room and asked me if Florence acknowledged she was sorry. I said that she had done nothing wrong, only resting in the afternoon, and I begged him to go down to her. About ten minutes afterwards he told me he had seen her and made it all right.

If troubled waters had been soothed on this occasion, however, according to Mrs Cox there were other disharmonies at The Priory. She went on:

> Three or four weeks before that there was a quarrel between them, I believe through a letter from his home, and he was very violent and said he would go. This was about ten or eleven at night. They usually go to bed early, and he went and unbarred the front door and went down the drive to leave the house.
>
> I followed him and entreated him to come back. He would not for some time and I said, 'Just fancy what a scandal it would be, and what will your mother say?' He said, 'Oh, my mother will be only too glad to have me back!' He seemed determined to go. I said, 'Do you think you are doing your duty as Florence's husband to leave her?' and he repeated, 'My duty!' and then he returned to the house. He went upstairs to his wife, and I rebolted the door myself for fear the servants should know anything about it.
>
> He often said how he hated Dr Gully and wished him dead. I always tried to make the peace between them. These sudden passions seemed to overtake him, because at other times he was quite pleasant. He was jealous of Dr Gully, though he knew everything before marriage.

Seeing that neither Florence's nor Mrs Cox's statements presented a picture of a man who was in any way at peace, their accounts might be taken as rather desperate bids to steer police opinion back to the theory of suicide. Certainly it was what they desired. They could not have realised, however, that the very same marital strife of which they spoke in support of a suicide theory provided equal support for a theory of murder.

When the preliminary inquiry was complete, Mr Stephenson sent to the Home Office all the papers relating to the case. From there the papers were passed to the Attorney-General, Sir John Holker, who, after carefully studying them, voiced concern over several aspects of the case – particularly Mrs Cox's statement to the Treasury to the effect that she had withheld Dr Gully's name while on oath at the inquest.

On 19 June Sir John applied to the Court of the Queen's Bench for a writ to bring about a Coroner's Inquisition, in order that the original inquest might be quashed, and that a rule *nisi* should be issued calling upon the coroner to show why a fresh inquiry should not be held.

The case came before the Lord Chief Justice, Sir Alexander Cockburn, and his learned colleagues Mr Justice Mellor and Mr Justice Field.

Before the tribunal Sir John Holker produced both the coroner's and John Reid's versions of the inquest, after which he presented an affidavit from Dr Johnson – who had changed his opinion – in which he now stated that it was his decided belief that Charles Bravo 'had not knowingly taken antimony or any other poison other than laudanum'.

Dr Johnson's affidavit also mentioned Robert Campbell's visit to him shortly before the inquest had been resumed, when the latter had said that he was confident that a verdict of suicide would be reached as he considered Sir William Gull's opinion to be beyond dispute.

The Attorney-General made reference to these factors in his appeal to the Court:

'Now my Lords, it is clear that Mr Bravo stated what practically amounted to a denial of suicide. The evidence on this important point was offered and not received. The coroner refused to receive important evidence and his doing so amounted to misconduct, which renders necessary the re-opening of the inquiry. I hope to show your Lordships that I make this application in the interest of public justice, and from a desire of ascertaining some facts which will enable the Crown to make a charge against someone.'

Sir John Holker then read Mrs Cox's statement – without mentioning the name of Dr Gully – adding that she had deliberately kept information from the jury.

After some consultation of the bench, Sir Alexander Cockburn told the Attorney-General that sufficient grounds had been shown to warrant granting a rule *nisi*.

A week later, on 26 June, the rule was made absolute, the inquest was quashed and the coroner, Mr Carter (who was absent from the proceedings owing to an attack of erysipelas), was directed to hold a fresh inquiry with a fresh jury. Said the Lord Chief Justice, who spoke on behalf of the learned gentlemen:

'It is true that the summoning of a fresh jury will involve the painful exposure of the body, but it appears to us, nevertheless, to be the best course we can adopt.'

So it was done. That most unsatisfactory inquest into Charles Bravo's death had been quashed and a new inquiry was set to take place, due to open in just two weeks.

Apart from the dramatic developments that had taken place in legal circles there had been changes, equally dramatic, in Florence's household.

Following her return from her visit to the Treasury on 1 June Florence had become very ill.

What the cause of this illness was can only be surmised, but it is known that it was of such a nature that both Dr Dill and Mrs Campbell were quickly summoned. After attending the patient, Dr Dill told Mrs Campbell that Florence was in the throes of a 'brain fever' and that her collapse was due to a severe attack of hysteria or delayed shock. Later the doctor was to tell Chief Inspector Clarke that 'she was in a most excited state and for a time had lost her reason, partly arising from drink and excitement upon the inquiry'.

It seems almost certain, however, that Florence's heavy drinking, hysteria and general collapse on that particular day had a cause involving Mrs Cox. Something had happened concerning the two women. Whatever had taken place, when Mrs Campbell went to 38 Brunswick Terrace that day she found her daughter in a state of almost total collapse and Jane Cox gone away. The companion was no longer in Florence's employ or resident in her house.

For some reason, after returning from the Treasury, Mrs Cox left Brighton and, after returning to Balham to collect her belongings from The Priory, departed for the anonymity of a lodging house in Handsworth, Birmingham. The close relationship between the women had ended, and with no obvious reason. There can be no question, though, but that the cause of the rift was a serious one; the hitherto solicitous and caring Jane Cox would never have left Florence in such a sick and vulnerable state without good reason. Or had the cause of the rift also been the cause of Florence's break-down?

Florence was later to say that it was while she was in Brighton that she was told by Mrs Cox that Charles said he had taken poison 'for Dr Gully'. If this was so, then it seems a reasonable hypothesis that it was following the return from making their Treasury statements that Mrs Cox gave Florence the information. It must have come as an enormous shock to Florence, and if, as seems likely, Mrs Cox also told her that she had spoken of it in her Treasury statement, one can imagine Florence's reaction. She would have been horrified. Not only had her friend and companion introduced Dr Gully's name into the case, but she had introduced it as the cause of Charles's suicide. Hearing such news, Florence could have had no doubt that in the event of a new inquest all her past would be exposed. Small wonder then, if, seeing Jane Cox as being respons-ible for her threatened shame and humiliation, she regarded her act as a betrayal.

While the tribunal debated the matter of the inquest during that early summer of 1876 Florence found no respite from her night-marish situation. After her collapse in Brighton she had returned with her parents to Buscot Park where, they hoped, she might regain some of her strength and start to repair her shattered emo-tions. Then, however, there came word of the decision to quash the inquest and open a new one. The news must have thrown her into the greatest despair.

While Florence, at Buscot, lived in dread of the coming inquest, Jane Cox, in her lodging house in Handsworth, felt compelled to write to Mr Harrison once more:

48, Villa Road,
Handsworth.

Dear Mr Harrison,

I am much obliged by your kind note. I wanted you to tell
me about the stomach pump. Mrs C. Bravo has told me
several times that she thought had the stomach pump been
used, Mr C. Bravo's life might have been saved. I told her you
told me afterwards it was impossible to use, and I know long
before Dr Moore arrived we could not get the strong coffee
down, his teeth were so clenched. Mrs C. Bravo said that Sir
William Gull said it might have been used, but I told her that
Sir William Gull could not know as you and Dr Moore did, the
state that Mr C. Bravo was in.

Of course this has grieved me dreadfully, and I should be
obliged if you would kindly write to me on the subject and
give me your opinion.

I remain, dear Mr Harrison,
Yours very truly,
Jane C. Cox

The underlying anxiety in the letter is plain. Clearly the writer
could not resist begging the doctor to absolve her from any blame.
Mrs Cox must have felt very much alone during those weeks of
early summer as the time of the second inquest drew nearer.

She was to see Florence just once more – that occasion being on 7
July at a meeting called in London by the Campbells. As Jane Cox
was so closely bound up in the interests of Florence it was essential
that she attend and she travelled down from Handsworth for the
purpose. There was also the matter of legal representation to discuss, which Jane Cox would need also, and which, in spite of the
estrangement between the two women, Florence's father offered to
pay for.

Also present were Henry Brooks, Mrs Campbell, James Orr and
Florence's brother, William. Rowe, the butler, was also there and
afterwards he was said to have told Mr Willis, proprietor of the
Bedford Hotel, that he had seen Mrs Cox at the meeting, adding,

'Ah, the poor old woman has got herself into a good deal of trouble from not telling the truth.'

Whether Mrs Cox had got herself into trouble remained to be seen. The new inquest was due to open, so perhaps it would not be long before the truth behind the mystery was at last exposed.

10

The Second Inquest Begins

Both the first and second inquests into Charles Bravo's death were extraordinary, but for different reasons.

The first inquest was remarkable for the fact that it was as near as could be to a private inquiry. Held in The Priory's dining room (refreshments by kindness of the widow), not only were members of the press cleverly excluded but so also was almost every other outsider. Not only that, but the coroner was extremely selective in regard to the evidence he allowed, to the extent that important testimony was not heard.

Such a discreet and almost private inquest into the death could not happen twice, however. By the time of the opening of the second inquest there was not a newspaper reader in Britain who did not know of the case, and now, with the press out in force, those millions of readers were looking forward to further developments in the fascinating case. Further, in contrast to what had taken place at the first inquest, when only the barest information had been elicited, now it seemed that every fact, both relevant and irrelevant, would be brought to light. In addition, every involved person would be examined; none would be allowed, out of misplaced consideration for feelings, to escape giving testimony.

It is sufficient to say that the coroner, having had his knuckles soundly rapped for his misconduct at the first inquest, was intent on avoiding making the mistake a second time. Consequently at the second inquest he allowed everything – the result being that with all its attendant voiced suspicion, scandal, publicity and razzmatazz, the inquiry must at times have given the appearance of an extremely bizarre and chaotic full-blown trial.

Not the least aware of this factor were those two opposing factions in the affair, the Campbells and the Bravos, the hitherto masked antipathy between whom was soon to be exposed in all its bitterness.

The Campbells in particular, with Florence being very much, if obliquely, under attack, must have felt extremely pressed, and Robert Campbell set out to hire for her the best legal representation available. In the event he hired the services of Sir Henry James, QC, and Mr Biron, QC. Sir Henry James, one-time Solicitor-General and Attorney-General, demanded a fee of 100 guineas a day.

Florence's father also enlisted the services of Mr Murphy, QC, on behalf of Jane Cox – at the cost of a further 50 guineas a day.

Acting for Joseph Bravo was Mr George Lewis, a young lawyer fast making a name for himself in legal circles. A ruthless examiner, he was to receive a fee of £1000 for his services, his participation serving as the springboard for a very successful legal career.

Dr Gully took the precaution of instructing Mr Serjeant Parry to watch the proceedings on his behalf.

The Crown was represented by Mr John Gorst, QC, and Mr Harry Poland,* assisted by no less a person than the Attorney-General, Sir John Holker.

As for Mr William Carter, the coroner, he – probably in view of the incompetence he had previously shown – was allocated the assistance of a legal assessor in the shape of Mr Burleigh Muir.

So, on the morning of 11 July, with a more impressive array of legal talent than was likely to have been found at the Old Bailey, the participants in the case converged on the billiards room of the Bedford Hotel for the extraordinary legal confrontation that was to take place.

The Balham Mystery, a contemporary broadsheet devoted to the case (released in seven parts, price 1d each), described the venue for the proceedings:

> The accommodation presented by the Bedford Hotel at Balham is unusually ample. Not only is the inquest room of much larger dimensions than one might expect to find in so

* John Gorst, Harry Poland and George Lewis subsequently received knighthoods.

comparatively quiet a locality, but the Hotel affords the additional advantage of a series of rooms for separately locating the
various classes of witnesses summoned to give evidence; as
well as others of the jury and the numerous members of the
legal profession who are engaged in this remarkable inquiry.

From the moment that the Coroner's officer announced to
Mr Charles Willis, the proprietor of the Bedford Hotel, that it
was decided to hold the second inquest there, no pains were
spared to make every possible provision for the general comfort of all.*

Outside the hotel that morning, well before the doors were open
to the public, many had gathered hoping to gain entrance or to catch
glimpses of the various individuals as they arrived to take their parts
in the proceedings. Once the doors were opened there was much
pushing and shoving to get inside. Even though the accommodation was spacious, many were turned away, and instead of having
ringside seats they had to be satisfied with the reports that were
brought out, or with the accounts that appeared in the newspapers
the next day.

Those spectators fortunate enough to gain access to the billiards
room found it already congested with legal gentlemen and repor-
ters. The rope-rack along one wall of the room was strewn with
black top hats, three deep in places, and there was hardly enough
space for a weary elbow between the hats and Gladstone bags that
were spread over the massive table in the centre. At the same time it
was noted that in the crowded and informal setting much of the
solemnity of the Law was lost.

The jury of seventeen was made up of local tradesmen, of
whom one Mark Cattley had been appointed foreman. Once order
had been established among the spectators the coroner addressed the
jury, urging them to dismiss from their minds all that they had read
and heard on the subject and to base their judgement purely on the
evidence they would hear upon oath, and, thereafter, 'without

* Mr Willis was not so accommodating after the inquest. He wrote to the Home
Secretary demanding compensation for the damage done to the Bedford Hotel. He
said that the seats had to be re-upholstered and the banisters replaced; even the
brickwork was crumbling, he said. The Home Secretary suggested that the money
Mr Willis made on the increased sale of food and drink was compensation enough.

favour or affectation to anyone' to give their verdict truly upon their conscience, 'upon the evidence of the different witnesses'.

He then informed them, in compliance with the law, that they had a duty to perform, that they must needs go by train to Norwood Cemetery 'where everything will be provided ready for you to see the person whose death we are about to inquire into'. After seeing the body, he added, they would return and begin to hear evidence with regard to the circumstances attending the death.

On arrival at the cemetery the jury found that under a temporarily erected screen of wood and canvas the coffin had been raised above the ground and placed on trestles. The lid had been removed and part of the lead lining cut away. A panel of glass had been inserted into the opening and through this the coroner and the jurors, one by one, viewed the head of the corpse. Wrote the reporter in *The Balham Mystery*:

> The morning was exceedingly sultry, and the closeness of the atmosphere was rendered still more oppressive by the pungent odour of the disinfectants used in order to enable the coroner and jury to perform their sad task with comparative immunity.

It proved to be an even more unpleasant task than had been anticipated. It came as a great shock to those present to find that in spite of the costly coffin and the leaden inner shell the flesh of the corpse was blackened, and so badly decomposed that the features were almost obliterated. As reported in *The Balham Mystery*:

> It was a remarkable fact that while the oak coffin and its ormolu handles presented to the eye . . . all the freshness of polish and lustre of their pristine condition, the head of the deceased gentleman exhibited every sign of the most rapid decay. The face had acquired the dark hue of a mummy, and the teeth were almost entirely black. This rapidity of decay was much remarked upon by those who were present.*

---

* Yseult Bridges, in her book *How Charles Bravo Died*, states that Charles's body was serene, 'as though life had just fled'. This was not so. Since Charles's death there have been a few recorded cases of death by *slow* antimonial poisoning where the bodies of the victims have been remarkably preserved – for instance in

When the melancholy and gruesome task was complete, the jury returned to the Bedford Hotel and the examination of the witnesses began.

Before presenting an account of the various examinations it should be established that a full transcript of all that passed at the inquest would take up far more space than the present authors have at their disposal. Certain newspapers of the time did publish daily verbatim accounts which, often covering a full, large page, sometimes ran to more than 20,000 words. When it is realized that only four such pages used more words than one would find in the average novel and that the proceedings covered twenty-three working days it will be fully understood why it is necessary to present here an edited version of the inquiry.

The first witness called was the undertaker, Mr Mold, who stated that the remains seen by the jury were indeed those of Charles Bravo.

The next witness, Mr Joseph Bravo, was then called.

After the coroner had asked him a series of rather perfunctory questions, a juror asked whether it was Sir William Gull who had told Charles that he was going to die. Joseph Bravo replied:

'He was told he was going to die ten or twelve times before he saw Dr Gull.'

There then followed a long-winded interchange between Sir Henry James and the other learned gentlemen as to the order which the questioning should take. When the matter was settled to their satisfaction Joseph Bravo was examined by his representative, George Lewis, who established that Charles had become Joseph Bravo's stepson when he was four years old. Said Bravo:

'I brought him up and I educated him, and at the age of twenty-one he desired to assume the name of Bravo.'

The jury heard then that Charles had been very fond of his family, especially his mother who, they learned, was 'in a state of very great mental stress and quite unable to be seen by anyone'.

Charles Bravo was an intellectual man, Joseph Bravo stated. He

---

the case of Mary Chapman, who died in 1897, and whose body was exhumed in 1902. But this was not so in the case of Charles Bravo, for he died of a concentrated dose of antimony.

had been educated at Oxford and was very fond of debate. He was very interested in medicine and often attended the operating theatres at King's College Hospital (of which Joseph Bravo himself was a governor). He was a man of courage and showed no tendency towards self-destruction and as far as his stepfather was aware was in no need of money.

Between the time of his son's marriage and death, Joseph Bravo said he had given Charles about £1100. And, furthermore, he said, his stepson knew 'he had only to apply and he got what he wished, in reason, and he had done so all his life'. Added the witness, 'I told the manager [of Charles's bank] that his account should never run down under £100 and that he should always have £100 to his credit.'

Having established that Charles had no apparent money worries, George Lewis produced three letters that Charles had sent to his parents shortly before his death. They were written in a light-hearted vein, concentrating on domestic matters and seemingly free of any hidden worries. In one of the letters, written on 16 April, just two days before he was poisoned, he had written:

> . . . poor Florence is still very weak. Royes ordered her to stay in bed which she is unwilling to do in this beautiful weather. She's to go to the seaside as soon as she is well enough. Mrs Cox is very kind and useful. I drove yesterday to Norwood to see Mrs Harford whose husband I think you know. He has been good enough to get some oats at the wholesale place where they are not only cheaper but better than they are here. Our fields are to be bush-harrowed and rolled tomorrow with a view to our getting a good crop of hay from them . . . Our third gardener is too good for us and cannot touch his cap or carry a parcel to the station, so I am going to give him a chance of bettering himself. I will never keep a servant who finds that it is 'not his place' to do what he is ordered to do . . .

Joseph Bravo told the court that Charles was always in good spirits and full of fun. He had last seen him, he said, on 15 March, at a charity dinner where he had appeared in good health and spirits, having brought along several friends to dine with him. The witness then said that he and his family had gone to stay at St Leonards-on-Sea, and he had not seen Charles again until he was called to his bedside on Wednesday 19 April. When he arrived at The Priory, he said, he was told that Charles was seriously ill, and was instructed 'to keep him as quiet as possible and to feed him as much as he could take, as those were the only means to restore his life'.

In answer to further questions the witness stated that Florence Bravo had made no attempt to account for her husband's illness, and that when Mrs Cox told him that Charles had said that he had taken poison he had declared that it was 'nonsense'.

Asked about the friendship between Charles and his cousin, Royes Bell, Joseph Bravo said, 'They grew up from boyhood together with great love and affection.' He then told the jury that after Sir William Gull had left the sickroom Charles had called out 'with a voice louder than I had any idea he possessed' that he wanted to speak to Sir William, and that when Sir William had come back into the room Charles had said to him very earnestly that what he had told him was the truth.

The witness then told the court that Charles had been a truthful man, believing suicide to be an act of cowardice, a point he had often debated with his stepfather. Asked about Mrs Cox, the witness said he had known her since 1868 and had assisted her in placing her children in school when her fortunes had been low.

When a juror asked Joseph Bravo the exact nature of Mrs Cox's position at The Priory he replied:

'Mrs Cox was Florence's companion. She had a salary and she had a seat at his table. She had certain expenditure in relation to travelling when they moved about and in one way or another my son estimated the probable cost to him would be £300 or £400 a year. I agreed with him that it was not a wise thing to tax his establishment with that charge. I suggested that she should go to Jamaica but she declined to go.'

George Lewis then turned to Charles's emotional state before his death, asking:

'Did your son at any time by speech or manner indicate that he had any feelings of jealousy towards anybody? Did he ever mention the name of Dr Gully?'

Said Joseph Bravo, 'Never,' and added that Charles and his wife seemed very happy together. However, when George Lewis asked if Florence 'seemed much grieved' during the time he was in the house, the witness replied, 'Not particularly so,' and went on to

complain that the Campbell family had consumed large dinners as
Charles lay critically ill upstairs.

Florence's letters to Joseph Bravo after the funeral were then read
to the court, and there was further analysis of Charles's financial
credit at the time of his death. The court was told that Charles's
professional income varied but that he averaged £200 a year. Joseph
Bravo admitted that his son was 'quick in temper' but denied that he
had violent outbursts of temper.

A juror then asked about the woman in Maidenhead who
Florence believed had been pressing her husband for money, to
which Joseph Bravo replied that until his son's death he had not
heard of her. On the subject of Charles's finances he said that on his
marriage he, the witness, had made a settlement of £20,000, to take
effect on the death of himself and his wife. He added that Charles
knew that if he was pressed for money he could always approach his
stepfather for 'any amount of money within reason'.

Questioned by Sir Henry James (for Florence), the witness was
asked if there was any reason why Charles had been unable to talk
freely to his family and friends during his illness. Joseph Bravo
replied:

'Certainly. He was ordered to keep quiet,' adding that because of
the doctor's strict instructions Charles had spoken very few words
to his parents.

Asked if Charles would have seen antimony in the stables at
Palace Green, Joseph Bravo said that although he had kept horses all
his life he had never used antimony in his stables.

Joseph Bravo was then questioned about the mysterious bout of
sickness that Charles had suffered early in March. In reply he said:

'On the morning that he came to my house at Palace Green, and
was ill, he said he was sick between Balham Station and his house;
and he was afraid the persons along the road must have thought he
was drunk the night before. When he got to Palace Green a sharp
attack of the bowels took place. It was between nine and ten when
he got there, and he looked very ill. His mother suggested various
remedies, all of which he refused. He took a glass of Curaçao, which
seemed to relieve him, and he left, saying he was going to chambers.
He never before his marriage suffered or complained of nausea or
sickness. He had been with me to Jamaica several times, and never
suffered from sickness even on the voyage.'

'Can you say what was the cause of that illness?'

'No. I never knew him to suffer from vomiting and purging at the same time.'

Later, on the subject of Charles's fatal illness, the witness added: 'My son died in the most dreadful agony, there is no doubt of that.'

At one point a juror asked Joseph Bravo if he had spoken to Charles about Mrs Cox's alleged poison statement. Bravo said:

'No, for this reason, that I was told by his medical men to keep him perfectly quiet and I did not desire to agitate him in any way.'

When asked by Mr Gorst (for the Crown) if Charles had about £1000 at his command when he died, Joseph Bravo replied that 'he had a great deal more than that'.*

The inquest being adjourned at this point, it was announced that the court would sit from 10.30 to 4.30 each day; it was also estimated that the inquiry would last a week.

So the first day of the second inquest was over, and during it Joseph Bravo had given the jury the impression that Charles had been entirely free from emotional and financial problems before his death and was, without doubt, a most unlikely man to commit suicide.

So far, in spite of the general air of anticipation, the nature of the proceedings had been calm and controlled. There was no hint of the fact that the inquiry, estimated to run for a week, would run well into the next month. And no one could foresee that during that time, with the drama and emotions running at their highest, certain witnesses would leave the packed courtroom with their reputations stripped bare, their lives in ruin from which they would never recover.

* Charles left £14,000 in his will.

A Very Capricious Poison

With so many people crowding into the billiards room of the
Bedford Hotel there was concern over whether the floor could
withstand the weight, and before proceedings began on Wednesday
12 July one of the jurors, who was a surveyor, was consulted. After
giving his opinion that the floor would bear the load the inquiry was
resumed.

Before any witnesses were called, George Lewis (for Mr and Mrs
Joseph Bravo) brought up the matter of the 'woman in Maidenhead'
and whether the £500 received from her sister had been a loan or had
been entrusted to Charles for investment on her behalf. In respect of
this he read – taking care not to reveal her name – a letter written by
the sister about three weeks before Charles's death, and which had
been taken from the deceased's chambers:

> Dear Charley,
>
>   You can keep the money as long as you wish. What made me
> write, I fancied you thought it troubled you to keep it any
> longer. I know you give me more interest than I could get
> elsewhere. God knows that every £5 is a consideration for so
> small an income as mine.
>
> >   I trust you and your wife are well,
> >   believe me, yours ever . . .

Clearly, the letter did little to support Florence's insistence that her
husband was being pressed for money by his former mistress. Two

other letters from the woman's sister were read to the court and they contained no hint of malice or antipathy regarding the return of the £500.*

Florence's solicitor, Mr Henry Brooks, was called as the first witness of the day. Questioned by Mr George Lewis he confirmed that he had advertised a reward of £500 for the discovery of the chemist who supplied the antimony, that the advertisement had appeared in twelve newspapers on seven consecutive days, but that there had been no occasion to pay the reward.

After Mr Brooks had stepped down his place was taken by Dr Joseph Moore. After being sworn the doctor, in reply to various questions, gave the following testimony:

'I am a doctor residing in Balham. I was requested to go to The Priory on the night of April 18th last. I found Mr Bravo in his bedroom leaning back in the armchair. Mrs Cox was rubbing his chest with liniment. He was totally unconscious. The heart's action was almost suspended. I was apprehensive it would cease every moment. He looked as if under a narcotic poison, but I could not find the usual symptoms. I detected no effluvia from him, only the mustard from the plasters he had on him. I did not think he would live an hour. This was about half-past ten. Mrs Cox told me she gave him mustard to make him vomit. I did not see any vomit. The butler and I put him on the bed to relieve the heart as much as possible. I endeavoured to give him some brandy to stimulate the heart's action, but he was unable to swallow. Mrs Bravo and Mrs Cox were both in the room, or in and out constantly. I remained with him until five o'clock in the morning. Mr Harrison was the next doctor who arrived, about three-quarters of an hour after I did. The symptoms all pointed to the giving out of the heart but the body was well-developed with no appearance of heart disease. I made a search of the room – we found chloroform and laudanum and a strong liniment of ammonia and camphor, but we found nothing to account for his symptoms. There was a gaslight burning in the room, and a fire. I noticed no fragments of paper or any indication of anything having been destroyed by burning in the fire. Mr Bravo in no way said in my hearing anything to account for his condition. Mr Royes Bell and Dr Johnson arrived at half-past two.'

* Mr Joseph Bravo later made it known that if the sum of £500 was owed to the sister of the woman in Maidenhead he would see that it was repaid to her.

Dr Moore then told the court that although the doctors had questioned Charles about what he had taken, he only repeated that he had used laudanum for his toothache. When asked by a juror if Mrs Cox had mentioned Charles's alleged statement regarding having taken poison he said that she had not mentioned it to him at all.

He went on to say then that when he arrived at The Priory, Mrs Cox had been in ordinary dress and Mrs Bravo in her dressing-gown. Accounting for her husband's condition, Mrs Bravo had told him that he had been shaken and fatigued by a bolting horse. Mrs Bravo, he said, 'was very much grieved' at her husband's condition.

George Lewis rose here to ask whether at this stage the doctors had talked openly of poison. Dr Moore replied:

'I do not remember that we did. They saw us examining the bottles. We discussed the matter of poison between ourselves but whether they could hear us or not, I do not know. While this was going on Mrs Cox made no communication to me that the deceased had told her that he'd taken poison, nor did she state anything which could account for his condition.'

The doctor then said that he and Mr Harrison had only searched the sickroom. He had noticed a water bottle in the room, he said, but did not remember seeing a glass or tumbler over it. He added that Charles Bravo had suffered 'very great pain indeed', pain which was 'very shocking'. After describing the patient's return to consciousness, he said that Charles 'treated his wife with affection'. 'I saw no trace of temper between them,' he said, 'and from the time he recovered consciousness to the time I left, I saw nothing but affectionate intercourse between them.'

Further questioning brought from the doctor the information that Mrs Bravo had burst into tears when she learned the seriousness of her husband's condition. 'Her grief and whole conduct appeared quite natural and real under the circumstances,' he said, after which he told the court of the pathetic spectacle of Florence falling asleep with her arms around her unconscious husband.

He went on then to say that if Charles, after regaining conscious-ness, had 'entertained any suspicion of foul play towards him' he had been 'quite able to give expression to such a suspicion'.

Continuing with his testimony, Moore stated that when he returned to The Priory at eleven o'clock the next morning Charles had seemed a little better; he had shaken the witness's hand and thanked him for coming the night before and said that he hoped to see him again when he was better.

·Later, with regard to the use of antimony as a poison, the doctor told the court that he had never had a case of poisoning with antimony in his life. 'Very few medical men have,' he said, adding, 'I cannot say I have ever heard of a case of suicide by antimony.' As to the effects of antimony on different persons he stated: 'The quantity which will destroy life depends on the condition of the person taking it. There are cases on record of a person taking a very large dose and recovering afterwards.'

There followed further evidence concerning antimony and its various effects, in the course of which the doctor stated that ten grains in water would induce vomiting in fifteen minutes, and that the mixing of such a quantity in water would have no perceptible effect on the appearance of the water. He further stated that if tartar emetic was stirred up to effect a solution 'there would be *nothing observable* to the eye'. He emphasised, however, that antimony would not be soluble in wine or other alcohol as the tannin would produce 'a muddy appearance quite perceptible to the eye'.

George Lewis then asked him what would be the effect of mixing ten or twenty grains of antimony in solid food. Dr Moore replied firmly:

'Oh, it would produce vomiting at once.'

Asked if he ever prescribed antimony in water in the course of his medical practice, the doctor said that he did, adding that although it was soluble in *cold* water, 'it was infinitely more soluble in *warm* or *hot* water'. To emphasise this point he said that whereas thirty grains of antimony would dissolve in a quantity of cold water, four hundred and eighty grains would dissolve in only two ounces of boiling water.

Questioned regarding chloroform and laudanum, he said that the very small amount of antimony that would dissolve in either of those medicines would be quite harmless.

Dr Moore's evidence was most important. The information he had given concerning the effects of tartar emetic indicated not only that the poison had not been contained in the bottles of chloroform or laudanum, but also that it had not been in the food or the wine which Charles had consumed at dinner. If it had been in either of the latter he would have vomited much earlier, probably while still in the dining room.

With no further questions Dr Moore was allowed to step down and after a short adjournment the next witness Mr George Harrison, was sworn in.

After telling the court that he was a surgeon, resident in Streatham, he said that shortly after ten o'clock on Tuesday 18 April he had been met at his house by the Bravos' servant, Parton, and summoned to The Priory. On arrival there, he said, Mrs Cox had given him an account of Charles's seizure, but without mentioning that he had been sick out of the window. She told him that she was sure that he had taken chloroform. On being shown to the sickroom he had found the patient in a state of collapse and Dr Moore in attendance. At two-thirty, he continued, Mr Royes Bell and Dr Johnson arrived and the four doctors discussed the patient's condition, whereupon it was decided that Dr Johnson should take charge of the case. Before regaining consciousness, he said, the patient had vomited and passed a bloody fluid.

George Lewis then asked him if these symptoms had given 'rise to the suspicion that he was labouring under the effects of an irritant poison'. Mr Harrison replied that they 'confirmed it'.

Asked about the water bottle in the sickroom, Harrison said, somewhat surprisingly:

'My impression is that the water bottle was on the centre of the table and that the water had been used by Dr Moore in trying to give the patient brandy and water, and I used it for the same purpose.'

Regarding Charles's alleged admission of having taken poison, which Mrs Cox had related to Dr Johnson and himself, Harrison said, 'I asked her why she had not told me before, and she said she thought she *had* told me. I believe my next words were, "You certainly did not; you told me you were sure that he had taken chloroform."'

Questioned further by Mr Lewis, Mr Harrison said that he was positive that Mrs Cox had not mentioned poison, and he was sure she was 'mistaken altogether'.

The witness then told the court that he was the family physician and had treated Florence before her marriage to Charles. He had also attended her during her miscarriage in January of that year.

Asked if Florence had displayed anxiety over her husband's condition, Mr Harrison said that she most certainly had, and that it was at her request that he wrote to Royes Bell asking him to attend Charles and bring a colleague of his choice.

Following this there was further reference to Florence's lapse into sleep beside her unconscious husband, added to which Mr Harrison said there was 'no sign of feigning on her part' and that 'her grief seemed quite genuine'.

A juror asked the witness then if he had informed Charles of Mrs Cox's statement about his having admitted taking poison. Mr Harrison replied:

'No, I did not, because at the time I considered Dr Johnson had taken management of the case and that he would have done so if he considered it necessary.'

The final chapter of Mr Harrison's testimony concerned his own experience of antimony, when he revealed that he had once accidentally taken a dose of tartar emetic. The quantity, he estimated, had amounted to no more than five grains. The effect, however, had been dramatic; he told the court:

'I began to feel very queer and vomited. The vomiting and diarrhoea went on for several hours until I was exhausted.'

This ended Mr Harrison's evidence and the court was adjourned until the following day.

The jurors were left with an interesting fact to dwell upon. Mr Harrison's estimate that *his* accidental dose of tartar emetic had comprised no more than five grains made one point very clear: if someone had administered upwards of forty grains to Charles Bravo such a massive dose had been surely meant to kill him.

At the resumption of the inquiry the next morning, Thursday 13 July, it was noted that Mr Murphy QC was in court to watch the proceedings on behalf of Mrs Cox.

The first witness to be called was Royes Bell – full name Hutchinson Royes Bell – who stated that he was a surgeon residing at 44 Harley Street, and was a cousin of the deceased. He said that soon after Charles had regained consciousness he had been sent for. Then: 'Mrs Cox made a statement to me,' he said. 'She gave me to understand that my cousin had taken poison.' He said he had been annoyed with her, saying to her, 'It's no good sending for doctors if you don't tell them what is the matter!'

Questioned further, he stated: 'I went out of the room and called Dr Johnson immediately. I made no further remark to Mrs Cox. I did not take any notice of Mrs Cox. Dr Johnson was in the sickroom at the time with Mr Bravo, and he accompanied me to the end room where Mrs Cox made the statement to me. She told Dr Johnson that my cousin had taken poison. I cannot tell the precise time but it would be between three and four in the morning.'

He added that when Mrs Cox was asked to comment on the cause of Charles's condition she suggested that he had taken chloroform.

Further questioning drew the information that after making her poison statement to Royes Bell and Dr Johnson, Mrs Cox did not return to the sickroom when the latter confronted Charles with the statement she had made.

'We went back into the sickroom,' Royes Bell said, 'and Dr Johnson told my cousin, "Mrs Cox says that you have taken poison." Charles replied that he hadn't taken anything but laudanum. Dr Johnson said that laudanum wouldn't explain his symptoms but Charles said he could give no other explanation.

'We looked around the room and made a search. We found a blue-fluted chloroform bottle which was empty and a laudanum bottle that was not quite empty. There was a bottle of Condy's Fluid and a bottle of camphor liniment. I observed nothing more.'

The witness confirmed his long friendship with Charles, describing him as a man of good health and spirits, and a truthful man – in fact rather outspoken. They were like brothers, he said, adding: 'When his parents went to Jamaica, he used to live with us, so there was no reason why he should not have spoken frankly at all. From my knowledge of him of twenty-five years I can certainly say he was not a likely man to commit suicide. During the three days I was with him before his death there was nothing in his conduct, demeanour or language which could induce me to believe that he had committed suicide.'

Royes Bell then told the court how Charles had asked him to read some prayers at his bedside but because he was too overcome with emotion his (witness's) voice 'was not quite strong enough'. He continued: 'Charles then offered up a very nice extempore prayer of his own and said the Lord's Prayer. This was after the doctor had gone and we were alone. He was not a man of very strong religious feeling.'

Asked by Mr George Lewis if he had noticed any ill feeling between Charles and Florence he answered:

'Just the opposite. When she came in early in the morning he kissed her and used some French expressions. He appeared pleased to see her and commissioned me to ask his mother "to be kind to Florence".'

Concerning Mrs Cox, he said that he had not known her before Charles married Florence and that he knew nothing of her circumstances. However, he said, Charles treated her with great kindness and consideration. He knew this was so as Charles was 'a man who was very communicative to his friends about his private affairs – rather *too* communicative, as he told everything'.

The witness then told the court that when the doctors tried to give Charles some laudanum to deaden his pain, he objected violently and spat it out.

The final piece of Royes Bell's testimony was particularly interesting, and perhaps significant. Asked about the post-mortem results in which the upper part of the alimentary canal had been found to be 'surprisingly free from inflammation', he said that 'supposing the poisonous dose was the very first one that Mr Charles Bravo had ever taken', he would have 'expected to find the stomach and small intestine highly inflamed'.

It seems clear: Bell was suggesting that judging by the condition of the stomach and small intestine of the deceased, the dose of tartar emetic that had proved fatal to him was perhaps *not the first dose* he had taken.

The first witness after lunch was Dr George Johnson who stated that Royes Bell had called at his house at 11 Savile Row about half-past one on the morning of 19 April and asked him to accompany him to The Priory. The witness described the patient's condition and then told of Royes Bell coming to fetch him to hear a statement which had just been made by Mrs Cox. Said Dr Johnson:

'What she said to me was this: "When Mr Bravo was taken ill he said to me, 'I've taken some of that poison, but don't tell Florence.'"'

Dr Johnson continued: 'I immediately went back to the patient's bedside, and said, "Mrs Cox tells us that you have spoken to her of having taken poison. What is the meaning of that?" His reply was,

"I do not remember having spoken of having taken poison." I said, "Have you taken poison?" He replied, "I have rubbed some laudanum on my gums for neuralgia and I may have swallowed some." I said, "That will not explain your symptoms."'

The doctor then described the search of the sickroom and listed the various bottles found. At this Mr Lewis asked if the court might see the bottles but Chief Inspector Clarke said he only had the laudanum bottle; the other bottles had been destroyed following the closing of the first inquest.

Dr Johnson continued: 'I did not notice any glass or tumbler containing any sediment. We particularly looked for that, and there was no residue of poison anywhere. I was nearly three hours with him that night and he suffered terribly, passing blood and vomiting. I suspected that he might have taken arsenic and I took away some fluid to test for arsenic without finding any. Arsenic was the only thing we looked for.'

The doctor then proceeded to outline his subsequent visits to The Priory during Charles's illness and described the manner in which Sir William Gull had tried, unsuccessfully, to elicit a confession from the sick man.

Mr Lewis then asked the witness if at any time Charles had made inquiries as to the cause of his illness. The doctor replied that he had not, but that he, witness, 'was not much surprised at this'. He added, 'You must remember that he was terribly ill the whole time. He was like a patient suffering all the horrors of sea-sickness with the addition of the torturing effects of an irritant poison on the stomach – and that makes a man very indifferent to many matters, which otherwise he would think very much of. I was not surprised at his not asking questions. I had directed him to be quiet.'

Questioned further, Dr Johnson told the court that he thought Mrs Cox knew that Charles had denied her poison statement. He said that he had inadvertently mentioned poison in Florence's hearing and turning to Mrs Cox she had asked if Charles had said he had taken poison; the companion said firmly that he had. Dr Johnson had been surprised at this dialogue. He told the court:

'My first feeling was one of regret that I had referred to the subject. Then I was a little surprised that Mrs Bravo did not appear more astonished on hearing it for the first time. The remaining part of the time I saw nothing that led me to suppose that she was otherwise than most anxious for her husband's recovery.'

With regard to the use of antimony as a poison, Dr Johnson said: 'It is remarkable how few cases of fatal poisoning by antimony have been recorded. Its violent emetic action prevents its destroying life. It is soon rejected from the stomach. The sooner the poison is thrown off the stomach the less likely it is to be absorbed into the blood. Mr Bravo was killed *not* by the local irritant action on the stomach, but by its becoming absorbed into the system where it produced fatal results. Unquestionably, during those four hours of unconsciousness, the poison was being absorbed into the circulation and it was that which killed him.'

He went on: 'The proper antidote for antimony is a vegetable astringent which would render antimony insoluble and therefore less active. Such an astringent would be wine or burgundy. It would be much more active in a solution of water, being soluble and more easily absorbed into the system.'

He estimated that there were between thirty and forty grains of antimony in Charles's body, and repeated his opinion that tartar emetic mixed with burgundy would make it very turbid and the precipitation would be easily seen, especially to someone like Charles who 'knew his wines'.

A juror put the final question to Dr Johnson:

'Did you ask Mrs Cox how it was that she concealed so long the fact that Mr Bravo had taken poison?'

No,' replied the witness, 'I did not.'

Mr Frederick Haynes MacCalmont was called next. After stating that he was a barrister-at-law, and that he had occupied business chambers with the deceased at 1 Essex Court, Temple, he described his meeting with Charles on the day he was poisoned.

'We went to Victoria Station where he took the 4.05 train to Balham,' he said. 'I was with him nearly half an hour. He was in excellent health and spirits; not in any way depressed; rather the reverse.'

MacCalmont described their arrangement to play lawn tennis on the Wednesday, then went on: 'I knew both him and his wife. I thought they were on excellent terms as man and wife. In my opinion he was the last man in the world who would be likely to commit suicide. I can only say that he was truthful to a fault; that is to say, he was more outspoken than was always judicial.'

MacCalmont said that Charles had always spoken quite freely

about his marriage, appeared to be very happy and had never shown any form of jealousy towards anyone. As far as he knew, the lady in Maidenhead had been very reasonable about Charles's marriage and had made no demands on him whatsoever. Charles, he said, had been free from financial worries of any kind, and knew that he could always ask his father for money if he needed any.

At this point, after the witness's deposition had been read, the court was adjourned for the day.

Next day, Friday 14 July, the inquest began as usual with the prompt assembly of the legal gentlemen, at which time it was noted that Dr Gully's solicitor, Henry Kimber, was also present.

The courtroom was extremely crowded that morning, with people jostling each other for the most advantageous places, for word had spread that Sir William Gull would appear and there was much eagerness to see the celebrated man. And the spectators were not disappointed, for Sir William was called as the first witness of the day. Both his appearance and his reputation were impressive and when he entered the courtroom he seemed to be fully aware of the rapt attention he commanded. He began his evidence with confidence, stating:

'I am a physician residing at 74 Brook Street. On April 20th last I received a request in writing to see the late Mr Bravo. I have the letter with me.'

Florence's letter was then read to the court, after which Sir William said that in consequence of it he went to The Priory. He received the note from Mrs Cox, he said. She brought it to his house and delivered it personally to him in his study, though she made no statement as to the cause of the illness. 'Finally,' he said, 'an arrangement was made for me to go with Dr Johnson and we drove down together in my carriage.'

On the way to Balham, said Sir William, Dr Johnson had given him the details of the case, including a description of the symptoms displayed. Sir William said that finding the patient in a very serious condition he had urged him to account for his illness, but the patient had spoken only of laudanum.

Asked if he had been told that Charles had denied taking anything but laudanum, the witness seemed confused and said:

'He spoke to me of nothing of what he had communicated to the medical men, that I can remember. I could not swear that Dr Johnson made no such statement to me, as far as I can remember, that is, as we drove down, or before we went into the room.'

This rather incoherent reply was followed by a lengthy debate on the exact words used by Charles during his conversation with Sir William Gull. However, the witness seemed very unsure of details and began to show signs of irritation. Undaunted, George Lewis (for Joseph Bravo) began a heated exchange with him in an attempt to encourage him to be more precise in his answers. As a result Sir William became angry and told the coroner that he strongly objected to Mr Lewis's attitude. The young lawyer, though, refusing to be intimidated by the illustrious witness, asked him again for the exact words used by the dying man. Sir William answered truculently:

'I do not remember the words.'

Sir Henry James (for Florence) glossed over this inadequate reply by asking the witness if Charles had shown surprise when told he was dying. Sir William said that he had been 'much astonished' that Charles had shown 'no expression of surprise'.

Sir William was now showing obvious signs of unease and throughout the questioning that followed stubbornly avoided giving a direct answer, especially when asked the exact time that he knew about Mrs Cox's poison statement. He was uncommunicative about Florence too, saying:

'I saw her, I should think, for twenty seconds. She came into the room. I just saw her come into the room and embrace her husband for a moment. I do not remember that she spoke to me.'

As the inquiry progressed Sir William was repeatedly asked to reconsider his recall of events. It seemed, however, that anything other than suicide was contrary to his brief, while it also became clear that he was finding his present situation extremely difficult. On one point, adamantly and defensively, he said:

'I was taken to his bedside to see a man dying of poison. I should never have been sent for for that. People do not send for me if people are lying dying of poison. I think Mrs Bravo would hardly have written to me to see her husband had she been informed he was dying of poison. She would have said, "My husband is dying of poison – pray see if you can save him."'

After repeating that Mrs Cox had delivered the note to him but had made no statement as to the cause of Charles's illness he was asked by Mr Lewis – who was not satisfied that Sir William had not known about the poison until he reached The Priory: 'Had not Dr Johnson told you as you drove down that it was an irritant poison of some kind?'

Sir William replied: 'He said he *thought* it was an irritant poison.'

Mr Lewis then made way for Mr Gorst (for the Crown), who asked if it was possible for a man to be 'so ill that, although his mind is perfectly clear, he feels indifferent to his surroundings and even to his own life, as with seasickness'.

'I think it is likely,' conceded Sir William.

'Is that the kind of state that tartarised antimony produces?'

'I think it is likely.'

Thus, Mr Gorst cleverly demolished the value of Sir William's statement that he had been surprised that Charles had seemed indifferent to the cause of his agony.

Next to be called was Professor Theophilus Redwood, who, unlike the previous witness, was sure of his facts and answered throughout in a direct manner. He began by stating that he was an analytical chemist and had been Professor of Chemistry to the Pharmaceutical Society for thirty years. Over a period of three days, 21 to 23 April, he said, he received certain bottles and jars containing various matters from the body of the deceased. Among the substances were vomit and a bloody fluid emitted by the dying man. Another container held part of the stomach and liver of the deceased. Another, a bottle, held a quantity of laudanum. The professor stated that he had found no antimony in the laudanum, but it had been present in the vomit, the bloody fluid and the liver. Ten grains of tartar emetic were found in the vomited matter alone, which was a fatal dose for the average person. 'From the evidence,' he stated, 'the quantity taken by the deceased could not have been less than twenty grains, and probably ranged between twenty and forty grains.'

George Lewis then asked: 'Would antimony in water be practically tasteless?' to which the professor replied: 'Almost so, practically tasteless,' and added, 'I have some here; anyone may satisfy themselves. I have a solution of forty grains. I don't think you'll be able to detect a taste in this. You may hold it in the mouth for two or three minutes.'

With the unnecessary warning from Mr Muir: 'I would not advise that you swallow it!' several of the jury agreed to sample the solution, after which came the general opinion that it was indeed tasteless.

Following this experiment Mr Lewis asked the professor: 'Supposing a man had been in the habit of drinking water out of a bottle, do you think if it contained thirty or forty grains it might be drunk without attracting attention?'

'Yes, I think it might pass without attracting any special attention,' came the reply.

On the effects of antimony, the professor stated: 'Antimony is considered one of the most uncertain of drugs in its effects.' However, he added, 'Its emetic effects are more certain than those of almost any other drug; usually sickness follows in half an hour.' He then went on to state that he knew of many cases where small doses of antimony had been added to alcohol to deter excessive drinking habits. Further, he said it would be a simple matter to make a solution of tartar emetic by adding the crystals or powder to water and shaking it up. It would dissolve easily and the solution would be imperceptible to the eye.

Continuing on the subject of antimony, the professor said he thought that it was *black* antimony, or liver of antimony, that was used in stables, which was quite different from white antimony, or tartar emetic. He added, 'I do not think that any chemist would be justified in supplying tartar emetic to a stableman. Liver of antimony as used by grooms is *insoluble* in water.'

This information was followed by an account of the search of The Priory and its grounds made by the witness and Chief Inspector Clarke on 22 and 23 May. Nothing had been found that might solve the mystery of the deceased's death. All medicine phials and empty wine bottles had been examined for traces of poison but none had been found. Some thirty-four different remedies had been found in Mrs Bravo's room, besides the medicine chest containing thirty-five common homeopathic treatments. A further eighteen bottles were found in her dressing room, two of which did contain antimony but in such minute proportions as to render them perfectly harmless. A medicine chest in Mrs Cox's room had contained twenty-three bottles of medicine, most of them with their stoppers still secured. Many of these preparations had been tested, but none had proved harmful. There were also several bottles that had once contained medicine, which Mrs Cox had kept for some reason.

Professor Redwood ended his testimony by saying that there was 'nothing in Mrs Bravo's house in any way indicating the source from which [deceased] received the antimonial salt which caused his death'.

With this the fourth day of the inquest ended.

Despite the amount of testimony given so far, the jury could be certain of only one fact – that Charles Bravo had died from a huge dose of tartar emetic, taken in a diluted form shortly before his collapse. Furthermore, it seemed very likely that the vehicle for the fatal dose had been the water bottle in his room.

Who, though, had put it there, and where had it come from?

12

Not in Front of the Servants

The first witness to be called on Monday 17 July was Frederick Rowe, the butler from The Priory.

Asked during his testimony about relations between his mistress and late master he said that they had never quarrelled in his presence. 'I saw a great deal of Mr and Mrs Bravo and they appeared to live very happily together', he said. 'I never heard them quarrelling. The nearest approach to anything like unpleasantness was that sometimes they would be speaking about writing cheques for bills and Mr Bravo didn't seem willing to write them.'

Remarked the coroner, 'That's a frequent occurrence between husbands and wives', which drew laughter from the assembly. When the laughter had died Rowe went on to recall some of the events of the fateful Thursday. He had waited at table that evening, he said, assisted by the footman, Edward Smith. Earlier in the day, at about four-thirty, he had opened the door to Mr Bravo on his return from town. Afterwards, about five o'clock, Mr Bravo had come to him for his riding breeches.

Rowe then related how, following Mr Bravo's return from his disastrous ride on the common, he went into the sitting room to stir the fire. He 'opened the door gently', he said, adding, 'I saw Mr Bravo in an armchair by the side of the fire. Mrs Bravo was on the sofa in the inner room. I should think it was about half-past six. Mr Bravo didn't appear to notice me. I closed the door quietly, afraid of disturbing Mrs Bravo. Mr Bravo looked ill – he was pale and his mouth was drawn down. He rang the bell for me to get him a hot bath and told me to tell the housemaid to leave the water as it would

do for the next day. He took a bath. I lit the fire in his bedroom. This
was before seven o'clock. He cried out loud with pain and put his
hand to his side when he rose from his chair, which was a very low
one.'

Shortly before seven-thirty, Rowe continued, Mrs Cox returned
to the house. He opened the door for her, and 'she went directly to
the morning room and looked in'. He added, 'At that time Mr
Bravo was there. She bowed herself out and went upstairs. I don't
think she spoke.'

It was only a few minutes later, Rowe recalled, that dinner was
served, during which Mrs Cox tried to interest Mr Bravo in the
house she had rented in Worthing. Dinner lasted rather longer than
usual and Mr Bravo and the ladies went into the morning room at
about twenty minutes to nine.

'I next saw Mr Bravo in his bedroom about half-past ten', Rowe
said. 'I had been sent in the meantime by Mrs Bravo to fetch
someone from Balham to attend Mr Bravo.'

When asked to recall the night of 18 April in more detail, Rowe
said that he had heard running up and down but had stayed at the
foot of the stairs because the housemaid had told him that Mrs
Bravo was in her nightclothes. 'Some time after that Mrs Bravo
came downstairs and cried out very loudly for me to fetch someone . . . She was running screaming along the passage with the
housemaid.'

The butler recalled that later his master seemed to be in great
bodily pain and cried out a great deal, but although he spoke of
death he 'did not at any time in his hearing account for his condition
or speak of poison'. Added Rowe: 'He only spoke of laudanum.'

At this point, at the instigation of Sir Henry James, extracts from
The Priory's cellar book were read to the court and it soon became
apparent that a great deal of alcohol was consumed by the inhabitants of The Priory. Charles usually drank burgundy, the two ladies
preferring sherry or Marsala. The butler said that Mr Bravo generally drank one bottle of burgundy a day, over lunch and dinner –
which was about six glasses in all – whereas Mrs Bravo and Mrs
Cox could easily accommodate two bottles of sherry each day.
Furthermore, between them they consumed two bottles during
dinner on the evening Mr Bravo became ill.

Rowe maintained that Mr Bravo always appeared lively and

cheerful in company but sometimes used to look sad when he was quite alone. He treated all his servants with kindness and considera- tion, he said, and they were fond of him. Asked about the status enjoyed by Mrs Cox, Rowe said that she was 'treated with great consideration by Mrs Bravo'. He added, 'From first to last I never heard a harsh word addressed to her. Mrs Bravo sometimes called her Janey, I believe, and Mrs Cox sometimes called the deceased Mr Bravo and sometimes Charlie.' As for the deceased, said Rowe, although he sometimes called the companion by her first name he usually addressed her as Mrs Cox.

Questioned about Mrs Cox's duties, the butler said that she didn't really have any in particular – only 'getting anything that Mrs Bravo wished for'. 'She used to be always in attendance on Mrs Bravo and going out shopping in the carriage,' he added. 'She was always with Mrs Bravo.'

In answer to further questions Rowe stated that Mr and Mrs Bravo often went to bed as early as nine-thirty, in which case Mrs Cox would either go up to her own room, or sit in Mrs Bravo's dress- ing room plying her needle and generally making herself useful.

Referring to Charles's illness, the witness said that Dr Johnson persistently asked him what he had taken but he always answered 'laudanum'. At one stage, said Rowe, his master became very angry with the doctor and snapped, 'If I knew what I was suffering from, why the devil should I send for you?'

Rowe went on, 'Mrs Bravo kept asking us to pray for him. He was in the most excruciating agony and seemed grateful for the attention he was given.'

After a brief adjournment Rowe was asked by Sir Henry James whether he knew Dr Gully. The butler replied:

'I've heard the name since Mr Bravo's death, but not before. I've never seen the gentleman in my life.'

The consumption of wine at The Priory was referred to once again, and also Charles's love of entertaining. In illustration of the last an extract from one of Charles's letters, written shortly before his death, was read to the court. First from a letter of 3 January:

. . . We are expecting half-a-dozen people, and with children we shall have thirty-one guests in the house besides ser- vants . . .

And on 22 March:

> . . . There has been a great slaughter of cocks and hens for the feast. I wished a goose on the table but Florence would not hear of it. The gander is *bon père de famille*, and his wives are either sitting or expecting shortly to be in the same interesting position . . .

There was laughter in the court at this. When it subsided Rowe – still on the subject of Charles's entertaining – told the court that Charles had told him 'never to stint the wine'. 'He lectured me once for not passing the wine and champagne more than I did. He told me never to spare the wine and always keep the glasses well filled up.' The Priory, he added, was a liberally run establishment.

Asked whether both Mrs Bravo and Mrs Cox had seemed very upset by Charles's collapse that evening, he replied that 'both ladies showed great anxiety'. When asked to recall the conversation over dinner, he said that Mrs Cox spoke of the trip to Worthing and that Mr Bravo muttered something to the effect that 'he wasn't going' or he 'wouldn't be there'. Mrs Bravo had been looking at the witness when this remark was made and 'didn't seem to hear him, but Mrs Cox did and looked up sharply'. Added Rowe: 'She stared at Mr Bravo in a questioning manner and said, "Oh." She continued to look directly at him in a scolding way over the rim of her spectacles.'

At this point there came a request for an adjournment, with which the coroner concurred. The weather that day was exceptionally hot and by the afternoon the air in the crowded room had become unbearably stuffy and oppressive. Upon the court reassembling, only a little refreshed, Mr Gorst, for the Crown, resumed the examination of the butler who, in answer to various repetitive queries, reiterated his previous evidence. Then, at four-thirty, he was allowed to leave the court and the proceedings were adjourned until the following day.

The maid, Mary Ann Keeber, was the first witness to be called the next day, Tuesday 18 July. She stated:

'For the last three months I waited on Mrs Bravo, in addition to my other duties as housemaid. I had to see that the rooms were properly settled. I used to leave water in Mr Bravo's bedroom in the water bottle which was kept on the washstand and I had to see that the bottle was kept full at night. There was a tumbler on top of the bottle. It appeared to me that some of the water was used occasionally in the daytime.' Asked whether she had noticed any difference in the character of the water in the bottle on the Tuesday in question, she said she had not. Questioned about Mr Charles Bravo she stated:

'On the evening of Monday April 17th he complained to me of toothache; he was then in Mrs Bravo's bedroom and said: "Mary Ann, I feel very cross. I have a toothache like you have sometimes." He was sitting by the side of the fire with his hands up to his face as if suffering pain. Mrs Bravo was in bed but she got out to him. They had been occupying separate beds at this time in consequence of Mrs Bravo's illness.'

The maid went on to relate that on the Sunday night when she returned from church Mrs Bravo asked her what she could give Mr Bravo for his toothache. She, Mrs Bravo, had already given him laudanum and chloroform, she said, but they had not relieved the pain. The maid suggested that he might try brandy and hot water.

The maid then gave the court her own version of the evening Charles collapsed, stating:

'I saw Mr Bravo at half-past nine going upstairs. Mrs Bravo was in her dressing room. Mrs Cox was with her. She very often went upstairs with Mrs Bravo to assist her in undressing. I went upstairs with two little cans of hot water. I went to the dressing room and rapped on the door. I went in and Mrs Bravo was undressed. I set one little can of water in the basin as I usually do and the other one I set on the landing to take up to Mrs Cox's room afterwards. Mrs Bravo said to me, "Will you fetch me a little Marsala?" and she gave me a very small tumbler to go and fetch it in. I fetched it out of the cellarette in the dining room. When I came out of the dining room Mr Bravo came out of the morning room.'

She then spoke of Charles's silence when they met at the foot of the stairs, and how he had turned to look at her twice, without speaking. She told the court that after being told to take the two dogs downstairs she asked Mrs Cox where one of them had gone, at which the companion said, 'I believe he has gone up to my room.'

Mary Ann continued: 'I shut Mrs Bravo's door and went to the bottom of the flight of stairs leading to Mrs Cox's room and called the little dog. As I stood at the bottom of the stairs, Mr Bravo opened his bedroom door in his nightshirt and called, "Florence" twice, and "hot water" very loud.'

Her testimony continuing, she told how she summoned Mrs Cox, how they tried to revive the unconscious Charles and how, at Mrs Cox's bidding, she hurried off on her various errands. It was while going into her mistress's bedroom in search of the bottle of camphor, she said, that she decided to awaken her. 'I said to her, "Will you get up? Mr Bravo is ill." She replied, "What is the matter?" I said, "I don't know; he seems very ill." I helped her on with her dressing gown and she said again, "What is the matter?" and I said, "I don't know." '

After relating her finding of the camphor Mary Ann told how she mixed mustard and water in the wash-hand-basin and put Charles's feet in it. She went on: 'Mrs Cox told me to rub his feet as hard as I could. She was then rubbing his chest with camphor. I said to her, "What is the matter with him?" and she said, "Rub him as hard as you can, Mary Ann." Mr Bravo was not conscious at this time and Mrs Cox said, "Wake, Charlie," or "Try and wake," or something to that effect. She then sent me for more hot water and when I returned with it she said, "Mix some mustard and water in the glass." I said, "How much shall I mix?" She seemed very impatient and said, "Oh, make haste, Mary Ann." I said, "You'd better mix it yourself." Mrs Cox mixed the mustard and water and gave a little of it to Mr Bravo, but he could not swallow much. So then she told me to get a strong cup of coffee. I went down to the kitchen and made it. We tried to give him some of the coffee, but he could only swallow very little of it. Mr Bravo was sick in my presence but I can't tell whether it was before or after the coffee. Mrs Cox said, "We'd better try and get him up on his feet." We couldn't get him up, and I called the other housemaid and asked her to help us to lift him into the easy chair.'

Mary Ann Keeber's simple words paint a grim picture of the desperate scene – the three women, Florence, Jane Cox and Mary Ann trying in vain to lift the dead weight of the unconscious Charles; then Mary Ann rushing off and returning with the other housemaid, with whose help they eventually managed to lift Charles into the easy chair.

'We got him into it,' Mary Ann said, 'and Mrs Cox told me to fetch more hot water. While I was gone for it they changed his nightshirt.'

On entering the kitchen, she continued, the other housemaid asked her what was the matter. Said Mary Ann to the court: 'I said, "I don't know, but Mr Bravo looks as if he would die." '

She went on to say that while she was in the kitchen Mrs Bravo came hurrying down crying out to Rowe to fetch someone, that Mr Bravo was so ill she was afraid he could die. Rowe replied that Mr Harrison had already been sent for, at which Mrs Bravo cried out to him to get someone nearer. 'Shall I get someone from Balham?' he asked her. 'Yes,' she said, 'I don't care who it is!' Added Mary Ann, 'She was very much distressed.'

After the doctors had arrived, said the maid, she heard Mrs Bravo ask if Mr and Mrs Bravo senior should be sent for. Her mistress said, 'If anything happens I know they will never forgive me.'

The following morning, Wednesday, Mary Ann continued, she went to tidy the sickroom in preparation for the arrival of Mr and Mrs Joseph Bravo, and as she entered the room Mr Bravo asked her how she was. She replied, 'Very well, sir. How are you?'

'Not much better,' he answered. Then, after saying that they would not have their trip to Worthing, he turned to his wife who was near his bed and said, 'What a bother I am to you all, Florrie.'

At this Mrs Bravo had said tearfully, 'Oh, don't say that, Charlie. It's no trouble, is it, Mary Ann?'

Continuing with her evidence after an adjournment for lunch, Mary Ann said that on the Thursday afternoon she had gone to change the bedlinen in the sick room, but this time Mr Bravo had not seemed to recognize her. The next morning, she said, after being awakened and asked to make tea, she was told by Mrs Bravo that Mr Bravo had died.

Mr Lewis, turning attention to Dr Gully's visits to The Priory before Florence had married Charles, asked whether the doctor had been a regular visitor. The maid said he had been, adding that he 'used to come to dinner and go away between nine and ten'. However, she said, he had never visited The Priory after her mistress was married.

Questioned further, Mary Ann made it clear that she thought Charles and Florence had lived very happily together; she had seen no sign of jealousy between them.

Asked if Mrs Cox had mentioned Charles's poison statement at all during the evening he collapsed, the maid replied that she had not. She said that when she went to Florence's bedroom to fetch help, Mrs Cox was sitting by her mistress's bed, still in her outdoor clothes. She was not talking or reading. She often sat like that after Florence had fallen asleep, she said.

Questioned regarding Charles's water bottle, the maid said that when she tidied his room on the Wednesday morning she refilled the bottle; but she had not noticed it after he collapsed the night before. She said that Mr Bravo always cleaned his teeth with plain water and never used tooth powders.

Mary Ann told the court that she never went into the dressing room if Mr Bravo was there, unless requested to do so. That night she had waited in the bedroom with the wine because she could hear Mr Bravo's voice in the dressing room, though she could not tell what he was saying. When Mr Bravo had gone to his own bedroom and Mrs Bravo had gone to hers, she, the maid, had begun to tidy the clothes in the dressing room.

She said that throughout Mr Bravo's illness Mrs Cox had seemed very anxious to assist his recovery. She also said that she was not the least bit surprised that she had had to wake Mrs Bravo to tell her about her husband's collapse, as she was still very weak from the miscarriage and had been going to sleep by seven-thirty each night.

After seeing Mr Bravo so ill, she said, Mrs Bravo had become very upset and at no time did she seem anything but genuinely concerned for his recovery.

On Wednesday 19 July, before resuming the inquest for the seventh day, the coroner and jury visited The Priory to see for themselves the close proximity of the rooms on the first floor. During the visit they noted the fact that Charles Bravo must have been standing no more than four feet from his wife's bedroom door when he shouted for help.

At the resumption of proceedings at the Bedford Hotel at ten-thirty, Mary Ann Keeber was recalled and asked whether she could give any reason why Charles's cry had not been heard by Florence and Mrs Cox when he had been so close to them. She said she did not know why they had not heard, adding: 'He called out so loud.'

Mary Ann then told the jury that as far as she knew Mr Bravo's
water bottle was not changed or emptied on the night he collapsed –
but she had refilled it the next morning. Each evening she took up
the cans of hot water for washing. That Tuesday, she said, on
entering the dressing room she had found Mrs Bravo sitting near
her dressing table, and Mrs Cox standing by the fire with her elbow
on the chimney shaft. 'Mrs Bravo was all ready, her hair was
finished and she had her dressing gown on.'

The maid told the court that a little tray was always taken to Mrs
Bravo's room and that it consisted of a teapot, two cups and saucers
and some bread-and-butter. On one point, however, her memory
failed her; she could not remember whether she had closed both the
inner and outer doors of Mrs Bravo's bedroom before going in
search of the dog.

Asked if the poison involved in Mr Bravo's death had been
discussed at Brighton after the funeral, Mary Ann said that it had
and that Mrs Bravo had said she did not know 'where he had got it
from'.

This statement sparked off a heated exchange between Sir Henry
James and Mr Gorst over the term 'got'. The temperature of the
packed billiards room, added to the noise from the railway station,
was beginning to try the patience of the learned gentlemen and some
were becoming irritable. When things were calmer Mary Ann said
that Mrs Cox ordered her to fetch mustard for an emetic but gave
her no reason for its use; nor, she said, was the word poison ever
mentioned. Said the maid, 'She simply told me to mix the mustard
and water and the poor man was to take it. At that time he was
insensible.'

Attention was then drawn to the hair-dyes that Mrs Bravo used,
and Mary Ann admitted that her mistress changed the colour of her
hair to a deep shade of red when she went to Brighton in the autumn
of 1875.

At this stage the proceedings were adjourned while a servant of
the court was dispatched to fetch the bottles of hair-dye from The
Priory. When they were brought into court a few minutes later Mr
Lewis declined Sir Henry's sarcastic offer to have them analysed
and, following some discussion, the idea that Mrs Bravo had used
hair-dye to poison her husband was duly dismissed. After Mary
Ann had emphasised that at no time did Mrs Cox tell her to wake

Mrs Bravo after Charles had collapsed, her deposition was read to her and she was dismissed.

The next witness was Parton, the coachman, who gave evidence about the drive to town on the morning of 18 April. As to the disagreement Florence said she had had with Charles during the journey, neither Parton nor the footman had heard raised voices or sounds of quarrelling from the carriage.

Parton said that when Mr Bravo returned to The Priory at six-thirty that evening after the cob had bolted with him, he had looked pale and shaken, saying that he 'could scarcely lift a limb'.

Replying to Mr Lewis, the coachman said that although he had heard of black antimony, he had never used it on his horses. He was in charge of two hired horses as well as Mrs Bravo's own cobs, Victor and Cremorne, and when he took over from Griffiths, the previous coachman, all the horses were fit. There had never been any rat poison in the stables to his knowledge, he said, though the gardener had said that he had used some 'a long time ago'.

The next witness was the footman, Edward Valentine Smith, who told the court that he had accompanied Parton on the trip to town on 18 April. He had also helped to serve the dinner that evening, he said, though he had not noticed anything unusual about his master during the meal. He said that all three people at table were talking about the trip to Worthing and looking at a photograph that Mrs Cox had brought with her. As to Dr Gully, the witness said that he did not even know where he lived, and he had never heard of Mrs Cox going to see him.

George Younger, the groom at The Priory, was called next and said that he had advised Mr Bravo not to ride the cobs that day. He had never used antimony on his horses, he said, but he had seen liver of antimony used at other stables. He had been employed by Mrs Bravo after Griffiths had gone to Herne Bay. He also said that he had never seen Dr Gully in his life. Following his testimony the court was adjourned until the following day.

13

Poison in the Stables?

On Thursday 20 July Amelia Bushell was sworn as a witness. She told the court that she was Mrs Joseph Bravo's personal maid, and the wife of the Bravos' butler, and that she had known Charles since he was fifteen.

After arriving at The Priory, she said, she had remained in the sickroom until the deceased's death, leaving it only to take her meals and short rests. The witness completed her evidence by stating that Charles had been an extremely truthful and outspoken man and, in her opinion, most unlikely to commit suicide.

The next witness was Anna Maria Bell, Royes Bell's sister, who told the court how she had come to The Priory bringing with her Charles's sister, Alice. While talking to Florence in the conservatory, she said, Florence told her that she and Charles had been very happy. Asked whether Florence had said anything about a coppery pan being responsible for Charles's illness, the witness said she had not; nor had she accounted in any way for his condition. Florence, she told the court, had said that her husband's death was 'very mysterious' and that she thought 'it would always remain a mystery'.

Asked to recall the meeting between Charles and Sir William Gull, Anna Maria said that the latter had made it quite clear that Charles was going to die. Throughout all the questioning, however, she said, Charles had insisted that he had only taken laudanum, saying: 'If it wasn't laudanum, so help me God, I don't know what it was.' She went on: 'His wife asked him what he had taken and he said, "Laudanum." "What did you take it for, Charlie?" she asked. "To do me good, of course," he replied, and when asked where he got it from, said "From your bottle, Florence." '

Concerning Dr Gully, the witness said, 'Until public attention was directed to this matter, I never did hear anything about him. Mrs Bravo never mentioned one word about him then.'

The next witness was George Griffiths, the handsome young coachman then employed by Lady Prescott at Herne Bay in Kent. After saying that he had worked for Mrs Ricardo at The Priory before she married Mr Bravo and that he had left her service on 3 January 1876, he surprised the assembly by saying that while working for Mrs Bravo he had been 'in the habit' of giving her horses tartar emetic, adding, 'I kept it in the stables.' Then, in reply to a query as to the type of antimony he used, he replied calmly: 'The white. I could get it at any chemist's.'

The court was further surprised when he said he had bought some at Robinson's shop in Streatham, at Smith's in Balham, and that he had also bought some when he was working for Florence at Leigham Court Road four or five years before. He had returned to her service in May 1875, he said, after she had moved to The Priory. He had used a lotion of antimony on her horses for sores and infestation – and also to make their coats shine. He had bought a quarter of an ounce from Smith's in Balham, but could not remember if he had signed the poisons register.* He said he 'just walked into the shop' and paid for it with his own money. The quarter-ounce of antimony had cost him 4d or 5d. He had learned about its beneficial effects from a book his father had given him called *The Pocket Farrier*. A quarter-ounce of antimony, he said, would make up to fifty treatments; he had mixed a pint and a half of the lotion in a bottle, stuck a *Poison* label on it and kept it in the cupboard in the stables of The Priory. When he left The Priory, he said, he 'poured the remainder of what was in the bottle down the drain in the yard', adding, 'I broke the bottle and threw it on the dung-heap.'

Griffiths went on to say that when he left Leigham Court Road to marry Fanny Plascot he had taken his stock of antimony with him.

* In 1869 a law was passed that required a chemist to keep a register recording sales of poisons.

TOP: Buscot – with Victorian additions
ABOVE: Alexander and Florence Ricardo at Folkestone, about 1864 *(Bernard Taylor)*
LEFT: Lieutenant Alexander Ricardo, about 1860 *(Bernard Taylor)*

Florence Bravo, photographed on her honeymoon at Brighton in December 1875 *(BBC Hulton Picture Library)*

Dr James Manby Gully *(BBC Hulton Picture Library)*

Jane Cannon Cox
(BBC Hulton Picture Library)

Charles Delauney Turner
Bravo, photographed on
his honeymoon at
Brighton, December 1875
(BBC Hulton Picture Library)

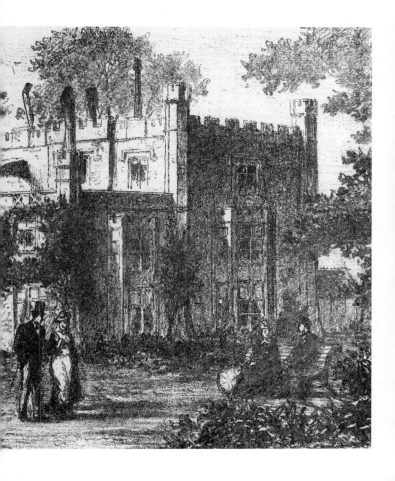

ABOVE: The stairs and first floor landing at The Priory; from a contemporary drawing. (A: Stairs to upper bedrooms. B: Room wherein Charles Bravo died. C: Bedroom in which Florence Bravo slept. D: Dressing room) *('Balham Mystery' BL)*

BELOW: The bedroom in which Charles Bravo died; from a contemporary drawing *('Balham Mystery' BL)*

OPPOSITE ABOVE: The locality of the inquest, showing at left, the Bedford Hotel, and A: The Priory, and B: Orwell Lodge *('Balham Mystery' BL)*

OPPOSITE BELOW: Orwell Lodge, Dr Gully's residence; from a contemporary drawing *('Balham Mystery' BL)*

ABOVE: Sir William Gull
being cross-examined by
Mr George Lewis *(Bernard
Taylor)*

Servants from The Priory
sketched while giving
evidence. FAR LEFT:
George Griffiths;
LEFT: Mary Ann Keeber;
ABOVE: Frederick Rowe
(*'Balham Mystery' BL*)

Mrs Cox under examination at the inquest. From a contemporary engraving taken from a drawing made in the courtroom. *(BBC Hulton Picture Library)*

Four of the physicians who
attended Charles Bravo.
TOP LEFT: Dr Moore;
TOP RIGHT: Dr George Johnson;
ABOVE: Mr Royes Bell *('Balham Mystery' BL)*;
LEFT: Mr George Harrison

TOP LEFT: Mr William Carter, the coroner, with Mr Burleigh Muir, the legal assessor;
TOP RIGHT: Mr Joseph Bravo;
RIGHT: Mr George Lewis with Mr Poland *('Balham Mystery' BL)*;
ABOVE: Sir William Gull *(Bernard Taylor)*

PRICE THREEPENCE.

THE PICTORIAL WORLD

AN ILLUSTRATED WEEKLY NEWSPAPER

No. 128. Vol. V. (Registered at the General Post Office as a Newspaper)   SATURDAY, AUGUST 12th, 1876.   THREEPENCE. Per Post, 3½d.

THE PRIORY

MR. CHAS. BRAVO

EXAMINATION OF MRS. CHAS. BRAVO

MRS. COX

DR. GULLY

THE LATE MR. CHAS. D. T. BRAVO, BARRISTER-AT-LAW

THE "BALHAM MYSTERY": PORTRAITS OF THE LATE MR. BRAVO, MRS. C. BRAVO, MRS. COX, AND DR. GULLY.

The Bravo poisoning mystery was front page news *(Bernard Taylor)*

Charles's grave in West Norwood Cemetery as it appears today, with close-up showing the engraving on the headstone *(Bernard Taylor)*

Before going to work for Mrs Ricardo, he said, he had been in Dr Gully's service in Malvern for eight years; he had left Malvern when the doctor had given up his horses.

The coachman then said that he had treated the doctor's horses with tartar emetic as well and had bought it from Clark's chemist shop in Malvern for that purpose. He could not remember, however, whether he had signed the poison book.

Griffiths's memory was soon aided when Mr Gorst produced the register of poison sales kept by the Malvern chemist, Mr Clark. The coachman's purchase was recorded very clearly indeed:

DATE: June 11th, 1869
NAME AND PURCHASER: Dr Gully
NAME AND QUANTITY OF POISON SOLD: 2 oz tartar emetic
PURPOSE FOR WHICH IT WAS REQUIRED: Horse Medicine
SIGNATURE OF PURCHASER: George Griffiths
SIGNATURE OF PERSON INTRODUCING PURCHASER: R. Bridges

The entry left no doubt and Griffiths had to admit that the signature was his own, though he insisted that he could not remember whether Dr Gully had given him a covering note.

As Dr Gully had kept only two horses, Griffiths was asked why he needed to buy enough antimony for *two hundred* treatments. He replied that he 'liked to keep some in hand', adding that both Mrs Ricardo's and Dr Gully's horses had suffered badly from worm infestation.

He went on to admit that Charles Bravo had instigated his dismissal from The Priory because of his careless driving. Until eight weeks before the marriage, he said, he had driven Mrs Bravo, Dr Gully and Mrs Cox in the carriage three or four times a week. He had not seen Charles Bravo again after his marriage, but he had seen Dr Gully quite often. 'I used to see him every day. I saw him up and down the road opposite my Lodge. He only acknowledged me, that's all; never stopped to talk.'

Griffiths had, however, kept in closer touch with Dr Gully's butler, Pritchard – 'my fellow servant during the whole time I was at Dr Gully's' – and told the court that he had had dinner with him at Orwell Lodge on the previous Sunday, 16 July.

Throughout his examination Griffiths proved himself a very

unreliable witness, contradicting himself more than once. At one point he told the court that he was using tartar emetic at Lady Prescott's stables in Herne Bay – a statement he obviously regretted, for he was to retract it the following day. His recall of detail also left a great deal to be desired, yet when his examiners remarked upon this fact he told them that 'he had enough to do with his work, let alone thinking about such things'.

Nevertheless his evidence contained some interesting facts and the entry in Mr Clark's poison book was undeniable. Without a doubt, Griffiths had bought a large quantity of tartar emetic whilst in Dr Gully's employment in Malvern. The question taxing the minds of the jurors was whether any of that poison had reached the stables of The Priory – with or without Florence's consent.

When the court reassembled on Friday 21 July, two more legal gentlemen swelled the illustrious number. They were Mr Serjeant Parry and Mr A. L. Smith, both instructed by Dr Gully's solicitor. It was a move which was hardly surprising, the reason for which Mr Smith made clear in an address to the coroner, saying in the course of it that the witness, Griffiths, had had put into his hand 'a document some seven years old, suggesting that antimony which was then bought in Malvern in some way has a connection with the death of Mr Bravo'. Added Mr Smith, 'Now the charge is undoubtedly made against Dr Gully, and Mr Parry and myself have come here to watch the evidence on behalf of Dr Gully.'

Replying to this address Mr Gorst repeated an earlier insistence that the purpose of the inquiry was not to make a charge against anyone but to hear all the evidence and ascertain the truth concerning Mr Bravo's death. This said, the examination of George Griffiths was resumed.

His memory had not improved on this second day of his examination and the answers he gave Mr Lewis showed that he was unsure of dates and past events, and appeared to be incapable of distinguishing truth from falsehood. Asked yet again if he remembered buying antimony for Dr Gully in Malvern, he shouted:

'No! not the time, nor the date, neither the month, nor the week, nor the day, nor yet the year!' adding that his mind was 'a complete blank as to the whole transaction and to anything that happened those years back'.

Under continuing fire from George Lewis, however, he did admit that as Dr Gully's horses were rarely ill, two ounces of tartar emetic *was* a large amount to buy at one time. He had taken the remainder with him when he went to work at Warwick Square, he said – but when his children were old enough to walk around he had destroyed it, thinking it too dangerous to keep in the house. Yet he once again insisted that when he left The Priory the second time he had poured the antimonial lotion down the drain in the yard and then smashed the bottle.

Attempts were made to ascertain how often Griffiths had used tartar emetic on his horses over the years but little was gained. Asked if Mrs Bravo ever went to the stables at The Priory, he said that she sometimes 'came in the mornings to look at her cobs' and that 'she took an interest in all the horses'.

In answer to a question from a juror, Griffiths said that he had earned £28 a year as Dr Gully's coachman, and that two ounces of tartar emetic would have cost 3s 4d. It was pointed out that this sum constituted a large proportion of his weekly wage, but Griffiths dismissed this by saying that he could 'charge it in other ways'.

With Griffiths's evasive replies the examination seemed to be leading nowhere, but then Mr Lewis surprised the court by producing Charles Stringer, the barman of the Bedford Hotel – the man to whom Griffiths had made his uncannily accurate prediction of Charles Bravo's death.

With a dramatic gesture George Lewis demanded: 'Will you swear that you did not tell the man who stands there: "Poor fellow, he will not live four months"?'

The confused witness denied that he had stipulated four months and said that his remark was made in temper because of his dismissal, adding: 'It didn't matter to me whether he was dead or alive. I had to go somewhere else for my living.'

Lewis asked Griffiths again why he had been able to predict Mr Bravo's death with such accuracy and, floundering, Griffiths said he had thought that Mr Bravo might die from a bite he had received from one of Mrs Bravo's dogs.*

Mr Lewis then drew attention to the meeting in the Lower Lodge

---

* Dr Moore had examined the wound and said it was not serious. Florence, however, was very upset and ordered Griffiths to shoot the dog. Charles had tried to dissuade her, but she had insisted and the dog had been shot.

between Florence and Dr Gully, shortly before the marriage. Griffiths said that his wife, Fanny, had been in the other room during the rendezvous, adding that she was on very friendly terms with Dr Gully, who often called at the Lodge to chat to her about the children.

'Mrs Ricardo was there sometimes when he came,' he said, 'before she was engaged to Mr Bravo, but never after. Sometimes they used to come down together across the lawn.'

Still on the subject of Dr Gully, Griffiths said that although he had heard Dr Gully was a married man, he was not sure if his wife was still alive. At this it was announced that she was 'alive and living in Brighton', and that she had 'lived there for years and years'.

With this Griffiths was allowed to step down and the court was adjourned for lunch. Afterwards Stringer, the barman of the Bedford Hotel, was called as a witness. He said that Griffiths had been drinking in his bar on the morning of Mr Bravo's wedding, and when asked why he was not celebrating with the rest of the household, said that he was going to Wandsworth County Court to pay a summons. Then, as he was leaving, he had said:

'Mrs Ricardo is sure to have a lot of brandy in her this morning before she goes to the wedding. Poor fellow, I shouldn't like to be in his shoes. He will not be alive four months.'

'That was all that passed between us,' Stringer said. 'He then ran off to catch the train.'

The witness then told the court that it struck him at the time that the words were said from spite because Griffiths had been dismissed from The Priory by Mr Bravo.

The next witness was Mr Henry Barnes Clark, the chemist from Malvern. He said the sale of two ounces of tartar emetic in 1869 had been conducted by his assistant, Mr Meredith, adding that Dr Gully had 'dealt very little' with his shop, preferring to use a homeopathic chemist. Asked if there were any papers relating to the sale, he said as far as he could recollect there 'was a short note on half a sheet of notepaper from Dr Gully'.

He said that tartar emetic came in the form of a white powder which could be stored for a considerable length of time, retaining its potency for many years. He had never known such a large quantity of tartar emetic bought by a private individual, and he would not have sold Griffiths such a large quantity of antimony without a letter from a medical man.

Mr Percy Smith, a chemist from Balham, who was called next, denied that he had ever sold any tartar emetic to Griffiths. His testimony finished the day's proceedings and the inquiry was adjourned until the following Monday.

Much of the evidence produced that day had been conflicting and the jury must have left the Bedford Hotel somewhat perplexed by what they had heard.

Griffiths had stated that without Florence's knowledge he had doctored her horses with tartar emetic at Leigham Court Road and at The Priory. He had estimated that the two ounces bought for Dr Gully was sufficient for two hundred treatments for worms, yet he said he had purchased even more tartar emetic from chemists in Balham and Streatham. What had become of the surplus tartar emetic? Had Griffiths destroyed it as he claimed?

Although the chemists rebutted Griffith's claim that they had sold him tartar emetic, it must almost certainly have been realized by the jury that any chemist would have denied such a transaction. If there was no proof of such a sale then it was probably the safest course to deny that it had ever taken place. To admit a sale without obtaining a signature was to admit that one had broken the law – and in this case the breaking of the law might well have led to a murder.

14

Loyalty and Laurel Water

Surgeon Mr Joseph Frank Payne, of 6 Savile Row, was the first
witness to be called on Monday 24 July. He stated that he was a
Fellow of the Royal College of Physicians and assistant physician at
St Thomas's Hospital, and that on 22 April he had been asked to
execute a post-mortem examination of Charles Bravo's body. Present at the examination, he said, were Dr Johnson, Mr Bell, Dr
Moore and Mr Harrison. He went on:

'The body was well-made and muscular and perfectly well
nourished. There was no external wound, bruise or other injury.
There was no outer appearance of disease in the body and there was
no indication of any natural disease which could have caused death.
With regard to the appearance of the stomach, I think it would show
that the poison was in a much diluted state.'

Further testimony on the results of the post-mortem took up a
considerable time, after which a member of the jury addressed the
witness:

'Mr Bravo is stated to have vomited almost immediately on
entering the room; he fell down insensible and remained so for a
long time. Would that be consistent with his taking a large dose
shortly before?'

Mr Payne agreed that this would be consistent with the deceased
having drunk thirty or forty grains of antimony in a tumbler of
water shortly before his collapse.

The next witness was John Meredith, assistant to the chemist
Clark in Malvern. Regarding Dr Gully's two ounces of antimony,
he said he had no recollection of the sale, although he admitted that
it was his own signature in the Sale of Poisons register.

Charles Matlocks, assistant to Smith, the Balham chemist, was called next. He said he knew Griffiths by sight but had never sold him any tartar emetic. In the autumn of 1875, however, he added, there had been a temporary assistant working in the shop who might have sold him some without entering the sale in the register.

George Griffiths was recalled after the lunch recess and, asked about his friendship with Dr Gully's butler, Pritchard, said they were very old friends. He had dined with the butler and his family at Orwell Lodge on the previous Sunday, but had not seen Dr Gully during the visit. After dinner, he added, the conversation had naturally turned to Charles Bravo's death and Pritchard had said that it was a sad case and that he fully expected to be called as a witness.

At this the jury decided they would like to hear the butler's evidence and an officer of the court was sent to fetch him. As Orwell Lodge was close by, Pritchard arrived in court within a short time.

After stating that he had been in Dr Gully's service since 1855, Pritchard, questioned by Mr Lewis, recalled that on the Thursday before Mr Bravo died Mrs Cox had come to the front door of Dr Gully's house and asked if the doctor was at home. The butler had replied that he was, after which he had led her into the drawing room. He then told the court:

'But I was very sorry afterwards, as I had orders from Dr Gully never to let Mrs Bravo or Mrs Cox into the house.' This remark prompted considerable laughter. When it subsided the butler went on to say that Mrs Cox had said, 'Mr Bravo is very ill. I am afraid he is dying,' to which, said Pritchard, he had replied: 'Oh, dear me; is he really?'

Hardly surprisingly this laconic response brought more laughter, bringing Mr Parry (for Dr Gully) to his feet, saying angrily:

'Mr Coroner, let me ask that there should not be this unseemly laughter in court. I notice it on the part of Mr Gorst, who is learned counsel conducting the prosecution on behalf of the Treasury, and I call particular attention to it.'

It was Mr Gorst's turn to protest, and he said sharply, 'I beg to say that I was not laughing!'

Mr Parry: 'You were smiling on two occasions.'

Mr Gorst: 'May I be allowed to say that I certainly do plead guilty to having smiled. And I beg to say that this is not a prosecution and I am not here to prosecute. I certainly smiled, as my friends opposite have smiled, and as Mr Parry himself has smiled, and I hope he may smile several times during the course of this investigation.'

This last brought renewed laughter, followed by applause. Mr Gorst went on:

'If I am to sit through the whole of this long investigation with an impassive and wooden face, I am certain I shall not be able to do so – and I shall certainly smile if evidence is given which is amusing.'

There were loud cries of 'Hear, hear!' from the jury and more applause from the crowd. The coroner, incensed, threatened to clear the room, in which move he was supported by Mr Parry, who accused counsel for the Treasury, Mr Gorst and Mr Poland, of being there for the purpose of 'fixing guilt upon three individuals' when, he said, the actual object of the inquiry was 'the cause of death of this unhappy young gentleman'.

After a call of 'We don't want speeches!' from a member of the jury, followed by more laughter, Mr Gorst rose to his feet and told the court that his instructions 'were not to bring charges but to *elicit the truth*', to which several of the jurors muttered, 'Quite right.'

Examination of Pritchard continuing, the court heard that after Mrs Cox's arrival at Orwell Lodge he showed her into Dr Gully's study and saw her leave the house a few minutes later and walk towards The Priory. Questioned further, he said that he had known about the 'great attachment between Mrs Ricardo and Dr Gully'. He added, 'He had a latchkey to Mrs Ricardo's house, so I should think that Mrs Cox was aware of the attachment existing between them. I've not seen Mrs Bravo at the house since November. I knew Mr Bravo by sight. I saw him but once passing, when I was leaning on the gate one evening – but he did not look across at me.'

Mr Murphy then asked Pritchard how old Mrs Cox was, to which the butler replied, 'I couldn't tell you.'

At this Sir Henry James remarked, 'I daresay she will not either,' to which Mr Gorst retorted: 'You had better not smile.' Said Sir Henry: 'But I am not smiling at what the witness says but at what I have said myself, and that is a very different thing.'

Continuing his testimony, Pritchard said that when Dr Gully had told him that he had met Mrs Cox a couple of times at the station he had advised his master to have nothing to do with her. Indeed, with regard to both Mrs Cox and Mrs Bravo he told the court that he did not want the doctor 'dragged up any more by them'.

Concerning Mrs Cox, Dr Gully's loyal butler was asked if he had known her before she went to work for Mrs Bravo. He replied unequivocally:

'I never saw her before in my life, and I should not be sorry if I had never seen her.'

The fascination of the case seemed to be increasing, with several daily newspapers feeding the voracious appetites of the public with verbatim accounts of the proceedings in the courtroom, in addition to publishing correspondence relating to the mystery. And there was no shortage of such correspondence. In addition to that received by the editors of the various newspapers, the coroner, the jury and leading counsel also received a daily influx of hundreds of letters from the public, apparently the most popular recipient being Mr Lewis, closely followed by Mr Gorst and Mr Poland.

Understandably very few, if any, of these letters exist today. However, the text of a particular one has survived – like other letters by virtue of its being published in the press. It appeared in *The Daily Telegraph* on the morning of 24 July, the tenth day of the inquiry. In it the correspondent stated:

. . . Captain Ricardo, it may be remembered, died and was first buried abroad but his remains were subsequently brought over to England, and can be exhumed by an Order from the Secretary of State. Without entering into details, you will perhaps allow me to suggest that an analysis of the remains of Captain Ricardo might, or might not, let considerable light upon the present inquiry.

To read such words must have been very disturbing for Florence and her family, for it clearly implied in which area certain suspicions were focused.

In the meantime the inquiry was continuing.

The first witness to be called on Tuesday 25 July was Dr Johnson.

There being little satisfaction with Sir William Gull's testimony as to his not having been told of Charles's condition before he arrived at The Priory, Mr Lewis asked Dr Johnson whether he had

William any information on the way to Balham. Replied
n:

'I described the symptoms and Sir William Gull said, "That looks
like poison," and I said, "There can be no question as to that. It is
clearly a case of poison, and there are only two doubtful points.
First, what was the exact nature of the poison, and secondly, how
did it get into the patient's stomach?"'

Denouncing Sir William's statement that he had thought he was
going to see a case of disease, and not poison, Dr Johnson said: 'It
astonished me. I couldn't believe it until I read it in *four* newspapers.
I could not believe it. I gave him the whole history of the case.'

After Dr Johnson had stepped down Frederick MacCalmont was
recalled. Examined by Mr Murphy, he was asked:

'Did you ever have any conversation with Mr Bravo as to the
position that Mrs Cox occupied in the house?'

The witness replied that one evening in February the question of
Mrs Cox's remaining at The Priory had arisen and Charles had
spoken of her as being 'very useful in doing the household work'
and helping his wife. They seemed, said MacCalmont, on the best
possible terms at that time.

Asked if Charles had ever mentioned Dr Gully, the barrister said
that he had first 'heard his name mentioned three or four days after
Mr Bravo's funeral'.

This ended MacCalmont's testimony, his place being taken by
another barrister, Mr Edward Hope, who stated that he and Charles
had been members of the same circuit. 'I knew him intimately for
four years,' he said. 'He was of a remarkably cheerful disposition,
and I should think very high spirited. He was full of anecdote and a
charming companion. I should have thought that he was a remarkably courageous man.'

Relating to the court how he had gone to The Priory on 22
March, when he had dined and slept there, he said:

'Two or three people were staying in the house: there was a party.
Mrs Cox was in the house with Mrs Bravo when I arrived there,
with Mr and Mrs Campbell. Mrs Cox and Mr Bravo seemed on
the most excellent terms. He had talked to me of the Campbell
family with great regard – I had known two of the sons at school. He
showed me over the grounds, the stables and the lawn-tennis
ground, and seemed very pleased with everything. When I first

went I asked who all the company were, and he said the old lady in spectacles was Mrs Cox, his wife's companion.'

The witness went on to say that Charles's remarks about Mrs Cox had always been complimentary. 'He said she was very useful – that she used to go up to London shopping for them, and that they sent her up in the carriage.'

The last time he saw Charles, he said, was on 11 April. After describing him as being in his usual health and spirits he said: 'He was sitting beside me in one of the courts; he'd got a piece of paper and a pen in his hand, and seemed to be calculating, and he said, "After all, Mrs Cox must be costing about £300 a year."'

Said Hope: 'I laughed and said, "You might keep another pair of horses for that, and they might be more useful than Mrs Cox."'

Hope then told the court that Charles – whom he spoke of as 'a very liberal fellow' – appeared to be very happily married. He did not seem to have any money problems and although he often spoke of his father's generosity he was not over-concerned with money matters.

Mr Carlyle Willoughby was called next and said that he had known Charles for about six years. In his opinion Charles and Florence were happily married and he thought Charles had been a most unlikely person to commit suicide. Indeed, it was this conviction of the witness that had led to his interview with the police at Scotland Yard two days after the funeral.

Following an adjournment for lunch, Florence's mother, Mrs Anne Campbell, was called to testify.

Questioned first by Sir Henry James, she spoke of her daughter's early marriage to Alexander Ricardo, saying that 'for some years they lived happily together but after the death of his mother Captain Ricardo appeared to be drinking excessively'.

After recalling Florence's visit to Malvern, and Alexander's rapid deterioration, Mrs Campbell told the court that she had taken Florence away from Malvern in November 1870, from which date Florence had remained with the family at Buscot until February 1871.

On the matter of Florence's subsequent move to Leigham Court Road in Streatham, she said that Dr Gully's frequent visits to her daughter had met with her 'entire disapproval' and that Florence's refusal to terminate the scandalous affair had resulted in an estrangement from her family that lasted four years. When asked if she considered her daughter's attachment to Dr Gully to be a criminal (i.e. adulterous) one, she indignantly retorted:

'Certainly not. I thought she entertained an extraordinary infatuation for Dr Gully, and as her mother I so regarded it.'

She went on to say that when she first met Charles she broached the subject of Florence's affair with the doctor, but Charles said that Florence had 'told him everything' and that he was 'quite satisfied'. When she had later urged him to tell his mother about Florence's past he refused, saying: 'We are old enough to judge for ourselves. The name of Dr Gully will never be mentioned by me to her.'

In response to further interrogation from Sir Henry James the witness said that after the family reconciliation she had visited her daughter at The Priory and found her surrounded 'with every comfort'. She felt that her daughter's marriage to Charles was a very happy one, notwithstanding that during their stay at Buscot he had discussed with her the matter of Florence's drinking habits.

The proceedings for the day ended with the reading of three letters written by the young couple shortly before Charles's death, the contents of which gave the impression that all was well at The Priory before the tragedy.

Wednesday 26 July. As on previous days, said *The Daily Telegraph*, 'the public attendance was large, especially after lunch when a considerable number of ladies assembled in the billiards room, forming yet another faction of the fascinated audience'.

As soon as the day's proceedings were begun Mrs Campbell was recalled.

Many of those present must have felt great sympathy for the dignified, kindly matron who came before them once more. Throughout her testimony so far she had quietly supported and defended the daughter whose scandalous behaviour had caused her so much unhappiness. But, sadly, any anguish she had known in the past was as nothing to what she was to suffer during the next few days.

Now, in response to questions from Sir Henry James she stated that she and her son William had arrived at The Priory about four-thirty on the day before Charles's death; they had been met at

Balham station by Mrs Cox who told them that Charles was very seriously ill and that there was little hope of saving him. From what Mrs Cox had said, Mrs Campbell had gathered the impression that he had deliberately taken poison.

The witness said that although her daughter had been very distressed throughout his illness she had tried to appear as composed as possible whenever she was in the sickroom so that Charles was not upset still further. After his death, though, her composure had crumbled and she had 'cried very much, appearing to be stunned'. Mrs Campbell went on to say that newspaper articles about Charles's death had contributed to Florence's distress – added to which she had also received a number of anonymous letters, some of which were very wicked and 'she was losing sleep because of them'.

On the subject of Florence's insomnia, the witness was asked about the laurel water prescribed by Dr Gully. In reply she said that her daughter had written on 16 April to say that she was sleeping naturally with the help of the sitz-baths and spinal washes. She had not mentioned Dr Gully or the laurel water, Mrs Campbell said, indeed, she (witness) had first heard about it on the day after the funeral. She felt sure, she said, that Florence and Mrs Cox were the only people who knew that the laurel water was in The Priory; she felt sure that Royes Bell and Charles were unaware of its presence.

Asked if Mrs Cox had left Florence's household for good, the witness said that she had, adding:

'She is going to Jamaica as soon as this inquiry is over. She was going before the death of Mr Bravo.'

Mrs Campbell went on to say that her daughter and Mrs Cox were on 'quite good terms' but that after Florence's collapse in Brighton Mrs Cox was no longer needed. She went on to say that she had last seen Mrs Cox at the Campbells' meeting on 7 July. Asked when she last saw Dr Gully, she said that she had seen him on a train, adding, 'He went out of it very quickly when he saw me.'

Asked if Florence's infatuation for James Gully had already begun before Alexander's death, she replied:

'Captain Ricardo made some rumour about it, but he made so many rumours when under the influence of drink that I did not regard it.'

In defence of her daughter the witness went on to say that until

Alexander's death she thought Florence 'liked Dr Gully as a friend'. She added, however, that in May 1871 she became aware of the attachment between them. 'It was at that time that I ceased to receive her,' she said.

Mr Lewis approached the next question with caution:

'Much as you disapproved of that intimacy between Dr Gully and your daughter,' he said, 'were you under the firm impression that impropriety had *not* taken place?'

Mrs Campbell: 'I am, and I was then. When I had that interview with Mr Bravo I did not refer to the connection with Dr Gully as having been a criminal one. We both looked on it as an extraordinary infatuation. He always told me he was very proud of her, and very fond of her.'

She went on to say that she and Charles had become firm friends during the five months they had known one another. Shortly before he died, she said, she had tried to question him about the cause of his illness; she had touched his arm, saying, 'Charlie, what did you take?', but he had turned his head away impatiently saying he did not know.

That afternoon Mr Murphy rose to examine the witness. In answer to his first question she said that Charles had disliked Dr Gully very much and 'wished that he could annihilate him'. She also said that she had heard of Mrs Cox's proposed visit to Jamaica before Charles became ill, adding that 'he did not wish to have her back after she came back from Jamaica, to save the expense'.

Back on the subject of the laurel water, she was asked to recall the conversation she had had about it with Florence. In reply she said that they were in Mrs Cox's room after the funeral and Mrs Cox had drawn attention to the bottle of laurel water. Florence had said again that she did not need it and that it should be thrown away. Mrs Cox did not, however, remove it from the medicine cupboard during this conversation, but left it where it was on the shelf.

George Lewis then asked Mrs Campbell: 'Didn't you think it was very strange when Mrs Bravo told you that this laurel water was from Dr Gully? Didn't you think it most extraordinary that her resolution should have been broken, and that she should have been in communication with Dr Gully and getting laurel water from him?'

Mrs Campbell: 'My daughter had nothing to do with it. It was

Mrs Cox who made the communication. I thought it would have been much better had she not done so. I should rather she had nothing to do with Dr Gully.'

The witness then said she had forgotten to mention the laurel water to the police – owing to Mrs Cox's having told her that she had thrown it away. Florence's solicitor, Mr Henry Brooks, however, had warned her that she might be questioned about it during the second inquiry.

Concerning Mrs Cox's meetings with Dr Gully before the tragedy, Mrs Campbell said:

'I heard she'd met him going to the station two or three times. It was no affair of mine what Mrs Cox did with Dr Gully. I saw very little of Mrs Cox. I told her I was sorry she had gone to him on the Thursday to inquire for any remedies.'

Asked if she thought her daughter was happy in her marriage she said: 'I am quite sure she was. She liked Charles as a companion. He was an intellectual man and she liked him very much. She married him, as far as I can tell, for love.' The witness did admit, however, that the couple did quarrel over his mother's interference in their domestic affairs.

Referring to the 'grave charge' against Charles of which Florence had spoken to Chief Inspector Clarke, Mr Lewis asked Mrs Campbell if her daughter had made any complaints to her after Charles's death. Mrs Campbell said that her daughter had made no complaints at all, adding that 'she was more in grief than anything'.

Asked to recall Alexander Ricardo's condition in 1870, she said that a doctor in Malvern found him to be comatose and apparently suffering from an overdose of a narcotic. She had assumed that his condition was due to alcoholic excess.

George Lewis then asked her: 'Did the doctor tell you that Captain Ricardo had great debility of the stomach and almost uncontrollable vomiting, and that the coats of the stomach were "worn out"?'

Mrs Campbell replied, 'Yes, I remember that I had seen him so in our house whenever he took a quantity of spirits.' She added, 'He remained at Buscot nearly five months, and off and on he was sick night and day.' She had, she said, known him to vomit sixty times in one day and that he had said he was 'used to it'.

At this point the Attorney-General rose to ask the witness if either

Florence or Mrs Cox had suggested that Charles had killed himself on account of Dr Gully. She said that both women had told her that 'it made Charles unhappy whenever he passed Dr Gully's house', and that although they both thought it was a case of suicide, she, for her part, 'had never supposed such a thing'.

Mr Murphy then rose to ask the witness if she felt that, once married, Florence still needed the friendship of a mature person like Mrs Cox. She replied:

'No, not after her marriage, but as Mrs Cox was going to Jamaica and she had no home to go to, my daughter kept her more from kindness, I think.'

Questioned by a juror she said it was not arranged till after the wedding that Mrs Cox should go to Jamaica. In reply to another juror who wished to discover whether Florence would benefit financially by her husband's death, the witness said that the £20,000 settled on her daughter was not to come to her till after the death of Mr and Mrs Joseph Bravo, adding, 'There was no immediate advantage.'

Mrs Campbell ended her testimony by saying that her daughter had brought a surprise gift of 'dark blue ties and other things for her husband, he being an Oxford man'. Said Mrs Campbell, 'She showed them to me after his death.'

On Thursday 27 July there was an unusually large crowd hoping to gain admittance to the Bedford Hotel. Word had spread that Mrs Jane Cox was to be called that day, and everyone was eager to see her and hear her evidence. To the general disappointment, however, the first witness of the day turned out to be Mr Joseph Bravo, recalled for further questioning.

He was asked to repeat his account of the assistance given to Mrs Cox in the past, which he did, and after saying that he believed her to be a 'very respectable woman', he continued:

'About two months after my son's marriage she called at my office and informed me of the serious illness of Mistress Margaret Cox, in Jamaica. Knowing as I did the surroundings of the case, I expressed a strong opinion as to the propriety of her going at once to Jamaica. She urged that it would be inconvenient and she knew not what to do with her boys. I urged her in all ways, but it was all in vain.'

Referring to Charles's earlier mysterious bout of sickness, he said that 'it was early in March'.

This ended the testimony of Mr Joseph Bravo, but the spectators were to be disappointed once again, for the first witness called after the luncheon adjournment was one John Atkinson, a barrister who had known Charles since their Oxford days in 1863. After telling the court that they had shared rooms for a period of two years he made this highly significant observation:

'I noticed that he always drank a very large drink of cold water. In fact, I have never seen him go to bed without doing so. He very often took it from the water bottle in his room and almost invariably without using a tumbler. This was his inveterate habit.'

Describing Charles's character, he said:

'He was the last man on earth to commit suicide. He was better acquainted than any barrister I know with medicine and medical jurisprudence. He was a very clear-headed man with a great deal of common sense and very little sentiment. No feeling for any woman would make him take a painful and uncertain poison, the effects of which he was thoroughly acquainted with. I also know he was in no money difficulty.'

This precise and articulate statement seemed to settle the matter for the Attorney-General, who suddenly interrupted the witness to pronounce that he 'thought it was arranged to call Mrs Cox'.

Mr George Lewis, clearly annoyed by the interruption, produced yet another witness – Mr Meredith Brown, a stockbroker. This gentleman testified that Charles was financially astute and very prudent in money matters, but not obsessively so.

As the stockbroker left the room the excitement amongst the spectators rose again for they sensed that the witness they had come to see was about to enter the court. And then came the words they had waited for:

'Call Mrs Cox.'

15

Scandalous Revelations

Mrs Jane Cox, dressed entirely in black and wearing a rather pert, feather-trimmed hat, was escorted into the room by Mr Harford, the husband of her old friend.

Although appearing outwardly composed during the examination that followed, at times she stroked the surface of the table, her gloved hand moving in tense, compulsive movements.

In response to her counsel, Mr Murphy, she began to tell of her life before she had become Florence's companion. She spoke in such a low voice, however, that Mr Murphy had difficulty in hearing her and asked her to speak a little louder. At this Mr George Lewis rose to say that he, too, was having difficulty in hearing her replies. This brought Mr Parry (for Dr Gully) to his feet, saying that during Mrs Campbell's evidence Sir Henry James had repeated her answers so that the court might hear them clearly. He now suggested that Mr Murphy did the same for Mrs Cox. Mr Lewis responded to this by saying that if the witness 'could speak over a dinner table she could speak loud enough' for him to hear when he was sitting opposite her. This brought loud applause from the crowded court, which angered Sir Henry James who exclaimed, 'Really, this is monstrous!' His words were swiftly endorsed by Mr Parry – clearly keen to make his mark and never slow to protest – who said, 'This is terrible in a court of justice – applause, and of *that* kind. It's something fearful. This kind of terrorism is enough to intimidate the most courageous.'

Calm was restored by the coroner threatening to clear the court if there was 'a repetition of that kind of thing', after which Mr Murphy continued his examination.

Answering now in a more audible voice Mrs Cox finished recalling her history, after which she was questioned on the relationship between Florence and Charles – and very quickly stretched naïveté to its limits by saying that the reason Charles had sometimes stayed the night at The Priory before his marriage was because his mother had objected to his going home in the cold night air.

After she had stated that both Charles and Florence had wished her to stay on at The Priory after their marriage the inquiry was adjourned for the day, by which time considerable crowds had gathered outside the hotel. As the legal gentlemen, witnesses and spectators left the building the crowd surged forward, eager to catch a glimpse of Mrs Cox. However she was swiftly propelled towards a waiting carriage that whisked her away to her lodgings at 7 Manchester Street, near Baker Street in London's West End.

Friday 28 July, and the crowds were there in force again, many people being turned away as the courtroom filled with spectators eager to witness Mrs Cox's continuing inquisition.

Resuming her testimony, Mrs Cox was questioned by Mr Murphy regarding an advertisement that had appeared in *The Times* of 17 January that year:

> £100 Reward. This is to give notice that the above reward will be paid to anyone who will give such information as will lead to the conviction of the writer of certain anonymous letters which have been for some time past sent to a lady in Kensington Palace Green reflecting upon the character of some of her near-relatives. Information to be sent to H. M. C. E. Messrs Ingle, Cooper and Holmes, solicitors, City Bank Chambers, Threadneedle Street, City, EC.

The advertisement had been shown to her by Charles Bravo, she said, who had 'no doubt' that it had originated from his stepfather, and that the anonymous letters referred to had come from Dr Gully. Said Mrs Cox: 'He was very much annoyed, and had said he thought it "a wicked thing of that old wretch".'

Questioned further, she told the court that in February of that year the tenant of her house in Lancaster Road had died and she had been obliged to make frequent journeys to Notting Hill to arrange another letting. On three of those trips, she said, she had chanced to meet Dr Gully. The first meeting had taken place outside the Army and Navy Stores in Victoria. Shortly after this they had chanced to meet again, which occasion had followed Charles's having himself received an anonymous letter accusing him of marrying Florence for her money and speaking 'in very vile terms' of Florence's relationship with Dr Gully. The letter, Charles believed, had come from the doctor. On meeting Dr Gully, she said, she had told him that Mr Bravo was 'very much astonished' that he should send an anonymous letter of such a vile nature. Dr Gully, she said, had indignantly denied all knowledge of it.

It was at this meeting, she stated, that she asked the doctor for a treatment for Jamaica fever which he had promised her as she was intending to visit the island on business. They had sometimes discussed family matters, she said, each having lost a daughter in childhood. Voicing her admiration for him, she described him as 'the greatest hydropathic doctor in the world'.

The written treatment for Jamaica fever, she said, had arrived soon afterwards in the post, and she told the court how Charles Bravo had stopped her in the street on her way to the station with two letters for her in his hand. He had met the postman and collected the morning post from him and, recognising Dr Gully's handwriting on an envelope addressed to the witness, demanded that she open it there and then in his presence. She told the court:

'I told him I could not do it; I was in such a hurry I should lose the train. He again insisted upon it. I was annoyed at that, because I thought he had no right to ask me to open my own letters. I told him if he liked to come with me to the station I would open them there. He said I could open them going along, which I did.'

She went on to say that one envelope contained a letter from her son, the other held three pages from Dr Gully on the treatment of Jamaica fever. The deceased, she said, examined the papers from the doctor.

Brought back to the subject of her chance meetings with the doctor, the ex-companion went on to say that the second time they met was while he was studying the timetable at Balham station. On this occasion she had told him of her mistress's pain and lack of sleep following her miscarriage and he suggested the use of sitz-baths and spinal washes. The next day, Saturday 8 April, she said, he had left a bottle of laurel water at her house in Notting Hill. This she had collected on the following Monday, 10 April, taking it back to The Priory – only to find, however, that Florence was sleeping naturally and did not need it after all.

'She asked me to put it in my room,' said Mrs Cox. 'It was a small white bottle with a glass stopper and a piece of white leather over the stopper.'

Questioned further, she told the court that she and Dr Gully had met on a third occasion and had travelled in the same carriage between Balham and Notting Hill, a journey of about half an hour. Florence, she said, had known about her meetings with the doctor.

Speaking of the deceased, she said that he hated Dr Gully so much that he said he wished he was dead and that he 'would like to see his funeral crossing Tooting Common'.

Questioned again on the matter of the anonymous letter which Charles had received and which he believed had come from Dr Gully, she said that Charles had later spoken of it again. Asked what had become of the letter she said, 'I saw him tear it up and throw it on the fire. He asked me if I thought there was any use in keeping it and I said, "No; I would burn it if I were you."'

The witness then gave an account of a quarrel between Florence and Charles that had arisen over his mother's interference in their domestic affairs. Said Mrs Cox: 'She wanted her to put down the horses and cobs, to dispense with a lady's maid, and retrench expenditure.' During the quarrel Charles had struck his wife, Mrs Cox told the court, after which he had stated his determination to leave. She, however, she said, repeating the evidence in her Treasury statement, had prevailed on him to stay and make it up with his wife.

After an adjournment for lunch Mrs Cox was questioned further regarding the marital strife at The Priory. In reply she said that on Good Friday, four days before the tragedy, Florence had come downstairs after lunch, and, still weak from her miscarriage and needing rest, had gone to lie down on the sofa in the morning room. Charles, who was also in the morning room, had been very restless, so much so that Florence had tried to persuade him to go for a walk around the garden, or go up to his room for a while. He would have none of it, though; said Mrs Cox: 'He was very restless – always in and out of the room. He was very angry about it. He said that if the servants lighted a fire in his room he would put it out.'

Going on to repeat her Treasury statement almost word for word, she said that later that evening he told her that Florence was 'a selfish pig', and that he despised himself for marrying her, that he wished he were dead and was quite determined to go away; 'he had made up his mind he would not live with her any longer'. It was by means of her remonstrations and mediations, she said, that the disharmony had eventually been dispelled.

Taken to the matter of her trip to Worthing on the fateful Tuesday of 18 April she said that on her return she had caught the five o'clock express train from Brighton. 'It was about twenty minutes past seven when I arrived at The Priory,' she said. 'I think I looked into the morning room first and then I went up to Mrs Charles Bravo's room. I was rather surprised to see her dressing for dinner and told her she ought to go to bed. I went upstairs to my room. I had not had time to dress so I merely washed my hands.'

She went on to tell the court that they retired to the morning room after dinner, and that she and Mrs Bravo went upstairs shortly before nine o'clock. Having fetched a glass of wine from the dining room, she said, she 'helped Mrs Bravo undress and take down her hair and replait it'. When Mrs Bravo had finished undressing, she continued, Mary Ann Keeber came upstairs with the cans of hot water and was sent down again to fetch more wine. While she was away Charles came into the dressing room and said to his wife: 'You have sent down for more wine; you have drunk nearly a bottle of wine today.'

'I do not think Mrs Bravo answered him,' said Mrs Cox. 'She was standing with her back to him, folding her compress. He went out of the room and we went into her bedroom a few minutes after.'

Mrs Cox concluded her evidence that day with details of Charles's collapse and the events that ensued. The day's proceedings were then brought to an end. Just before the court was adjourned it was estimated that the inquiry would last another two weeks – a prospect that must have pleased the public.

Even though the oppressive heat had given way to dismally wet weather there was a huge crowd outside the Bedford Hotel to watch Mrs Cox leave the court that day and hasten to the carriage that would bear her away.

On the following Monday, 31 July, the inquiry entered its third week.

The proceedings that day began with the recalling of Mrs Cox. Examined by Mr Murphy, she was asked why she had not given her poison statement to Dr Moore soon after Charles had collapsed. She replied:

'Because I was expecting Mr Harrison every moment and Dr Moore was a stranger to me. And coming from Balham I did not like to tell him such a thing. I thought it would be such a dreadful scandal in the place.'

She insisted, however, that she *had* told Mr Harrison that Charles had been sick out of the window, even though Mr Harrison was adamant that she had not.

Mr Murphy then asked her if it had been suggested to her that she should confront Charles with her alleged poison statement. She replied, 'I only wish it *had* been.' Asked if any of the doctors had said anything to imply that they doubted the truth of her statement, she answered: 'Never for a moment.'

Also concerning the events of the fateful time, she told the court, 'I never undressed from Tuesday night till the Saturday morning, except removing my dress and putting my dressing-gown on.'

In response to further questioning she recalled her meeting with Sir William Gull on the landing outside the sickroom when he told her that Charles was dying and that there was no hope for him. It was at this point, she said, that she told Sir William that Charles had been sick out of the window.

The witness was then asked by Mr Murphy if she knew that Charles was in the habit of drinking water every night before he got into bed. She replied that she did not.

In answer to questions about the water bottle in Charles's room, she said that as far as she knew nobody touched or emptied it that night, adding, rather disdainfully, that it was the housemaid's job to attend to water bottles, not hers.

Further examination led to the subject of the bottle of laurel water and Mrs Cox said that 'it was not disturbed' from the time she received it from Dr Gully. She said that in a brief note from Dr Gully, left with the laurel water at her house, he had written that she 'need not be alarmed at the word *poison* on the bottle'. Apparently she was not, for, as she told the court, while it was indeed poison, it was 'not anything strong'.

After the death of Mr Bravo, she said, Mrs Bravo asked her to throw the bottle of laurel water away 'in case people said it was poison'. Added Mrs Cox, 'I know why she said it – because Mr Joseph Bravo said there were poisons in every room in the house. He called all homeopathic medicines poison. I left it in the cupboard.' Later that day, she said, she had found Florence, her mother and aunt in Florence's bedroom. There, Florence had said to the witness: 'I have been telling Mama and Auntie about Dr Gully ordering the sitz-baths and spinal washes and sending me the little bottle to make me sleep. Auntie will throw the medicine away.' Mrs Cox, however, had replied: 'Oh, no, she needn't trouble to do that. I can do it.' Now asked what became of the laurel water, Mrs Cox replied, 'I am not sure as to the time I threw it away. I thought it was a useful little bottle so I put some vinegar in it. I left it on my dressing table at The Priory.'

At this point the Attorney-General rose and read aloud some of the evidence given by Mrs Cox at the first inquest. Afterwards he suggested to her that 'a great deal of it was not true'. Eyes lowered, her gloved palm stroking compulsive circles on the table surface, Mrs Cox replied:

'It – well – I cannot exactly say it was not true. I withheld the words "for Dr Gully". That was not true.'

The Attorney-General then questioned her about the relationship between Dr Gully and Mrs Bravo, but Mrs Cox answered evasively. Asked if the doctor was very intimate with Mrs Bravo she said that he often called to see her. She also told the court that at one time Florence had worn a locket holding a photograph of the doctor. Asked if Dr Gully had treated Mrs Bravo with 'a good deal of familiarity', Mrs Cox replied that he had treated her 'as a gentleman treats a lady'. When asked if she looked upon Dr Gully 'as Mrs Bravo's lover', she said that he was 'very much interested in her'.

'Did you look upon Dr Gully merely as a friend, or did you regard him as Mrs Ricardo's lover?'

Mrs Cox did not answer, but merely stroked the table top.

The Attorney-General began to lose patience with the witness. 'I must put it to you again,' he said. 'Did you know that Dr Gully was Mrs Ricardo's lover? You were there. You lived with her for four years. You must have had a shrewd idea. I ask you now, having had all the experience you have had, did you not know, sooner or later, that Dr Gully was Mrs Ricardo's lover?'

There was silence as the court sat hushed, then:

'Yes,' said Mrs Cox. 'I think I did.'

The Attorney-General resumed his questioning directly the court reassembled after luncheon.

'At the time they went to Kissingen in 1873,' he said, 'did you know that Dr Gully was Mrs Ricardo's lover?'

Mrs Cox replied that she did not know exactly what he meant by the term *lover*. Said the Attorney-General, his voice edged with sarcasm: 'I will try and explain.' He then went on: 'You knew *he* was exceedingly fond of *her* and *she* was fond of *him* – and he was not a mere friend? You understand what a lover is?'

'I think it is very likely that if Dr Gully had not been married she would have married him,' came the reply.

There then followed questions about the various trips made by Florence, Dr Gully and Mrs Cox, in answer to which the witness spoke of vacations in Italy – 'We went via Dover and Calais, to Paris, Mâcon and Turin' – and to Brighton, Matlock and Southsea, at the latter staying at 'a place nearly opposite the fort'. Asked if Florence and Dr Gully had ever lived together as man and wife on these occasions, Mrs Cox retorted:

'No, certainly not. I should not have been with them if they had.'

Describing the break between Florence and Dr Gully she said, 'There was no quarrel. Mrs Ricardo wrote to say that she wished to give up the acquaintance. I knew she was anxious on account of her mother's health. Dr Gully seemed much grieved and Mrs Ricardo had been very sorry at the parting.'

Regarding the night of the tragedy, Mrs Cox was asked how long she was in the room with Charles before the maid came back upstairs with hot water. She said:

'I should think it was quite ten minutes, because the mustard and water had to be procured.' She went on to say that she gave Charles the mustard emetic to make him sick as she thought he had been poisoned with chloroform.

The Attorney-General, however, was not satisfied. 'Mrs Cox,' he said, 'if that was your object, and Mr Bravo had stated to you that he'd taken poison for Dr Gully – I ask you, *why* did you order that the vomit be thrown away?'

'So that he should have a clean basin when he wanted it,' came the reply.

She was then asked by the Attorney-General if she could swear that she had indeed told Mr Harrison that Charles had told her that he had taken poison. She answered:

'My impression is that I told him, but of course, chloroform was so impressed on my mind that I really could not swear that I did mention the word "poison" to him.'

Then there followed another question about the laurel water: 'There were a great many inquiries about poison and a great deal of conversation about it, and you knew that Mr Bravo was supposed to have died from an irritant poison. Did it not occur to you, therefore, that it was a very foolish thing to throw the laurel water away?'

'No, I never thought anything of it,' said the witness, and went on to say that she had not bothered to tell Mr and Mrs Joseph Bravo about the laurel water. She had first mentioned it to Mr Henry Brooks at the Campbells' meeting on 7 July, she said, adding that she had not thought it important enough to mention in her Treasury statement.

At this point an adjournment was called until the next day – not, however, before Sir Henry James had urged the coroner to announce that in the future 'no ladies or children would be admitted to the courtroom'.

While the women present groaned in disappointment at the words the journalists must have heard them with pleasure for they implied a promise of even more scandalous revelations to come, which would ensure an even greater demand for the newspapers. And what further revelations might follow Mrs Cox's shocking admission that the gay young widow of Balham had travelled abroad with the ageing Dr Gully?

On Tuesday 1 August the coroner's ruling of the previous day was rigidly enforced and no females were allowed into the courtroom, the space allocated to the general public being 'densely thronged exclusively by the sterner sex'.

As soon as Mrs Cox had been recalled there followed several questions about her efforts to assist Charles after his collapse. Then the Attorney-General asked:

'Can you explain why, if you had told Mr Harrison already that Mr Bravo had said he'd taken poison, you should specially call Royes Bell to tell *him*?'

Mrs Cox answered this vital point by saying that she wanted to tell Royes Bell the *exact words* that Charles had used, though without mentioning Dr Gully's name.

Mr George Lewis then rose to question the witness on Mrs Bravo's relationship with Dr Gully. After receiving several evasive answers he tried a different tack and said to her:

'Will you answer my question, madam? Were you under the impression that Mr Bravo believed his wife had had a criminal connection with Dr Gully?'

Mrs Cox replied that Charles did not know at the time of the engagement – but after Florence had spoken to him about her past attachment and he had confessed his affair with the woman in Maidenhead he had been fully aware of the nature of the attachment. At the time of the engagement, though, Mrs Cox said, she herself had kept from him what Mrs Bravo had told her 'after she had given up her acquaintance with Dr Gully'.

Mr Lewis: 'What do you mean by that?'

'I suppose you can draw your own conclusions,' replied the witness. Pressed further by her examiner, she said:

'She told me of her intimacy with Dr Gully.'

'Criminal intimacy?'

'Yes.' And she swiftly added: 'But you must remember that I had no idea of that during Mrs Bravo's acquaintance with Dr Gully. Not the slightest.' She went on to say that the admission had been made to her before Florence's marriage, and that she had urged her mistress to tell Mr Charles Bravo. 'Did you hear her tell him?' she was then asked, to which she replied, 'No, I did not, but he spoke to me on the subject.'

'Did he tell you that she had confessed to him that her intimacy had been criminal?'

'Yes, he did.'

Under tenacious examination by Mr George Lewis, Mrs Cox admitted that she had revealed Florence's confession to two persons following Charles's death, neither of whom was named publicly in court, though it was clear that one was her friend, Mrs Harford. At this point Mr Murphy, Mrs Cox's counsel, became more than usually defensive on his client's behalf, and rose to take Mr Lewis to task for what amounted to his persistence in his examination of her. Said Mr Murphy:

'I really must interfere. This is following up the unnecessary annoyance which this lady has already experienced. Mrs Cox, I may tell the jury, came here with a series of letters containing representations of gibbets with the witness hanging from them, and this is a continuation of the terrorism which has prevailed here since that time.'

Mr Lewis, however, was not to be swayed from his course by appeals for sympathy. 'I should wish to make an observation as to that,' he said. 'I intend strictly to perform a duty here quite regardless of any consequences to anybody.' This was greeted with cries of 'Hear, hear!' from a juryman and a burst of applause which was swiftly quelled. Mr Lewis went on: 'I intend, as far as I can, to elicit the truth as to how this gentleman came by his death; and I am surprised that a Queen's Counsel should have spoken as he has done after the delicacy I exhibited.'

Mr Murphy, saying that he had observed no delicacy, passed the letter to the jury – 'There is the letter' – at which Mr Gorst rightly protested, saying that he objected to Mr Murphy addressing the jury 'not publicly'.

Mr Murphy: 'I have spoken publicly. Let the representative of the Crown look at it and see the letter sent to this lady to prepare her for giving evidence.'

Mr Gorst: 'I would not notice such things.'

Mr Murphy: 'Ah, you have never had one, and I hope you never will.'

Following Mr Murphy's attempts to foster a little sympathy for his client, Mrs Cox's examination by Mr Lewis was resumed, during which she had to extricate herself from a succession of tight corners, countering his tenacity with a feigned innocence as they shadow-boxed around her denial of complicity in the adulterous affair between Florence and the doctor.

Under questioning she said that the doctor had felt very bitter towards Florence for ending their acquaintance and had sent both women 'very angry' letters – which had since been destroyed. However, he had written to Florence shortly afterwards apologising for his outburst.

The witness's examination continued after the luncheon break, at which time she denied the suggestion that she and Florence had collaborated over their statements to the Treasury. On the subject of the relationship between her master and mistress she said that although they seemed happy together generally they were both quick-tempered – and when Mrs Bravo over-indulged in sherry she became rather irritable and awkward. With regard to her former mistress's drinking, she said she had 'acquired the habit during the lifetime of her first husband'.

Mrs Cox was certainly being thorough. Having presented her ex-mistress as a fallen woman she was now presenting her as a drunken one as well.

Asked if she had intentionally concealed from Mr Charles Bravo her meetings with Dr Gully and the presence of the laurel water she replied, 'It could do no good to tell him,' adding that Charles had known nothing about the prescribed sitz-baths or spinal washes either.

Questioned further about the events of the evening of Charles's collapse, Mrs Cox said that she and Florence had been alone upstairs for about twenty minutes while Charles was still down in the morning room. Pressed by Mr Lewis, she agreed that it would take only a few minutes to pass from one of the upstairs rooms to another.

Mr Lewis then inquired as to why Mary Ann Keeber had not heard Charles mention poison when she and Mrs Cox reached his side after he had collapsed. Mrs Cox said:

'He called out very loudly for hot water – but he spoke softly to me about taking poison.'

Under continuing pressure from Mr Lewis, she now insisted again that she *had* told Mr Harrison of Charles's having taken poison – but that she had withheld Dr Gully's name from her original statement in order to protect Florence's reputation.

Speaking of her ex-mistress, the witness stated that Florence had been 'kind and generous' to her. Further, she admitted that her salary at The Priory had been £100 a year, which was 'the principal support' of her boys.

With Mrs Cox giving her view of Dr Gully as a charming, intelligent man, 'able to exert a strong influence over women', the proceedings were adjourned for the day.

Wednesday 2 August. With the resumption of the proceedings Mrs Jane Cox was recalled and, dressed as usual in black, took her now familiar position at the table, her gaze lowered, her expression composed.

It was Sir Henry James who rose to question her, but throughout his examination she steadfastly refused to admit that Florence's illness after the Kissingen interlude had been anything but a 'natural' one. Keeping her eyes lowered, and with her gloved hand tracing the repeated pattern on the table's surface, she refused to acknowledge that Dr Gully had performed an abortion, preferring to see the operation as one for the removal of a 'kind of tumour'. Perhaps her reluctance to admit what she must have known to be the truth was the necessity not to compromise her position with regard to future employment; she would not wish to be thought of as a woman who had condoned such behaviour. Whatever her reasons, however, she made it very clear that whatever sins had been committed they had not been committed with her approval or even her knowledge.

Later, when questioned about her relationship with Charles Bravo, Mrs Cox said he had treated her with every consideration. When asked if she had borne him any ill-feeling she replied: 'Not the slightest.'

After admitting that she was no longer employed by Mrs Bravo, and that she was 'substantially without resources and had her children to support', she was asked by Sir Henry James whether she had managed to find other employment. She said she had not.

Following the luncheon adjournment Mr Serjeant Parry (for Dr Gully) asked the witness if she had ever discussed poison during her meetings with the doctor. She replied that she had done no such thing.

'The bottle of laurel water was taken to your house in Lancaster Road by Dr Gully,' said Mr Parry. Are you quite sure – and I ask you in the most emphatic manner I can – that the bottle was never *opened* or *emptied* in any way until after Charles Bravo's death?'

'I am quite certain about it.'

Asked about Charles's mysterious bout of sickness early in March of that year, she said:

'I never heard of it till I saw the letter in *The Daily Telegraph*.'*

Finally, Mr Parry had a very important observation to make and put the question:

'You have told us that Mr Bravo said, "I have taken poison for Dr Gully. Don't tell Florence." And yet the first person he appealed to was his wife, Florence, when he called for hot water. Does that not strike you as very strange?'

* See p. 86.

'It never struck me,' came the reply.

This simple statement concluded Jane Cox's testimony and she was free to go.

The jury had been given much to consider during her five days as a witness and many of her answers had been far from satisfactory. Whatever some of the jurors might have had in mind, however, they had yet to hear the evidence of Florence Bravo. Though extremely fragile in some ways, the young widow could be as strong-willed as the next person when she chose to be.

16

The Beautiful Young Widow

The morning of Thursday 3 August was taken up first by a discussion among the jury as to whether they should sit on the following Bank Holiday Monday – they agreed to do so – and afterwards by the reading of Mrs Cox's lengthy deposition. These matters completed, an adjournment for luncheon was called, after which the spectators had their patience rewarded by hearing at last the call they had waited for:

'Call Mrs Charles Bravo.'

As Charles Bravo's beautiful young widow appeared on the arm of her brother William Campbell every head was turned towards her. Florence Bravo knew well what had been said of her by Mrs Cox over the preceding days, and as she entered, well aware of the rows of avid eyes fixed upon her, her emotions can perhaps be imagined. For the moment, though, she gave nothing away. Wearing deep mourning, with a heavy veil, she was led to the table by William where she was sworn. She kissed the book, her hand trembling noticeably, then sat and lifted the veil from her face, revealing pale but composed features. Breathing a deep sigh, she prepared herself for the examination.

Prompted by Sir Henry James, her counsel, Florence told the court of her past, first of all speaking of her marriage to Captain Ricardo. In her evidence she recalled that he was constantly sick when intoxicated and had been stricken with delirium tremens three or four times. During their last visit to Malvern in 1870, she said, he was drinking heavily, adding, 'The habit had been increasing very much at this time. It grew upon him rapidly.'

She then admitted that on learning that he was in the company of another woman at the time of his death she had refused to pay his debts.

Speaking of Dr Gully she told the court that when he had left Malvern in 1871 he had moved into a house near hers in Leigham Court Road, and that when she and Mrs Cox had moved to The Priory in March 1874 the doctor had moved into Orwell Lodge, only a few minutes' walk away.

For the most part Florence related her earlier past with clarity and composure but when she came to describe her meeting with Dr Gully in Brighton after her dismissal of him, she became distressed and agitated – so much so that on several occasions the court was obliged to wait while she composed herself.

Such moments of drama, of course, only ensured the more rapt attention from the spectators, more and more of whom had pressed into the room as the young widow gave her evidence. Eventually the crush became so unbearable that the coroner gave directions that no more persons should be allowed in.

In the course of her questioning, Florence made the painful confession that she had travelled to Kissingen with James Gully, and that 'at one time there had been an improper intimacy' between them, which had resulted in a miscarriage. She told the court that she had suffered greatly at this time and owed her life to Mrs Cox's care. She stated that after this illness the improper intimacy between the doctor and herself had ceased.

'We know of your statement to the Treasury, Mrs Bravo,' began Sir Henry with some delicacy, 'in which you said that this intimacy was an innocent one. Of course you would be most anxious to keep back this knowledge of your error from the public and from everybody connected with you.'

In reply Florence said that she had promised Charles 'on a solemn oath not to divulge it', adding that she had not been under oath when she made her Treasury statement. Further to this, she said that her mother did not know her secret 'until two or three days ago'.

Later on, Florence gave an account of the meeting with Dr Gully in the Lower Lodge before her marriage. She had not spoken to the doctor since that day, she said, though she had 'seen him twice, at a distance, walking across the common', adding, 'I saw him from my window when I pulled up the venetians. I knew him by his dog.'

There followed some points about the marriage settlement, after which the inquiry was adjourned for the day.

Following Thursday's revelations it was hardly surprising that on the next morning, 4 August, the Bedford Hotel was once again besieged at an early hour as the common folk and the gentry rubbed shoulders in their eagerness to hear more of the testimony of Mrs Bravo.

When the proceedings began, Florence, again swathed in black crape, was once more escorted into the court by her brother. When she was seated and her examination under Sir Henry James was resumed, the assembly heard that she had changed her mind about part of her statement on the previous day. She had told the jury that improper intimacy between herself and Dr Gully had only occurred once – during the visit to Kissingen. Now Sir Henry asked her if there had ever been intimacy between them 'on any occasion before the visit to Kissingen'. The court was hushed as it waited for her reply. Then it came:

'Yes.'

As soon as she had spoken, however, her composure collapsed and she began to weep. Asked why she had misled her husband on this delicate matter she said that she had not wanted him to think that she had been the doctor's mistress for a long time. She continued to weep and again the proceedings were adjourned to give her the opportunity to compose herself.

In later evidence, she said that her mother-in-law had tried to curb her extravagance and that Charles was sometimes torn between his loyalties to his wife and his mother. Asked if Charles had been a difficult man to live with, she said that she did not want to say 'anything against him' and again began to cry. Questioned further regarding her husband's temperament she admitted that he had struck her once but that he had 'burst into tears immediately he had done it'. 'He was only like a child,' she said. 'He was excessively sorry for it afterwards.'

With regard to their disputes over money, Florence said: 'It was all through his mother. We never had a word between us as long as we were left to ourselves. While his mother was away at St Leonards we were happy as the day was long. He was kind and attentive and took an interest in all domestic matters.' She went on to say that they had been happy in each other's company. He often used to read to her, she said, and they frequently entertained his friends and members of his family.

Later in her testimony she said that she had offered to pay off the remainder of the lease of Orwell Lodge if Dr Gully would leave Balham. He had refused, however, saying that he had spent a good deal of money on his house and had no intention of leaving it.

Still on the subject of Dr Gully, Florence said that Charles often spoke of him in abusive terms and said that it angered him to pass his house every time he walked home. To ease the situation, she said, she had even considered leaving The Priory.

This evidence was followed by a detailed account of the happy Easter weekend at The Priory just before the tragedy, and of the trip to town on the fateful Tuesday. She told the court that she lunched alone and that after taking a little champagne she had retired to the morning room to rest until her husband's return.

'He came in and kissed me most affectionately,' she related, 'and said he had had a jolly lunch with my uncle. He was pleased with his presents and his anger of the morning had gone, as it always did . . . He called the gardener and asked him to lend him his knife to cut the pieces of tobacco and he told me he was going to have a smoke in the garden. A few minutes afterwards he came down dressed for riding, to my astonishment.'

The witness went on to say that when her husband returned from his ride with the runaway cob he seemed in pain and looked ill, so he took a warm bath. After Mrs Cox's arrival, she added, they went into dinner.

Continuing, Florence stated that after a rather uncomfortable meal they retired to the morning room, following which she and Mrs Cox went upstairs soon after half-past eight. Florence estimated that they were in her dressing room for about a quarter of an hour before Charles came upstairs. Asked if Charles had remonstrated with her about the amount of sherry she took, she said:

'Yes, he had. He had a horror of ladies taking too much wine.'

She went on to say that she had been 'utterly exhausted' that night and had fallen asleep within minutes. She had not heard Charles's screams for help. She wished she had; she would have gone to him at once. By the time she reached his bedroom, she said, he was already unconscious and Mrs Cox was doing all she could to assist him.

There came then the significant question as to why she had not shown any surprise when Dr Johnson said that Charles might have taken poison. In reply she said that she had assumed that he meant Charles had accidentally taken too much laudanum or chloroform.

After the luncheon adjournment, Sir Henry resumed his examination of the young widow. At one stage, when speaking of Charles's illness, she said he had cried out with fearful pain, saying: 'Lord have mercy on me! Oh, Christ!'

Asked when she knew for certain that Charles was poisoned, she said: 'When Sir William Gull came. I should not have sent for him if I had known he had taken poison. He would have been of no use.'

Questioned about Griffiths, the coachman, she said she did not know that he used antimony in her stables and that she 'totally disapproved of horses taking medicine'. She said that she often went into the stables in the mornings to see her horses and feed them with carrots and apples.

'Did you ever, Mrs Bravo,' asked Sir Henry, 'go to any cupboard and see or take away any medicine from it?'

'No, never. I had nothing to do with it. I did not know where it was.'

The witness went on to say that during her last miscarriage Mr Royes Bell had prescribed a sedative but she had not used it. Furthermore, she did *not* ask Mrs Cox to get any treatments from Dr Gully. As to the laurel water, she said, she did not need it anyway, as she was sleeping naturally.

'Mrs Cox took the bottle away immediately,' she said. 'I never had it in my possession.'

Sir Henry: 'Did you ever, at any time, take anything out of that bottle or use anything that was in it for any purpose whatsoever?'

'No.'

Sir Henry James then read to the court Florence's Treasury statement. Then he asked her:

'Have you the slightest knowledge of how your husband came by his death?'

'No.'

With this Sir Henry's examination came to an end and Florence, showing signs of extreme exhaustion, was allowed to retire to another room to rest for a short while.

When she returned to the crowded courtroom and took her place at the table once more she found herself faced by Mr Lewis. So far she had been examined only by her own counsel, Sir Henry James, who had carefully brought out in her testimony that evidence which he had thought it advisable to reveal. Now she was to be examined by the representative of Mr Joseph Bravo. It must have been a daunting prospect, and Florence must have felt some relief when the examination was temporarily postponed by Mr Lewis's requesting that a court messenger be sent to The Priory to fetch the letters Charles had written to her.

Following the request Sir Henry James suggested that the court adjourn for the day, adding that as the next day on which the jury was to sit was the coming Bank Holiday Monday it would be better, out of 'consideration for Mrs Bravo' and 'for the public peace in the neighbourhood' – there being horse racing held at Streatham – if Mrs Bravo's examination was postponed until Tuesday. Other witnesses could be examined in her place on Monday, he said. Mr Gorst, for the Crown, agreed with the proposal.

Qualms about the likelihood of disturbance on the Bank Holiday were shared by others, among them Mr Stephenson, Treasury Solicitor. He was concerned also about the safety of The Priory from the anticipated influx of curious visitors, and as a result had written to the Home Office requesting a special police guard 'on The Priory and its boundaries and fences to protect them from the curious and callous mobs'.

On Monday 7 August the inquiry entered its fifth week. This day was also the Bank Holiday which had caused concern in the court. However, the local people and the visitors must have converged on the betting booths at Streatham Races instead, for there were fewer spectators in Balham than the police had anticipated.

Among the by now familiar faces of the legal gentlemen who sat around the table that day was the unfamiliar face of one Mr Berger, solicitor, there to watch the proceedings on behalf of the relatives of the late Captain Alexander Ricardo.

The first witness to be sworn was Mrs Ellen Harford, who said she had been a friend of Jane Cox for twenty years, from a time when the latter had been the governess Miss Edouard. Mrs Harford said she had known of Mrs Cox's expectations in her aunt's will, and confirmed that Mrs Cox had received a letter from her aunt requesting her to travel to Jamaica. She had helped Mrs Cox to compose a letter, she said, to the effect that she, Mrs Cox, would make the journey if the cost of her passage could be forwarded. The witness went on to say that Mrs Cox intended to visit Jamaica and return to England when her business affairs were settled. The witness had assured her that while she was away she would care for her sons.

Mrs Harford was followed by Mr Charles Matlocks, assistant to Smith the chemist in Balham. He said he knew Dr Gully, who had called at the shop between eight and nine o'clock on Saturday 8 April. The laurel water was made up and a dark red label marked *poison* was put on the bottle. The sale had been entered in the poison register, which was then exhibited to the jury.

Next came Dr Joseph Moore who, speaking on the subject of the water bottle in Charles's room, stated, 'It was on the little table on which I mixed the brandy and water,' adding that he had seen Mr Harrison drink a tumbler of water from the bottle, though his 'attention at the time was not directed to the water bottle'. While he was present, he said, he was not aware of the bottle being interfered with by anyone.

Mr Lewis rose then to say that 'a very grave question had arisen as to whether the poison was administered through the water bottle'. Further questioning revealed, however, that Dr Moore had been far too engrossed in the treatment of his patient to notice the position of water bottles and other bedroom requisites.

Mr Lewis: 'It never struck you that it was possible he might have been poisoned through the water bottle?'

Dr Moore replied that it had not. Asked to identify the type of water bottle used in Charles's bedroom, he said that all water bottles looked alike to him.

After the luncheon adjournment Mr George Harrison was called to testify, and confirmed that he had indeed drunk from the water bottle in Charles Bravo's room about twelve o'clock that Tuesday. He was followed by Mr Henry Smith, surgeon at King's College Hospital and Fellow of the Royal College of Surgeons, who stated that his late wife was Mrs Joseph Bravo's sister,* and that he had known Charles Bravo since his boyhood. Asked if he thought

---

* Her death on 25 November 1875 had provided an excuse for Mrs Joseph Bravo to absent herself from Charles's wedding.

Charles could have obtained tartar emetic relatively easily, he answered:

'I think it is possible, with his knowledge. He was an acute, sharp fellow – as most barristers are.'

This remark caused some laughter, following which the witness said it was most unlikely that Charles had obtained antimony from King's College Hospital, as the drugs were never stored anywhere near the operating theatres which he had frequented.

He went on to say that although he had never heard of Charles writing a prescription, it would have been a simple matter for anyone with Charles's medical knowledge to obtain up to forty grains of tartar emetic from almost any chemist. He also said that it was a well known medical practice to put small doses of tartar emetic into alcohol to cure patients who drank to excess.

At this point, Sir Henry James proposed the theory that Charles had swallowed a large amount of laudanum, perhaps in a fit of pique, and had then taken a dose of tartar emetic to clear the laudanum from his system.* Asked his opinion on this suggestion, Mr Smith said that there was no positive evidence from the results of the post-mortem to prove or disprove the theory. In addition, the witness said that in twenty-eight years of experience he had never heard of any person taking laudanum and then a poisonous dose of tartar emetic to make himself sick. He added that the usual thing was for people to call for hot water when they wanted to be sick.

Questioned further, Mr Smith agreed that if a person were to take a large dose of antimony on a full stomach he would vomit profusely within a quarter of an hour. Asked by Mr Gorst if there was anything in the post-mortem results inconsistent with Charles Bravo 'having received the poison a quarter of an hour previously – from his water bottle', the surgeon answered that there was not.

Further, the witness told the court that he had never heard of a case of suicide by antimony – it was, he said, a drug more usually associated with murder.†

* Yseult Bridges expounds this theory in her book *How Charles Bravo Died*. It will be dealt with at a later stage in this book.
† Eleven years earlier, Dr Edward Pritchard had been condemned to death for the murder of two people with antimony. Pritchard and Henry Smith had been medical students together.

Mr Smith's testimony ended the proceedings for that day.

Over that weekend and the Bank Holiday Monday, with inquisitive thrill-seekers coming to gaze at The Priory, Florence Bravo must have felt besieged. Now, however, Tuesday had come, the day for the resumption of her examination, and on that morning of 8 August it must have been with renewed dread that she took her seat facing Mr George Lewis.

For the first part of her testimony under his questioning she kept her composure. She denied, as Mrs Cox had done before her, any knowledge that Charles had been in the habit of drinking a large quantity of water before he went to sleep. She was then questioned as to her own drinking habits, and asked if her husband had 'found fault' with her drinking. She replied untruthfully that he had not, adding, 'He merely said he thought I should be better if I drank burgundy instead of sherry – if I drank his wine.'

Following this, some of Charles's letters were taken up and extracts from some of them were read to the court:

'I hold you to be the best of wives . . . I wish I could sleep away my life till you return . . .' 'I miss you my darling wife, dreadfully, and I live only for your return. When you come back I will take such care of you that you will never leave me again . . .' 'I walked up and down the road for half an hour waiting for a letter from you, and the postman came whistling along, the light-hearted wretch, though he had no letter for me . . . I am as perfectly happy as I could be, barring your absence . . .' 'My own darling Wife, I have been thinking all this morning of the sweet old girl I left behind me. Although I pass the day in the fresh air I am not happy, neither shall I be till I regain you . . .' '. . . I cannot be happy in the absence of my best of wives. My only object in life is to make myself pleasant to you . . .' 'Life without you is not worth having; with you it is delightful.' '. . . you make sunshine wherever you go . . . I am always thinking of you, always longing for you.' 'I cannot bear to be away from you. My dearest wife, I shall never cease to love you. I can never love you more than I do. It is impossible for love to be greater than mine . . .' '. . . You are the foundation of all my happiness. Goodbye my sweet love . . .' 'I hope to see you tomorrow, and I have no intention of ever leaving you again . . .'

As the passages were read out Florence became very much moved and bent her head and wept. When she had recovered Mr Lewis said to her, 'Do you mean to say, after these letters, that you repeat to the jury that this gentleman was always speaking, morning, noon and night, of Dr Gully?'

Florence: 'I do.'

'Did you ever tell anybody so in his lifetime?'

Florence replied that she had told Mrs Cox and had also told her mother in January.

Mr Lewis then turned his attention to the period when Florence was staying at Malvern in 1870, during Captain Ricardo's lifetime. He asked her if there was anything that she wished to keep secret, but Florence replied that nothing had happened in Malvern that she would want to hide. Mr Lewis, however, was not satisfied with this answer and asked her if there was 'any sort of familiarity' between Dr Gully and herself that she wished to keep secret. Again she answered that there was not.

'Nothing that you wished your servants to conceal?'

'No.'

Mr Lewis's response to this denial was to hand her a letter, written from Buscot and dated 16 November 1870. The letter, which she confirmed was in her own writing, was to her former maid, Laundon, whom she had taken with her to Malvern in 1870 and later dismissed for impertinence. In the letter – written in response to a request for a reference – Florence had written:

Dear Laundon,

I am quite satisfied with your apology and, as I told you before, that had it not been for Field, who is not worthy of you, you would never have been rude to me. Nobody regrets more than I do the circumstances that compelled my parting with you for I like you personally, and you suit me in every way. I will do all I can to procure you a good situation and hope you may soon succeed in getting one. I hope you will never allude in any way to anyone of what passed at Malvern. Let it all be buried in the past and if anybody questions you, please refuse to answer any inquiries ...

With kind remembrances to yourself,
Yours truly,
Florence Bravo

BURN THIS.

Having read the letter, Mr Lewis adjusted his monocle and looked across the table at Florence.

'What was it you wished her never to tell anybody?' he asked.

She replied: 'That I had an attachment – but not a criminal one – to Dr Gully.' Then, turning angrily on her examiner, she said, 'But I do not see how it relates to my husband's death.' Her voice breaking, she cried out:

'Mr Lewis, I have been sufficiently pained and humiliated, and I appeal to the coroner and the jury, who are gentlemen and Britons, to protect me! I think it is a great shame.'

The sharp sound of loud applause echoed through the court, and the witness burst into tears. When she had calmed herself enough to speak, she said to Mr Lewis:

'I am willing to tell you anything to help you find out how Mr Charles Bravo met his death – but with Dr Gully you have nothing to do, and I refuse to answer any further questions. It seems to be impossible that a woman can love a man without doing what is wrong with him, according to you.'

After this outburst, Florence agreed to continue with her evidence, telling the court once again that she had not asked Mrs Cox to get any treatments from Dr Gully on her behalf and that the meetings between the doctor and the companion were quite unknown to her. She had not even heard of laurel water, she said, until Mrs Cox brought the bottle from Dr Gully.

Mr Lewis finished his interrogation at this point, and then the representative of the Crown, Mr Gorst, rose to continue the examination. Responding to his questions Florence told him that Dr Gully was in no way involved with her separation from Alexander, adding that he had known nothing about it. Mr Gorst, however, knew otherwise, and produced Florence's Deed of Separation of 31 March 1871. It bore the signatures of both Henry Brooks and James Gully. Florence looked at the document and said:

'I have no recollection of it, Mr Gorst.'

Having made his point, Mr Gorst turned his attention to Dr Gully's dismissal in the autumn of 1875. Florence here insisted that her affection for her ex-lover had not diminished in any way, and as she said this she broke into unrestrained sobbing once more. She said that she had parted from Dr Gully with 'a very painful interview', adding that she did 'not wish to remember the contents of the angry letter' he had sent to her.

Referring to the meeting with the doctor in the Lower Lodge shortly before her marriage to Charles, Mr Gorst asked if the doctor had said 'anything about the length of time Mr Bravo was likely to live'. Florence replied that he had said nothing of the sort – indeed, Dr Gully 'had never seen him', and that he had 'merely expressed his wish that we should be very happy'.

Florence then reminded the court that her statement to the Treasury had been *voluntary*, adding that had she known it would be made public she would not have mentioned in it the marital disputes. Having said this, she became tearful again, and was unable to continue immediately with her testimony. The coroner, taking advantage of the break in the proceedings, suggested that the court should be adjourned until after luncheon.

Mr Gorst resumed his questioning when the court reconvened, and began by asking Florence about the statement she had made about Charles to Dr Dill in Brighton after the funeral. Clearly somewhat discomfited at the question, Florence answered evasively, saying that she had spoken to Dr Dill about Charles's tragic death and nothing more. But Mr Gorst persisted, rephrasing his question:

'I mean, did you make any statement to Dr Dill to convey a very grave charge against your husband?'

Florence, still avoiding a direct answer, replied: 'I told Dr Dill, as I told everybody else when I heard my husband had been poisoned by antimony, that he must have taken it himself, because there was no antimony in the house, to my knowledge.'

Mr Gorst was still not satisfied, and asked her again if she had made a statement which involved a grave charge against her husband. In reply, she snapped:

'I told you what I told him. I can say no more.'

Questioned further, she agreed that Chief Inspector Clarke had called on her in Brighton and asked various questions about Charles's death. Mr Gorst, determined to delve further, asked her:

'Did you tell Mr Clarke to go to Dr Dill and ask him what you had said to him?'

Florence: 'I said for further information respecting my late husband he must go to Dr Dill. I could tell him nothing more.'

'Did you refer him to Dr Dill to tell him something particular that you could not tell him yourself?'

'Yes, but not in the way you mean. It was merely relating to my health, which I did not think I was called upon to talk about to Inspector Clarke.'

'I am not going to say a word about the nature of the communication,' said Mr Gorst.

'No,' retorted Florence, 'and I am not going to answer it either!'

Mr Gorst: 'Did you give him to understand there was something more that Dr Dill could tell him?'

'No, nothing very important, but he was asking questions which I did not choose to enter into with Inspector Clarke – or any other gentleman, except a doctor.'

'Did you know that what Clarke would learn from Dr Dill would involve a *serious charge* upon your late husband?'

Florence: 'No, I did not.'

It was obviously to Florence's great relief that this line of questioning ended and Mr Murphy rose to replace Mr Gorst. Now she was asked if she had ever heard Mrs Cox express anything but gratitude towards Mr Charles Bravo. She paused before answering, then replied:

'I did not hear her express gratitude to Mr Charles Bravo because I do not think she thought she owed it to him. I think she thought she owed it to me.'

'Was she, as far as you can judge, quite contented with the arrangement to go to Jamaica?'

'She did not like leaving me, but apart from that, she was.'

Then came a question that must have struck at the witness's heart.

'Do you,' asked Mr Murphy, 'extend the same kindly feeling to Mrs Cox at present that you have done during the whole of the years of your acquaintance with her?'

Florence became extremely agitated and paused for a considerable time before answering. Then, with dignity, she replied:

'I think she might have spared me a great many of these painful inquiries that have been made.'

This epitaph to the close friendship that had once existed between the two women ended Florence's evidence, and on the arm of her brother she left the room.

Her examination had been both long and turbulent, and the assembly in the courtroom had witnessed her confused emotional state in all its complexity. She had cried out pathetically over her husband's memory and had defended her ex-lover with spirit and loyalty. On the other hand, she had dismissed Jane Cox, with whom she had lived on the most intimate terms, with dignified indifference.

17

Final Witness

On Wednesday 9 August Florence Bravo made her last appearance before the court when she sat listening as her testimony of the previous day was read out to her. Forty-five minutes later when the reading had come to an end she signed her deposition and then, 'with an air of great relief', left the court.

At the request of some members of the jury Mr Murphy then put before the court some letters, two of which had been written to Mrs Cox by her aunt in St Ann's Bay, Jamaica. One of them was dated 26 March 1874 (see page 21); the other was dated 8 May 1876, and had evidently been written in response to Mrs Cox's letter requesting funds – 'presents' – for her return fare to be forwarded to her. Judging by the later letter Mrs Margaret Cox had grown increasingly concerned over the problem occupying her mind, fearing that in the absence of her banker, Michael Solomon, his representative might, on her death, take advantage of the situation and possess her house, Content, on which there was a charge. In her letter she wrote (her italics):

My dear Jane,

Mr Solomon *is going to America*, and is leaving all his business matters in the hands of the young man, Mr Chadwick, who you know is engaged to W. Stennett; and should anything happen to me they would get married and come here to live. No one has told me so, but I feel sure that would be the case. *Do not mention this to anyone. I really do think you ought to get out* *here as soon as you can to see after matters.* I am not able now to attend to anything, and as to seeing about presents, that is quite out of the question. *I am sure were you to ask Mr Bravo he would advance you the money to pay your passage out, and when you wish to return Mr Solomon would do the same, and charge it to this property. Tell him this from me.* I should like to see you again, and have many things to tell you that I cannot write about, so do come soon. Should you be able to manage this do not bring Leslie* with you; it would be the ruin of him to come here so young. *Dora will tell you the rest.* I am not able to write more at present, but do come.

With much love,
Your affectionate aunt,
Margaret Cox

The other letter, of the same date, had come from a certain Mrs Fox, a friend of Mrs Margaret Cox, who was known to Mrs Jane Cox. In her letter she wrote:

... Mrs Cox bids me tell you that she notes all you have said in your letter about coming out, and she hopes most earnestly you will try and come out as soon as you can ... It is very kind of Mrs Charles [Bravo] to promise to take care of the boys while you are away, which I suppose will make your mind more easy to think they will be with her while you are away. I hope you will try and come. If you have not already left when you receive this, try and hasten out, for I know poor Mrs Cox wishes to see you.

Fanny Griffiths had been called as a witness but she still had not arrived by the ending of the reading of the letters. Rising, one of the jurymen remarked, 'We might as well have five minutes, Mr Coroner, while there's nothing doing.' So saying he left the court-room, followed by eight of the others who, only too pleased to quit the stuffy atmosphere of the billiards room, took an impromptu stroll on the common. While they were gone Mr Parry, not one to

* Jane Cox's eldest son, John Leslie, was aged sixteen in March of that year, 1876.

keep silent for long, made a few sarcastic remarks to the effect that the Treasury had been too miserly to finance Mrs Griffiths's overnight lodging. Mr Gorst soon put him right, informing him that the travel arrangements had been made out of consideration of the needs of the witness's young family, and not from any desire to save on expenses.

There was still no sign of Fanny Griffiths when the jurors returned from their walk fifteen minutes later, and in her continued absence Elizabeth Evans, under-housemaid from The Priory, was called. After saying that she had helped to lift Mr Bravo into a chair when he was unconscious, she was asked whether she knew anything that would throw any light on the way in which he had come by his death. She replied that she knew nothing. After a few more questions which elicited no information of significance she was allowed to go.

Eventually, Fanny Griffiths arrived and was sworn in. Under examination she said that her husband had had some antimony when they were living in Warwick Square, adding, 'He had it from the time we were married. He used to keep it in a little box in a drawer. It was not locked up. It was in the sitting room. There was half an ounce to nearly an ounce. I destroyed it while we lived at Warwick Square. I was afraid of the poison being about, and I wanted the little box. I destroyed it by putting it on the fire.'

Although she insisted that she had never heard her husband say anything about Mr Bravo living only for four months she agreed that when he was annoyed he was apt to express himself 'pretty strongly'.

Her testimony finished, Fanny Griffiths was allowed to leave the court. As the learned counsel then proceeded to talk among themselves word quickly spread that Dr Gully was to be called. With the news a murmur of excitement passed through the ranks of the spectators, the locals now easily outnumbered by celebrities and city gentlemen. Moments later Dr Gully was called, and the assembly turned to see the last witness appear in the doorway.

Dr James Manby Gully, who cut a distinguished figure, entered the room smiling and with an appearance of self-confidence. He was invited by his counsel, Mr Parry, to sit, but this was objected to by the jury who said that the privilege of sitting was given 'only to ladies'. Although Mr Parry protested, the doctor had no choice but to remain standing.

Examined by Mr Parry, Dr Gully said that he had been in medical practice for forty-two years and had practised hydropathy at Màlvern for twenty-nine of those years. It was then clearly established that he had not been summoned to appear in court, but had come voluntarily. This having been stated, Mr Parry said:

'Now, Dr Gully, I ask you upon your solemn oath: had you anything to do, either directly or indirectly, with causing the death of young Charles Bravo?'

Replied Dr Gully: 'On my solemn oath I never had anything to do with it, either directly or indirectly.'

At this point the elderly physician was permitted to sit. His questioning continuing, he said that he knew nothing of Griffiths's purchase of two ounces of antimony in Malvern in 1869; in fact, he said, he had rarely used Mr Clark's chemist shop, preferring to deal with the homeopathic one in the town. Questioned further, he insisted that he would never have allowed his horses to be treated with antimony, saying that he used to treat them hydropathically, with 'marvellous results'.

'It is proved here,' said Mr Parry, 'that five times in March and April you saw Mrs Cox.'

'That is true,' said Dr Gully, and then went on to describe the second meeting on Friday 7 April.

'She was taking a ticket to Victoria,' he said, 'and I was taking one to Thornton Heath. While she was going towards the platform she told me of Mrs Bravo's state of sleeplessness, and asked if I could suggest anything. I hurriedly told her that I thought a cold sitz-bath and cold washing of the spine two or three times a day would be useful. I knew that Mrs Bravo was driven frantic with opiates, so I bethought me of laurel water. On my way back I stopped at Smith's, as my old allopathic knowledge was rather rusty, and asked him to show me the Pharmacopoeia.'

Mrs Cox, he went on, had told him that she was going to her house in Lancaster Road to arrange a letting and he decided to leave the bottle of laurel water there as he was going that way to his son's house in Bayswater the following day, Saturday the 8th.

Mr Parry's next question was to the point, but it had to be asked; it was the sum of all the questions so far asked about the laurel water. Said Mr Parry:

'I must draw your attention to the suggestion that is made. Did you put tartar emetic into that bottle of laurel water?'

'No, sir, I had no tartar emetic to do so with.'

Questioned further, the doctor went on to say that he had not sent the bottle directly from Smith's in Balham as he 'considered all communication with The Priory forbidden' to him 'entirely, in any way'. At this Mr Lewis spoke up, saying that if Mrs Bravo had been in such urgent need of the remedy, it would have been much quicker to have had the laurel water delivered directly from the local chemist. In this way she could have received it by midday on the Saturday, instead of having to wait until Mrs Cox had collected it two days later.

'Yes, very true,' agreed Dr Gully, 'but it did not occur to me.' He then said that Mrs Cox had been free to reveal the presence of the laurel water to Charles Bravo 'if she had thought it proper to tell him'.

After the luncheon adjournment, Mr George Lewis rose to examine the witness. In response to questions Dr Gully described his two visits to Brighton after his rejection and said that although he knew that Charles had been very attentive to Florence there, he first heard of their engagement in a letter from Mrs Cox, dated 10 November 1875. As to his second visit to Brighton, he said that Mrs Bravo had sent him a telegram asking him to make the journey with Mrs Cox, who would join his train at Croydon.

Referring to that meeting in Brighton with Mrs Bravo, Mr Lewis said, 'Let me ask you this. At the second interview did you not tell Mrs Bravo that you should die?'

' – That I should die?'

'If she separated herself from you?'

'No – nothing of the kind – not even in a poetic flight.' There was laughter at this, then the doctor added, 'I told her that I should be very unhappy for a while.'

'How old are you, Dr Gully?'

'I am in my sixty-eighth year.'

Speaking of the time when Florence had stayed in Malvern, Mr Lewis said, 'Will you allow me to ask you whether it was during the period when Mrs Ricardo was a patient of yours at Malvern in 1870 that this attachment between you and herself commenced?'

'Well . . .' began the doctor, smiling, 'it commenced after a fashion. It was a mere friendly understanding between us at the time. She was alone a good deal and I used to take tea with her.'

Mr Lewis then asked what it was that had passed between the witness and Mrs Ricardo before November 1870 that would 'induce her to write to her servant begging her never to allude to it, but to allow it to be buried in the past'.

Said Dr Gully, 'I cannot conceive what it was.'

'You cannot conceive anything that had passed which could justify a lady in such a position writing in that way to her maid?'

'No.'

Many questions proceeded then on the sacrifices Florence had made for the sake of the witness, it being suggested that she had 'sacrificed her honour' for him. Dr Gully resisted the suggestions and eventually Mr Parry got up to protest, saying that Mr Lewis was 'asking questions that were not relevant to the inquiry'. His interruption brought a mixture of applause and hissing from the crowded courtroom. Mr Lewis persisted, however, saying that the point of his questioning would soon emerge, and the coroner, afraid to deny anything, allowed the questions to continue. Clearly Mr Lewis was probing to see whether the doctor might have been humiliated through the love affair to the point where he had been driven to commit murder, for he said:

'You are aware that she had sacrificed her honour and her family to you during 1872 and 1873. Did there come a time when she asked you to sacrifice your house at Balham?'

But Dr Gully denied it. 'No,' he said, 'there did not come a time when she asked me to sacrifice my house at Balham.'

'Did she propose to pay the rent of your house at Balham?'

'No, she did not.'

Questioned then as to whether he thought that Charles had known about his affair with Florence, he said it was a matter of complete indifference to him whether he had known or not. He then said he had misunderstood the question, adding that during his conversation with Florence in the Lower Lodge, she had told him that Charles knew everything about their past relationship.

The witness then went on to say that he had borne no grudge against Charles Bravo and had only wished for Florence's happiness. He said that he knew nothing of life within The Priory after Florence's marriage to Charles and, in order to avoid meeting the occupants whenever possible, had 'even taken his walks differently'. After saying that he had never seen Mr Charles Bravo, he was asked if he did not remember seeing the young man raise his hat to Florence in Brighton. Dr Gully said he could not recall the occasion, adding:

'I should have liked to have known whom my friend had married.'

This remark ended his examination and Dr Gully, who had remained composed and in control throughout his testimony, was given leave to go.

The spectators immediately engaged in animated chatter while the learned counsel conferred in small groups. Forthwith it was decided that sufficient evidence had been presented and no further witnesses would be called. This decision precipitated yet more discussion, this time on the best way to conclude the proceedings. The coroner eventually suggested that he should present his summing-up on the following Monday – but this day was too far off for some, and Sir Henry James asked that it be earlier as the strain on the persons involved in such a lengthy inquiry had been considerable, and a further delay would be intolerable. The coroner's assessor, Mr Muir, agreed that he and Mr Carter would prepare the summing-up by Friday morning, and so received an expression of appreciation from Sir Henry.

A commendation of Mr Burleigh Muir for his handling of the case was then endorsed by Mr Lewis, Mr Poland and Mr Parry, the latter including the jury in his thanks and voicing the opinion that they had shown great patience.

After these formalities the proceedings were adjourned until Friday 11 August.

Although the jury was not yet required to present their judgement of the case, there can be no doubt that as the members left the Bedford Hotel that day they were already weighing up the evidence they had heard over the previous weeks in preparation for reaching a verdict.

For the three in the centre of the drama – Florence Bravo, James Gully and Jane Cox – those two days of waiting must have been very difficult. In the examination of each one there had been questions that had centred solely upon possible guilt of the crime of murder. But as yet the main questions remained unanswered. Like the rest of the population they would have to wait for the verdict.

*

On the morning of Friday 11 August the coroner was faced with a difficult task. He had before him a wealth of evidence, some of which was irrelevant, much of vital importance. Faced with the problem he offered to read the entire evidence, but the jury was strongly against such a course, and protested – 'Oh, no, certainly not!'

Persuaded against his proposal the coroner then went straight into his address to the jurors, during the course of which he urged them to 'weigh the evidence as to Mr Bravo's character and mental condition'. If they were then satisfied that he deliberately took antimony, he said, they should find accordingly. He further stated that in considering 'whether antimony was administered by any other person or persons', he was unable to point them to any direct evidence. He went on:

'Before you can bring in a verdict of murder against any person or persons you must be satisfied that that person or persons wilfully administered poison to Mr Bravo, or laid poison for him, and he took it and was killed by it. For if that poison was laid, the law will presume that the administration was malicious, although no particular enmity was proved...

'Lastly, if you should be satisfied that there is no evidence before you as to how the antimony came into the body of the deceased, you will find accordingly.'

At eleven-thirty, following the coroner's address, the members of the jury retired to a private room to consider their verdict. At two-fifteen that afternoon they emerged, whereupon the coroner asked their foreman, Mark Cattley, if they had agreed upon their verdict. He affirmed that they had and gave him a piece of paper on which was written:

We find that Mr Charles Delauney Turner (Bravo) did not commit suicide, that he did not meet his death by misadventure, but that he was wilfully murdered by the administration of tartar emetic, but there is not sufficient evidence to fix the guilt upon any person or persons.

The inquiry's cost had amounted to many thousands of pounds, and it had lasted twenty-three working days spread over more than four weeks.* Yet the cost, the duration, the number of witnesses and the sensational revelations had resulted merely in a verdict which most people had fully expected. As to who was guilty, that question was still to be answered, and the killer – or killers – was still free.

---

* Although the leading counsel commanded huge fees for their services at the inquest, each juror received only ninepence for his five-week duty. All the members of the jury felt that their loss of income during the period constituted considerable hardship and applied to the Home Office for additional reimbursement, as did Mr Carter the coroner. It is not known whether their applications were successful.

PART THREE

'. . . someone killed Mr Bravo
and somewhere in the tangled
story the motive was there . . .'

John Williams, *Suddenly at The Priory*

18

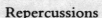

Repercussions

The purpose of an inquest is not the prosecution of a case against any person or persons, but to elicit from the witnesses the full facts of the case. If, as a result, there is guilt to be apportioned, then the jury should try to indicate where the guilt lies, so leading to a charge and subsequent prosecution.

Unfortunately, following the inquiry into the death of Charles Bravo the jury was unable to reach any conclusion other than that a murder had been committed. And, understandably, the lack of any resulting charge caused great dissatisfaction. Said *The Spectator*:

> The antimony has not been found in the cesspool for all the stirring ... A more unsatisfactory inquiry was never terminated in a more unsatisfactory verdict.

A great deal of dissatisfaction was voiced over the way the proceedings had been conducted. Said a writer to *The South London Press*:

> The proceedings were a disgrace to this country. Justice has not been administered and the dignity of the law has been insulted. It was a most iniquitous verdict.

And a writer in *The World*:

> There are many features in the way this inquiry was conducted that offend the public sense of propriety and justice ... The

scenes which took place in the court were the reverse of pleasant or creditable. Both the Coroner and the jury no doubt gave
every attention to the proceedings, but the latter failed to
display the taste and the temper which the subject and place
demanded – and the former was impotent to check either the
rude outbursts of the jury or the licence of the counsel...

And from *The Daily News*:

The Lord Chief Justice appears to have broken the spirit of the
Coroner ... and disqualified him to check certain of the counsel in a line of inquiry which has aroused public indignation...

The newspapers and magazines were not alone in voicing dissatisfaction. An anonymous pamphlet issued on the subject, entitled *The
Gay Young Widow of Balham*, also had harsh words for those who
had conducted the inquiry:

The mystery of the case seems to be very nearly as dense as at
the beginning; and it may be said that it would have been well
to have been content with the first inquest ... It should be
observed, however, that the failure of the first inquiry was due
to the incompetence of the Coroner ... and the mismanagement of the second inquest is also attributable to the same
cause. It is quite clear from what has happened that Mr Carter
has no idea of the proper way in conducting a judicial investigation...

The examination of Florence Bravo in particular brought its share
of protests. Wrote one reporter who had witnessed the scene:

It was a horrid spectacle to see a young woman to whom her
reputation was evidently dear, having wrung from her by
questions as cruel as the rack, an open confession of dishonour.

The Times joined in the chorus of disapproval, Florence Bravo
again the object of sympathy:

Public feeling has been revolted by the manner in which this investigation has been conducted. When the fact of a previous existence of a criminal connection between Dr Gully and Mrs Bravo had been established, the main object of the exposure had been gained, and it was a cruel and even barbarous act to subject a most unhappy woman to hours of cross-examination for the mere purpose of eliciting details of this connection. It was at this point that Mrs Bravo, with perfectly just indignation, refused to answer any more questions respecting Dr Gully ... That a cross-examination of a crushed and humiliated woman should have been pushed to the length it was at Balham is a disgrace to the court which allowed it, and to the manliness of everyone who was responsible for it.

Dr Gully had also suffered from Mr Carter's disgraceful handling of the proceedings. Where *he* was concerned, however, *The Times* clearly felt no sympathy. Said that newspaper of Dr Gully:

... In violation of the heavy responsibilities of his profession and with no excuse from the passions of youth, or even of middle life, he abandoned himself to a selfish intrigue, and he cannot complain of his present condition.

Others reserved their opprobrium for the medical men involved in the case. Said *The Lancet*:

... Any practitioner called to a case where such remedies [as the use of a mustard emetic] had been employed, would naturally send first for a stomach pump and then search for the vomited matter. Neither of these obvious and imperative steps were taken. The patient lay in a condition of collapse and all the time absorption was proceeding rapidly. Had the vomited matter been discovered at once, much of what happened might have been prevented. It is impossible to disguise that a grave omission was made in not applying the proper medical tests to the matter vomited and that passed by the intestines.

Echoes of dissatisfaction and accusations of bungling continued, while from the police there remained an ominous silence. However, notwithstanding the unsatisfactory verdict, the jury's words – that there was 'not sufficient evidence to fix the guilt upon any person or persons' – clearly indicated that suspicions were very strong.

And so the press and the public waited. But there was no news of any charge being made. Why? Was nothing being done? A rising young barrister with everything to live for had been cruelly murdered when supposedly in the company of those he trusted, and whoever had killed him seemed now to be sidestepping the law with remarkable dexterity and cunning. But surely after such a long inquiry the investigators must have found something to work with; surely justice would have its day.

Unfortunately for justice, however, many mistakes had been made and a great deal of time had been lost. Charles Bravo had died on 21 April, and it was 10 May before the police investigators had begun asking questions. By that time whoever was guilty had had more than three weeks in which to cover up any telltale tracks and dispose of any remaining poison.

The police, it appeared, had done as much as they could. On 11 August, the day the inquest ended, the Home Office had responded to a request from Scotland Yard and issued instructions for a reward of £250 to anyone who could assist the police in bringing about a charge of murder in the case. The police cannot have been hopeful, for the next day Chief Inspector Clarke submitted a report to his superior, officially informing him of the result of the inquest and adding the melancholy words:

I would respectfully call the Commissioner's attention to the fact that during this long inquiry nothing has been elicited to show by what means the deceased met with his death, other than is contained in my former reports . . .

Whether the police had suspicions in any particular direction is not known. In writing his reports Chief Inspector Clarke was surprisingly reticent when it came to noting his thoughts or opinions. Whereas police files on investigations into other murders often show clearly the directions of suspicion held by the investigators – even though those suspicions are not supported by a great deal of evidence – the police file on the Bravo case gives no such information.

Through the reports of Chief Inspector Clarke one gets the

impression that he was at a loss. Writing on 24 May, he had stated:

> He must have taken the poison after he retired to his room, but whether it was with his own knowledge, or whether placed there secretly by some other person, I refrain from giving an opinion ...

Also, going by this particular report, one gets the impression that for a time the Chief Inspector was tempted to believe that Charles had indeed committed suicide – though clearly he did not accept the motives for such an act as put forward by Florence Bravo. That he was not much impressed with Florence at that early time in the investigations he does make clear; he states:

> Mrs Bravo admits to me that on several occasions when he attempted to make any change in their domestic arrangements, she reminded him that she found the money, and does not appear to have had that sympathy and love for him that he might have expected, and she certainly shews no grief at his death.

Whether Mr Clarke harboured suspicion against any particular individual we do not know. Certainly no moves were made in any particular direction, and, surprisingly, none of the popular suspects in the case appears to have been questioned after Saturday 3 June when Mrs Cox was interviewed at Brighton.

In the meantime the offer of a reward by the Home Office brought no better response than had that similar offer coming from Florence Bravo. And in spite of continuing letters to the press and Scotland Yard on the matter, offering opinions and suggestions, no progress was made. So, as was to be expected, with no further developments in the case active investigations soon ceased, and the inquiry ground to a halt. The weeks went by and the main protagonists in the drama went their own ways unhampered, to their great relief able to leave the glare of the spotlight.

And the mystery remained.

19

Charles Bravo – Villain or Victim?

Was Charles Bravo indeed the victim of some cruel, merciless poisoner on that April night, or did he die by his own hand, as some writers have claimed?

Without question there were those at the time who supported the suicide theory, notably Florence Bravo and her family, the Campbells, and Jane Cox – though they were interested parties, having much to gain from the acceptance of such a belief. The alternatives to a verdict of suicide, an open verdict or a verdict of murder, threatened to (and indeed did) reveal so much to the public gaze, risking the exposure of all kinds of skeletons-in-cupboards – which exposure in the constrained days of the mid-Victorian era was far more to be feared than it is today. A verdict of suicide, therefore, melancholy though it would be, would have been infinitely more acceptable in the long run.

One who believed in the theory of suicide was the anonymous writer of the pamphlet, *The Gay Young Widow of Balham*. Said the writer:

> ... No evidence has been given to show in the slightest degree the connection of anyone with his death except Mr Bravo's own hand. All the direct evidence supports the hypothesis of suicide. Yet the jury tell us that murder has been committed, in the face of the deceased's declaration that he poisoned himself, and in the face of the fact that there has not been a tittle of proof to show murderous act or murderous design.

Which, of course, is nonsense. The writer seems to have based his case on an assumption that Charles did indeed confess to having taken poison, and therefore that Mrs Cox spoke truthfully to that effect. Needless to say, however, not everyone was impressed with the veracity of Mrs Cox's statements.

But what of Sir William Gull's statement regarding his belief in the suicide theory – a belief shared at the beginning by Dr Johnson? It may well be that Sir William Gull later felt that he had been mistaken – as did Dr Johnson – and that his judgement had been too hasty. Then, however, realising that in spite of his eminence his opinion had not been accepted, he found it impossible to back down and admit that he had been wrong.

In regard to the question of whether Charles Bravo did indeed commit suicide there are several points that should be noted.

First of all, antimony is *not* a poison one uses to take one's own life, and Charles would have been well aware of this fact. Being by its nature completely unreliable, it could never be swallowed with any certainty as to its effect; as it was Charles lingered in great agony for several days. It can be argued that the whole point of suicide is to escape pain of one kind or another, and to choose a painful means of dying would appear incompatible with that purpose. Suicides who have a choice do not choose slow, agonisingly painful deaths. It is not credible, therefore, that a suicide would choose to die by poisoning by antimony.

At no time could Charles's behaviour ever be seriously construed as that of a man who had set out to kill himself. He showed every sign of wishing to live, of being anxious to recover. Further, he denied having taken poison. 'I have taken *nothing*,' he said to Royes Bell, his much loved cousin. He repeated the statement *twice*, and then, trying the only way he knew how to account for his condition, added, 'I rubbed my gums with laudanum and I may have swallowed some.'

That he did indeed fear that he might well have poisoned himself with the laudanum was later demonstrated as he lay on his sickbed. In order to lessen his extreme pain he was given a dose of laudanum, but, on realising what it was he spat it out, refusing to swallow it.

One point used to support the notion of Charles's having taken his own life is that he asked no questions as to his condition, and is said to have shown no surprise at it. But these factors are easily accounted for. When almost every person who set foot in the sickroom was asking him what he had taken, it would have made little sense for *him* to have asked *them*. Also, his lack of exhibition of 'surprise' at his condition was accounted for by more than one of the medical men who attended him; they said in effect that the great discomfort from which he suffered without respite – 'Oh, Royes, must I linger long in such agony?' – would inhibit the curiosity of anyone in such a situation.

There is also the fact of his screaming out 'Florence!' and 'Hot water!' – which surely he would not have done if he had been intent on killing himself. His immediate reactions to feeling the first effects of the poison were of fear and horror.

Furthermore, why, if he had intentionally taken poison, should he have disregarded the doctors' warning that after his death some person – and obviously Florence was one person they had in mind – might well be suspected of being implicated? He could not help that, he said; he had taken only laudanum. Yet his treatment of Florence as he lay dying shows that he was genuinely fond of her. Would he willingly have condemned her to the misery, the humiliation and the suspicion that later came upon her?

Another point: if a man shoots himself dead or cuts his throat then one would expect to find the gun or the blade close by. Similarly if Charles had committed suicide one would expect to find the remains of the poison at hand, or at least some trace of it, or its container. There was no sign or trace of poison or a poison container in his bedroom. Likewise there was no trace of poison anywhere else in the house. If he did poison himself with up to forty grains of antimony he also managed, with remarkable efficiency, to destroy every trace of his possession of that poison.

Finally: Charles had no motive whatever for killing himself. The motives put forward – jealousy over Dr Gully, and pressure from his former mistress in Maidenhead – simply cannot be taken seriously.

We are left with the inescapable conclusion that Charles Bravo did not kill himself. There is far too much evidence against such a supposition.

As stated in an earlier part of this book, there have been two previous full-length factual books written on the case, the first of which, *How Charles Bravo Died*, was published in 1956, its author, Yseult Bridges, setting out to do what she could to salvage Florence Bravo's reputation and relieve her of the suspicion that has shadowed her name since Charles Bravo's death occurred. The writer attempted to do so by putting forward her own theory of how he died, which, she believes, was neither by suicide nor by murder, but was the result of *an attempted murder and an accident*.

In her book, Mrs Bridges puts forward the remarkable theory that Charles, very much the villain of the piece, governed by 'money mania' and having married Florence solely for her money, was slowly poisoning her.

While Mrs Bridges was a writer of great ability she also appears to have been one of those who, instead of reaching a conclusion through a study of the evidence, decide first upon a conclusion and then search for evidence to back it up – which process, sadly, often entails distorting the facts.*

Her book on the Charles Bravo case contains many flights of fancy but, even if they are accepted as fact, they do little to give any credence to her unlikely theory.

For a start, there is no evidence whatsoever that Charles was 'slowly poisoning' Florence with tartar emetic. Indeed, all the evidence is against it. For one thing, although much was made at times of Florence's various indispositions there is never, throughout all the many thousands of words written on her life with Charles – and their brief marriage seems well documented – any mention of her suffering from vomiting, or vomiting and purging – which would surely have been the case if indeed Charles had been feeding her regular doses of antimony.

Yseult Bridges puts forward such a theory, though, and, further, says that the 'grave charge' made by Florence to Dr Dill was to this effect – that Charles was regularly feeding her doses of poison. Mrs Bridges states, giving her theory *as a statement of fact*:

The 'grave charge' which Charles Bravo's widow brought

---

* It might be noted that in her earlier book *Saint – With Red Hands?*, dealing with the case of Constance Kent, she actually gave support to her astonishing thesis by 'rewriting' a vital statement made by one of the police officers in the case. Unfortunately for her theory, the statement concerned, that by Sergeant Watts and signed by his own hand, is still available for examination at the Public Record Office in London.

against him to Inspector Clarke at Brighton was that he had
been administering to her small and frequent doses of tartar
emetic, adding that 'if he wanted to know more he could go to
Dr Dill'.

It is an astonishing statement – particularly when there is nothing
to support it, and all the evidence is against such a theory. For one
thing Charles visited Florence's Brighton doctor, Dr Dill, to ask
him to use his influence to curb Florence's heavy drinking – on
which subject he sometimes upbraided Florence and also made
known his displeasure and concern to her mother. If he had wanted
his wife dead all he needed to do was to encourage her addiction to
the sherry bottle, not try to curb it. According to Mrs Bridges,
though – who astonishingly states that Florence had no drinking
problem whatever – Charles had Florence's murder all planned, and
was only waiting for the right time to give her the final and fatal
dose of tartar emetic while they were staying in Worthing. Another
point in Charles's favour is that he had Griffiths dismissed on the
grounds that he did not drive safely. If he had truly wanted Florence
dead, he might have done well to have kept Griffiths on and to have
encouraged Florence to drive out more often.

In looking at the matter of the 'grave charge', it must be emphasised that Florence made it in conversation with Dr Dill, to whom
she later told Chief Inspector Clarke he should go if he needed more
information. It must be clear, however, that it was not a *formal*
charge in any way, but in the nature simply of relaying information;
there was no 'charge' as Mrs Bridges implies, no formal accusation.

But can it be seriously entertained for one moment that if a
woman suspects her husband of systematically feeding her poison
she should wait until his death before she tells anyone of it? For this
is what Mrs Bridges would have one believe: that after Charles's
death Florence went to her *doctor* with the story that her husband had
been feeding her poison.

Had Florence indeed told Dr Dill that Charles had been poisoning
her the doctor would at once, of course, have informed the police.
Also, surely Florence would have spoken of it to her doctor while it
was happening; it is an extraordinary complaint to make of someone after his death. Further, if it *had* been the case it is astonishing
that Florence should have been so loath to discuss it with Chief
Inspector Clarke, referring him instead to Dr Dill.

It must be noted that Dr Dill was never called as a witness at the inquest, and surely there was a reason for this – not least being the fact that the communication made to him by Florence was not in any way relevant to the inquiry.

Another point: if Charles had been poisoning Florence, surely she would have told some member of her family. She certainly did not hesitate to complain loudly of other aspects of Charles's behaviour. Surely the matter of being fed poison is not a subject one is likely to be reticent about.

Florence's testimony at the inquest is very revealing – an examination of which should serve to demolish Mrs Bridges's preposterous theory for all time.

Mr Gorst, for the Crown, began his line of questioning by saying to Florence:

'Soon after going down to Brighton with Mrs Cox did you make a statement about your late husband to Dr Dill?'

Florence, clearly hedging, started to reply by saying, 'I really forget,' and then, with a sudden switch, began to answer a question that had not been asked: 'I spoke to Dr Dill about it naturally,' she said. 'I told Dr Dill what I told everyone else when I heard that my husband had been poisoned by antimony, that he must have taken it himself; because there was no antimony in the house that I knew of...' Then, still avoiding the question, she continued to speak on the possible source of the antimony that had killed her husband. It was not, however, what Mr Gorst wished to hear, and when she had come to a halt he said:

'Did you make to Dr Dill at Brighton a statement which involved a very grave charge against your husband?'

Faced with Mr Gorst's persistence, Florence tried to evade the question in a different way.

'I have told you what I told him,' she said. 'I can say no more.'

Gorst: 'A short time after you went to Brighton did Inspector Clarke call to see you?'

Florence: 'He did not call to see me, but I saw him at the detective office.'

'You knew he was making inquiries about your late husband's death?'

'Yes.'

'Did you tell Mr Clarke to go to Dr Dill and ask him what you had said about your late husband?'

'I said that if further information was wanted about my late husband he should go to Dr Dill – that I could tell him nothing more. That was all I said to Inspector Clarke.'

'Do you mean to say you did not send him to Dr Dill in order to have a particular communication made to him?'

'I told him that if he wished to have any further particulars regarding my late husband, Dr Dill would give them to him.'

'Did you not refer Inspector Clarke to Dr Dill in order that Dr Dill might tell him something which you could not tell him yourself?'

'Yes, I did. It was merely relating to my health, which I did not think I was called upon to speak about to Inspector Clarke.'

Then, obviously trying to put Florence at ease, Mr Gorst said:

'I am not going to say a word as to the nature of your illness –'

To which Florence burst out:

'And I am not going to answer you either.'

Mr Gorst continued:

'Did you not send Inspector Clarke to Dr Dill to gain a particular piece of information?'

'I did not send him. I told him he might go if he wished.'

'Did you lead him to suppose that there was something important which Dr Dill could tell him?'

'Nothing very important. He asked me questions which I did not wish to enter into with him – or with any gentleman except a doctor.'

'Did you know that what Inspector Clarke would learn from Dr Dill would involve a serious charge against your late husband?'

'No, I did not.'

It must be very clear to anyone who cares to make even a brief study of this particular section of Florence's testimony that she was not making any reference to being given poison by her husband. For one thing the nature of the 'grave charge' was clearly of a somewhat more delicate nature than that of poisoning, and was clearly something she could not bring herself to speak of to Chief Inspector Clarke or, later, in front of the court. Examine some of the exchanges a little more closely:

Mr Gorst had said: 'Did you not refer Inspector Clarke to Dr Dill in order that Dr Dill might tell him something which *you could not tell him yourself*?'

'Yes, I did,' answered Florence, and then: *'It was merely relating to my health, which I did not think I was called upon to speak about to Inspector Clarke.'*

The delicacy of the subject – which was connected with Florence's health – was hinted at in the next exchange between herself and Mr Gorst:

Gorst: 'I am not going to say a word as to the nature of your illness –'

Florence: 'And I am not going to answer you either.'

Clearly Florence was extremely embarrassed over the discussion. After further exchanges Mr Gorst asked:

'Did you tell Mr Clarke to go to Dr Dill and ask him what you had said about your late husband?'

'I said that if further information was wanted about my late husband he should go to Dr Dill – that *I could tell him nothing more.'*

And then:

Gorst: 'Did you lead him to suppose that there was something important which Dr Dill could tell him?'

'Nothing very important. *He asked me questions which I did not wish to enter into with him – or with any gentleman except a doctor.'*

A little later:

Gorst: 'Did you know that what Inspector Clarke would learn from Dr Dill would involve a serious charge against your late husband?'

Florence: 'No, I did not.'

Is one to believe that Florence Bravo was so naïve as not to know that wife-poisoning was an offence? Whatever the nature of the 'grave charge', Florence spoke of it to Dr Dill *without being aware that it constituted a criminal offence.* Also, as stated, it is a mistake to lay too much emphasis on the term 'grave charge' – in that clearly Florence did not make a charge, *per se*, against her late husband. The matter clearly came up during the course of conversation in consultation with her trusted doctor, Dr Dill. It was relating to her health, as she said, and, further, was something she was not prepared *'to enter into with any gentleman except a doctor'.*

The subject of the 'communication' that came out at Florence's meeting with Dr Dill, and of which she later refused to speak to the police inspector or to the examiners at the inquest, has mystified many devotees of the Bravo case. There can be no doubt that it was of a medical nature, and a very personal one. So delicate was it that it appears that she was unable to mention it to anyone, and vehemently refused to discuss it with either Chief Inspector Clarke or Mr Gorst. Neither could Mr Gorst, through delicacy and consideration for Florence's feelings, bring himself to name the specific nature of her communication to Dr Dill – which is surprising in view of the fact that there had been little reluctance shown so far in stripping her of her reputation in the inquiry. And as pointed out, nor was the doctor himself called as a witness, when obviously he could have shed much light on the matter – if light were needed; though it seems that it was not. As for Chief Inspector Clarke, he was just as reticent on the matter; in his official report of 5 June 1876 he wrote:

> I also saw Dr Dill who states that the communication made to him by Mrs Bravo was after the death of her husband, when she said that *'he was very persistent in that line of conduct'*.

It seems clear, through all the evident reticence and avoidance of naming the nature of the subject, that it must have been of a sexual nature. On the last day of the inquest it was insinuated by a member of the jury that Charles might have been suffering from a venereal disease. This was not so; the post-mortem on Charles's body showed that he had no disease whatever.

In any case, a venereal disease is ruled out if viewed in reference to the words in Chief Inspector Clarke's report: '. . . *he was very persistent in that line of conduct'*. Clearly, the charge involved some aspect of Charles's conduct.

Bearing in mind that in 1876 any deviation from a standard form of sexual behaviour between married couples was often ignored as if it did not exist, there appears to be only one conclusion to draw; only one answer that fits the whole picture as presented by the nature of Florence's words to Chief Inspector Clarke, her exchange with Mr Gorst and, later, those elliptical phrases in Mr Clarke's report. There is only one act which, in the view of the present authors, fits all the comments and statements made concerning Florence Bravo's 'communication' to Dr Dill. That is the act of buggery.

There is no doubt that buggery (or sodomy) is very much a taboo subject even in these times of permissiveness and verbal freedom, and one can imagine the constraints surrounding it in the far more repressed climate of the Victorian era. Examination of the Criminal Charge Registers of that time held at the Public Record Office reveal that many of the clerks could not even bring themselves to write the word *buggery* in full. As often as not, when a man was charged with the act it would be written in the register simply as *B.....y*. Although the act was, and is, more commonly associated with male homosexual practice, and constituted a criminal offence, it was also deemed a crime between men and women – notwithstanding that the couple might be married to one another. Not that the act when performed between men and women was commonly known. Although it took place often enough between married couples (indeed it was a common method of sexual intercourse where birth control was necessary), usually the only charges that arose concerned the act when committed between men.

As stated, however, and as sexual studies will verify, the act is commonly practised by married couples today (notwithstanding that in Great Britain it remains, for men and women, a criminal offence – though policy clearly dictates that criminal charges are rarely brought against the participants) – and the situation was surely no different in the mid-Victorian era.

(Assuming that it was this act which was the subject of the 'grave charge', one must wonder why it was referred to at the inquiry, causing, as it obviously did, so much pain to Florence Bravo. The only reason one can see for the matter being brought up before the court is the possible belief that in some minds it might have constituted a reason for murder.)

Whether or not buggery was indeed the subject of Florence's communication to Dr Dill, and it appears very likely, there can be absolutely no credence placed in the supposition that it was to the effect that Charles was systematically feeding her tartar emetic.

In charging Charles with such an act, however, Yseult Bridges suggests that he kept a secret store of antimony, ostensibly to 'cure' her drinking, but in fact in order to kill her. She continues her hypothesis by maintaining that on the night Charles collapsed he inadvertently swallowed some laudanum and then took a large dose of tartar emetic to make himself sick. (A similar suggestion had been put forward by Sir Henry James; see p. 173.) Contrary to this theory, though, is evidence showing that Charles was very familiar with drugs and their effects and was most unlikely to take antimony without due caution. Also, the surgeon Henry Smith said that in twenty-eight years of experience he had never heard of such a thing.

Furthermore, if Charles had just taken a dose of tartar emetic to rid himself of laudanum, why did he call for hot water? Hot water was the *mildest* domestic remedy to induce vomiting, yet according to Mrs Bridges he had already – and *knowingly* – taken one of the most violent emetics possible. And yet this is what Yseult Bridges states must have happened.

Even so, unable to find support for her theory in the knowledge of what took place she has to invent certain happenings. When Charles is first taken ill she finds it necessary to rewrite the scene between him and Mrs Cox, who, she says (conveniently), 'juggled with the truth, adding or subtracting to suit the occasion'. So Mrs Bridges invents a scene where Keeber goes hurrying off for hot water and Charles points to a packet of antimony on the mantelpiece and says to Mrs Cox, 'I have taken some of that poison; don't tell Florence; *throw it in the fire*.' And being an obliging little woman Mrs Cox obeys, while asking, 'How could you do such a thing?' to which he replies that he took it 'medicinally'. Continues Mrs Bridges:

> As she crouched by his side he made her vow to tell *no one* – neither Florence nor anyone else – what had happened. He would know that William Palmer had twice dosed John Parsons Cook with tartar emetic, and each time immediate vomiting had saved his life and left him little the worse next day. He would tell Mrs Cox that so long as he vomited copiously he would be all right, and to give him a mustard emetic to stimulate his circulation. He reckoned without the rapid absorption into the system that would naturally occur soon after a meal.

Apart from the *content* of the conversation that the writer has occurring between the pair, more surprising is the *amount* of talking she has going on between them – which is even more astonishing when one considers that no one else overheard one single word of it, and that Charles's jaws were locked.

To account for Charles's warmth to his wife while he was supposedly poisoning her, Yseult Bridges makes the astonishing claim that the slow poisoner 'develops a species of amnesia whereby he may, in effect, lose the consciousness of guilt and lead an apparently normal life'. This form of amnesia, however, she says, 'rapidly evaporated' as Charles regained consciousness and he was overcome by guilt and a desire to repent, 'under the influence of which he prayed and wept, bade his wife marry again, made a will leaving her every penny he possessed, and implored his mother to be kind to her'. The fact that he did not confess to having swallowed poison, says Yseult Bridges, was due to his egotism and vanity – 'which is part of the criminal make-up' – and because he still hoped for recovery.

This implausible theory was inspired by one expounded by Mr Arthur Channell, a retired High Court Judge, in a letter to Sir John Hall, after the publication in 1923 of the latter's book, *The Bravo Mystery and Other Cases*. Channell stated he had been present at the second inquest on Charles Bravo's death at which time he had apparently proposed his theory to Mr Murphy QC (for Mrs Cox). His theory was that Charles had been administering small doses of tartar emetic to Florence in order to cure her of her liking for sherry, that he had accidently swallowed some laudanum while treating his gums and that he took the tartar emetic – not knowing that it was a deadly poison – to rid himself of the laudanum.

In the postscript to the 1972 reissue of *How Charles Bravo Died*, Yseult Bridges extends Arthur Channell's original, and extremely improbable, hypothesis by producing a letter written to the police late in 1876. The writer of the letter was a Mr Ponsford Raymond who was eager to get his hands on one (or both) of the rewards offered in connection with the case. Mr Raymond claimed that he sold Charles Bravo six packets of his 'miraculous' Heymen's Remedy (a cure for alcoholism) through the post on receipt of 27/- in postage stamps.

For dubious reasons, however, Mr Raymond had not presented the information during the second inquest, despite the vast publicity. Instead he waited and then approached first the three suspects in the case – through their various legal representatives – Florence Bravo, James Gully and Jane Cox – in so doing claiming the £500 reward which Florence had offered on 16 May that year. Getting no satisfactory response from those quarters, he then approached the Metropolitan Police – where he met with no better success.

Nevertheless, Yseult Bridges had faith in Mr Raymond's claim, believing that several packets of his 'Heymen's Remedy' held the tartar emetic that led to Charles's death. There can be no truth in it. If each packet had contained as much as two grains, the compound dosage of all six packets would have fallen very short of the thirty to forty grains Charles swallowed that night. Further, any supposition that Charles somehow managed to purchase enough packets to make up the amount he took must promote more questions than it answers – for example, how did he extract the tartar emetic from the rest of the 'Remedy', whatever its constituents were? He would have needed the facilities of a laboratory, not to mention the fact that he would have been left with a great deal of the residue of the mixture, which surely would have been noticed at the scene. The supposition is too absurd. If Charles had wanted to procure tartar emetic he would not have relied on the dubious contents of patent medicines; with his knowledge and his contacts he could have procured any quantity of it by his own endeavours. Said *The Lancet*, speaking shortly after the closing of the second inquest of the ease with which one could purchase the poison:

> It is by no means difficult to procure. Without possessing the knowledge necessary to write a prescription, or the audacity to impersonate a medical practitioner, any man or woman may walk into a chemist's shop and procure a few grains of the drug, either as an emetic or a fever powder. Half a dozen such powders might be purchased without suspicion for domestic purposes and a very few investments of this character would result in the acquisition of quite as much tartar emetic as Mr Bravo took.

The evidence of the coachman, Griffiths, also made clear how easy it was to obtain the poison. According to his testimony he bought enough antimony for 4d or 5d to kill a dozen people – and he had no reason whatever to lie about it. The chemists questioned denied that they had sold him antimony – but they had reason to deny it. Clearly, if Charles had wanted tartar emetic he would have had no difficulty in procuring as much as he wanted.

A final note on Mr Raymond's claim: his letter to the police arrived at Scotland Yard in November, three months after the close of the second inquest. His letter and a police report were sent to the Treasury who replied that the Home Secretary did 'not think it necessary to take any action'. It would seem, therefore, that both the Treasury and the police doubted the reliability of the information, particularly as no proof of sale was ever forthcoming from him. It must be remembered with regard to Raymond's claim, that if Charles *had* furtively purchased the 'Remedy' using postage stamps and the collecting box at The Temple, as Mr Raymond stated, then that same anonymity also provided a convenient cover for Mr Raymond's enterprising attempt at extortion.

One fact must emerge from this examination of the events, and that is that Charles Bravo did not meet his tragic end through an act of suicide or misadventure. There can be no doubt that, as the second inquest found, he was most coldly and calculatingly murdered.

Which of course brings us to the all-important question: who was guilty?

20

Who Killed Charles Bravo?

One theory bandied about by the gossipmongers during the investigations was relayed by Chief Inspector Clarke in his report of 24 May. He wrote:

> A number of letters have been received (many of them anonymous) suggesting that the poison was administered to Mr Bravo by Mrs Bravo or Mrs Cox, or both, and supplied by Dr Gully for the purpose of getting rid of him to enable Mrs Bravo and Dr Gully to get married, but after careful inquiry I can find no evidence to support these suggestions.

Was Dr Gully guilty? There are those who put forward such a belief – though there is no evidence to support the thesis. Granted he was very hurt and angry at being dismissed by Florence – but it is generally only the young who believe that such feelings last through life; James Gully was no longer in the first flush of youth, and age and experience would surely have brought with it the knowledge that he would recover from his hurt in time. Besides, how would he have carried out the murder? He did not enter the house and therefore he would have needed an accomplice. Who? Florence? Very improbable. As improbable as a plot hatched with Mrs Cox; somehow one cannot see the eminent doctor getting together with the paid companion to plot the poisoning of his usurper. Notwithstanding his ill-advised affair with Florence, Gully comes over as far too sensible a man to have calmly plotted – at almost seventy – the death of another. On examination of the facts little credence can be placed in the notion – examined at the time – that he sent the tartar emetic to Mrs Cox in the bottle which ostensibly held the laurel water, and that with it she, carrying out his wishes, murdered her master.

For one thing – if Gully had been in league with Mrs Cox it is very doubtful that he would have mentioned his meetings with her in Victoria and at Balham Station, knowledge of which came from Gully himself. He volunteered the information to, among others, Pritchard, his butler. By doing so he clearly indicated that the meetings were innocent.

Once Dr Gully and Florence had parted he made no further attempt to contact her. He knew that he had lost her and there is no reason to believe that he thought that once Charles was out of the way he and his former mistress could pick up where they had left off.

A further, and very powerful, indication of Dr Gully's innocence is his obvious acceptance of Florence's new commitment as demonstrated by the events at his meeting with her in the Lower Lodge when she asked him to advise her regarding the terms of her marriage settlement, a matter which was threatening her proposed marriage to Charles. Clearly she was in much doubt as to what to do; had Gully wished he could have struck a blow for himself, encouraging her in her wish not to give in to Charles's demands. Such a move might well have led to the engagement being terminated – and therefore to the doctor being reinstated in Florence's affections. Instead, he advised her to go along with Charles's wishes – 'It's a small price to pay for happiness.' If he had been determined to rout his 'rival' then that day in the Lower Lodge he was faced with a relatively easy means of achieving his desire. He chose not to. It must be acknowledged, therefore, that it is not in the least likely that he would then opt for the commission of a murder.

A hypothesis embracing Dr Gully was carried in the words of a scurrilous little poem that was circulated during the inquest. Parodying lines of Oliver Goldsmith, it made Florence the instigator of the crime, saying:

> When lovely woman stoops to folly
> And finds her husband in the way,
> What charm can soothe her melancholy
> What art can turn him into clay?

> The only means her aims to cover
> And save herself from prison locks
> And repossess her ancient lover
> Are Burgundy and Mrs Cox.

There was no truth in the idea, however, that Florence ever wanted James Gully back in her life. She had seen the last of him that day at the Lower Lodge when she had sought his advice about her marriage settlement. She was never to meet him again, and there is nothing to hint at the notion that she ever wanted to.

Even so, disregarding love for James Gully as a motive for murder, was Florence Bravo guilty of causing her husband's death?

In examining the question one must first try to dispense with any irrelevancies in the matter, one of which is Griffiths's uncanny alleged prediction of Charles's demise: 'Poor fellow, he will not live four months.'

Some who would accuse Florence Bravo have snatched at Griffiths's words as if they hinted at a dark secret to which he alone was somehow privy. As he told the inquest, though, his remark was made in anger over his dismissal; also, he had *not* stipulated four months. If one does not accept that Griffiths shared a deadly secret – and the idea is preposterous – then the only alternatives are that he was genuinely clairvoyant, which is equally absurd, or that his melancholy prediction was, with a little help from hindsight, a strange coincidence.

Griffiths's prediction apart, however, two present-day writers in particular – John Williams and Elizabeth Jenkins – are firmly of the opinion that Florence was guilty, and their theories must be examined.

Elizabeth Jenkins, a previous writer on the Bravo case, believes that Florence, having suffered two miscarriages, unintentionally killed Charles in trying to ensure that she did not suffer a third. There is a belief in certain quarters that in the days before recognised contraceptives were in common use wives sometimes fed small doses of tartar emetic to their husbands to bring about feelings of nausea and so dampen their ardour. Accordingly, Miss Jenkins believes that Florence put tartar emetic into Charles's drinking water that night – not 'for murderous purposes', she stated on a recent radio programme (*An Infamous Address, BBC Radio 4, 1987*), 'but simply to make him violently sick'.

Notwithstanding that such measures might have been taken by some desperate wives, the present authors cannot accept that such a thing happened that night at The Priory. For one thing, it is known that Florence, recovering from her miscarriage, was sharing her bed with Jane Cox – as she had done for nearly a fortnight – while Charles was still sleeping in the spare room. Charles did have sharp words with Florence before they parted that night, but they were not over the sleeping arrangements, but because Florence had sent down for yet more wine after already having drunk so much at dinner.

But apart from the barrier of Mrs Cox in Florence's room there were still the physical states of Florence and Charles. Florence, not recovered from her miscarriage, was exhausted from her first day out, and had drunk a bottle of sherry into the bargain. Charles, on the other hand, had severe toothache and was a mass of aches and pains from his ride on the runaway cob.

Furthermore, the fact that the tartar emetic was placed in Charles's water bottle acknowledges that he planned to sleep in the spare room, and therefore would *not* be a threat to Florence's rest that night. Had Florence believed that he was going to insist on sharing *her* bed she would not have put the tartar emetic in *his* bedroom, for clearly that was the one place where he would not be.

The use of tartar emetic as a *successful* means of birth control is also very difficult to accept. Without doubt an attack of nausea will take the edge off a man's sexual appetite, but when was a wife to administer it? Not with the soup, for its effects are almost immediate. Certainly not in the wine, for it makes wine cloudy and would therefore be discernible. And if it were habitually employed surely a suffering husband (Charles not least) would soon get the message, for knowledge of such measures would obviously be known to him also. Furthermore, it being a very deadly poison, had it been in common use there would surely have been a great many husbands dying of antimonial poisoning. It must be acknowledged, though, that even were it the most common birth control method known there is not a shred of evidence to indicate that Florence ever used it.

Unlike Elizabeth Jenkins, John Williams, in *Suddenly at the Priory*, believes that Florence, 'ruthless, self-centred, supremely unsentimental', a woman who 'would go to any lengths to get what she wanted – or dispose of what she did not want', actually set out to murder Charles. Not only that, he asserts that she also poisoned Alexander Ricardo, who died in 1871 in Cologne. First, with regard to Charles Bravo, John Williams says:

> Florence killed Charles because she saw no other way of cutting short the married relationship with him which had become intolerable to her and which, had it gone on, would have meant her early death or permanent invalidism – or so, in her sick, unbalanced state of mind that April, she desperately believed. Only after marrying Charles had Florence realised to the full that physiologically she was tragically unfitted for normal married life and childbearing.

Williams then, in a demonstration of overkill, lists Florence's miscarriages and other ailments and gives a melodramatic picture of her lying exhausted after her trip to town that fateful Tuesday:

> As she lay on the sofa in the morning room after lunch, brooding in solitude on her broken health and the bleak future before her as the perpetually ailing wife of a husband whose attentions had become intolerable to her, the second fearful decision in her life took shape in her obsessed mind. She would get rid of Charles – just as she had set about ridding herself of Alexander.

John Williams then puts forward a sequence of events where Florence drops the tartar emetic into Charles's drinking water and then confesses what she has done to Jane Cox – who is aware of 'the misery' Florence has suffered through her miscarriages and 'the dark moods that accompanied her pain and restlessness'. According to Williams, therefore, Jane Cox invented Charles's 'poison' statement, and did it purely to protect her mistress. Afterwards, he says, Florence was stricken with remorse – which led to the rupture in her friendship with Jane Cox, 'her saviour'.

Larded with dark, melodramatic overtones, it is a most improbable scenario and does not hold up in the face of the known facts. For one thing there is no evidence for presenting Florence as being in a 'sick, unbalanced state of mind'. The picture that emerges from the contemporary reports shows her as anything but that. Where too is the evidence that she was prone to 'dark moods' and 'wild thoughts'?

And what of Mr Williams's absurd assertion that Florence also 'eliminated' her first husband? He uses such a thesis to support his theory that Florence murdered Charles. There is no question at all, however – as will be shown – but that Florence was perfectly innocent of the death of Alexander, and therefore John Williams's theory of her guilt in Charles's murder is predicated upon a lie.

It cannot be denied that there was rumour during the inquest to the effect that Florence had brought about Alexander's death, but that rumour only sprang from the suspicion that Charles had been murdered. It had never been whispered before his death and it never amounted to anything more than rumour.

A factor telling against any supposition of Florence's guilt in Alexander's death is the Deed of Separation she took out before he died. It was a major step in those days and one not entered into lightly by any party. Nevertheless Florence took that step which, in its fruition, would have cut her off from his fortune. As it happened he died before the deed came into effect and therefore his fortune became hers, but she could not have known that it would happen in such a way.

Nevertheless the rumours of her involvement in his death gained ground, given strength by the fact that Alexander, due to his consumption of alcohol, was continually vomiting. That his symptoms were a manifestation of his alcohol intake cannot really be questioned. He himself never questioned it, and neither did any doctor nor anyone else on the scene at the time. John Williams, however, states that Alexander and Charles manifested 'the same symptoms' prior to their deaths. This is quite untrue. They both suffered vomiting, but there the similarity ends. According to witnesses Alexander was vomiting continually, by his own admission sometimes as much as 'sixty times a day'. Charles is known to have vomited at two periods during the last months of his life; once early in March while on the way to visit his parents; and then in April after he had swallowed the fatal dose of poison.

John Williams writes as if vomiting is the only symptom of antimonial poisoning. It is not. An equally dynamic symptom is that of purging. Charles suffered from purging on both occasions when he suffered vomiting, but it has never even been suggested that Alexander ever exhibited such symptoms.

Furthermore, and astonishingly, those adherents to the notion that Florence poisoned Alexander conveniently ignore the fact that they were separated at the time of his death. She was living in Streatham while Alexander was living with his mistress in Cologne. She had last seen him in Malvern in November 1870 when, with her sister and her maid, she fled from his violence and was escorted back to Buscot by her mother. The next news she received of him was of his death which took place on 19 April the following year, when they had been apart for *five months*.

John Williams believes that Florence had been steadily poisoning Alexander with tartar emetic for so long that notwithstanding the couple's separation it was from the effects of that poison that he died. Such a supposition has no basis in fact, however. Dr Richard Shepherd, of the Department of Forensic Medicine, Guy's Hospital, London, recently stated to one of the present authors:

'Due to the mechanism of antimonial poisoning, which is similar to that of arsenical poisoning, its effects are usually reasonably acute. *Death by antimonial poisoning is related to when the antimony is administered.* If a man is still alive, say, a month after being given antimony then the chances are that he will recover. It would be extremely unlikely for a man to die of antimonial poisoning five months after taking the last dose.'

Nevertheless John Williams, in the face of forensic expertise, believes that such was the case. Further, he accepts a certain writer's assertion that Alexander's body was exhumed following the second inquest and that a post-mortem revealed antimony in the body.

The book he quotes, *Recollections of Forty Years*, published in 1910, has its author, Dr L. Forbes Winslow, stating categorically: 'Captain Ricardo died, and his body being exhumed, antimony was found.'

There is no truth whatever in the statement. Nevertheless Mr Williams has chosen to accept it at face value and, in the face of all the obvious evidence to the contrary, has used it to build up his case.

Both Dr Winslow and Mr Williams write as if an exhumation and post-mortem can be executed on the whim of any interested party. This is not so. An exhumation must be authorized by no less a government figure than the Home Secretary, usually on application from the police. If the post-mortem that follows the exhumation reveals death to have been due to unnatural causes, i.e. the administering of poison, an inquest must be opened. This procedure is *required by law*. Unfortunately for Mr Williams's theory the exhumation of Alexander Ricardo took place only in the minds of those who, seeking evidence of Florence's guilt, found it necessary to invent it.

The simple truth on any question concerning a post-mortem on Alexander's remains lies in the files of the Department of the Environment covering Brompton Cemetery, Fulham Road, London, where Alexander Ricardo's body was buried after being brought from Cologne. Says Mr G. S. Broom of that office, writing to one of the present authors:

> . . . with reference to ALEXANDER RICARDO, I confirm he was interred here on 24th April 1871, and was placed in the Catacombs. I also confirm that he is still here and *there has been no exhumation* (authors' italics).

The 'Author's Note' in John Williams's book offers thanks to, among others, the 'officials of Brompton Cemetery'. In view of the quotation from their letter above, however, one can only wonder at the nature of the 'help and advice' he received from them, for they could only have given him the same information – that Alexander Ricardo's body has never been disturbed since its burial there.

Whatever the case, Dr L. Forbes Winslow's presentation of fantasy as fact has, through John Williams's book, unfortunately been accepted as the truth in many quarters. In an article on the case published in *The Sunday Times* of 20 October 1968, reference is made to John Williams's book and 'the results of the exhumation of the body of Florence Bravo's first husband' – as if it actually took place. And more recently in his book *Murder Guide to London*, Martin Fido writes of Florence Bravo, an 'alleged' murderess, as 'twice bereaved of husbands who happened to have taken tartar emetic'.

Quite simply, it is nonsense. Furthermore, the incontrovertible evidence that Alexander's body was *never exhumed* gives some indication of the strength of rumour that followed the case, and which has led to misconceptions about it ever since. It must be acknowledged, too, that if the powers of the time had believed there was any truth in the rumour they would have acted upon it, and Alexander's body *would* have been exhumed. It stands to reason that the police, faced with no satisfactory results in their investigation into

Charles's murder, would have been glad of any lead they could get.

The absurd theories about Alexander's death apart, however, there is no denying that Florence has been named as the culprit – particularly during more recent times. This was the theory in a series of plays on the case produced and transmitted by BBC Television in 1975. The plays' writer, Ken Taylor, is quoted in *Radio Times* of 12 June 1975 as describing Florence as 'an egocentric hysteric'. He is also quoted as saying: 'She could reconstruct events entirely to suit her own needs and then believe herself unequivocally. At the inquest her honesty shines through answers that are complete fictions. She was incapable of a full appreciation of other people's reality.'

The present writers do not agree with this view. There is no doubt that at the inquest Florence did, on occasion, lie. She lied with regard to her knowledge of Charles habitually drinking water at night. She must have known that he did, and it was foolish to deny such knowledge. Her lie, however, clearly an act of self-preservation, does not indicate her guilt – only that she was conscious of her perilous position – and with the anonymous letters she was daily receiving and the coverage she was getting in the press, there can be no doubt that she felt her position most keenly.

She further lied, it appears, in the matter of the Deed of Separation, drawn up in relation to her marriage to Alexander. At the inquiry she said that Dr Gully had had no knowledge of her separation from Alexander. Yet the Deed was found to bear the doctor's signature. On its production Florence stated that she had no recollection of it.

Her lie in this instance is also understandable. Her shameful past – much of which was not relevant to the inquiry – had been exposed to the whole world. Not only had her examiners exposed her sordid affair with Dr Gully following Alexander's death, but some were intent on proving that it had begun during Alexander's lifetime. It is possible that it had – which supposition might be supported by Florence's letter to her former maid, Laundon (see p. 175). Whatever the truth, however, Florence denied it; understandably she did not wish it to be thought that she had had a sexual relationship with the doctor during Alexander's lifetime.

Even so, notwithstanding Florence's reasons for lying, was she guilty of the murder of Charles Bravo?

There is no evidence of her guilt, and those writers who believe in it present their beliefs in the face of the evidence *against* such a hypothesis.

Clearly there was no strong suspicion of her in the minds of the investigators – otherwise they would have applied to the Home Office for an exhumation order on Alexander's body. As records show, no such application was ever made and his body was never disturbed.

Nevertheless, Florence has often been named as the guilty one, and various motives have been assigned to her – one to the effect that she discovered that Charles married her only for her fortune; another – from John Williams – that she hated him, and wished to avoid a succession of miscarriages which she was afraid she would have to suffer in a continuing marriage to him.

With regard to the first motive attributed to her – if Charles *had* married her for her money it was not a factor that would have come as a surprise to her *after* her marriage. She had already considered it well before that time. She told the court at the inquest that when she and Charles were having disagreements over the marriage settlement she said to him that it could appear that he was marrying her for her money. Evidence that she did not truly believe such a supposition, however, is the fact that she went ahead and married him.

In further examining possible motives for Florence's guilt, one has to look at what is known of the marriage, at the couple's behaviour to one another and at Florence's conduct immediately after the crime.

It is not easy to determine the success of the marriage. Contemporary reports give conflicting pictures. On the one hand there is Florence's Treasury statement wherein she made reference to quarrels that had taken place arising from her association with Dr Gully. On the other hand there are the very affectionate letters Florence and Charles wrote to one another, their manner towards one another in company and their behaviour when Charles lay dying. Knowing that he was to die he spoke of Florence as the 'best and sweetest of wives', and asked his mother to be kind to her.

Florence during that unhappy time seems to have been truly moved by his tragic situation. Witness her shock on first discovering his condition – and it is hard to accept that it was anything other than genuine. Rowe spoke of her being 'sincerely anxious': 'Mrs

Bravo came downstairs and cried out very loudly for me to fetch someone. She was running screaming along the passage with the housemaid.' Also he said, 'Mrs Bravo cried out to me – screamed to me, "Go and bring someone. Fetch someone." Among the cries she used was, "Do something, Rowe."' Mary Ann Keeber, the maid, also spoke of Florence's distress on the morning of Charles's death, and, speaking of the earlier times, before Charles's collapse, said they had always appeared very happy together.

Further, the medical men called to Charles believed Florence's behaviour to be quite natural. Said Dr Joseph Moore, who was the first to arrive at The Priory:

'Mrs Bravo asked about the gravity of his condition. At once, on receiving my reply, she burst into a flood of tears. Her grief and conduct altogether appeared to me to be quite natural under the circumstances. She seemed entirely to reciprocate his affection. Whilst he was unconscious she was lying on the bed beside him and I did not notice one trace of assumed conduct or grief.'

Regarding the carriage being sent for Mr Royes Bell, Moore said: 'Mrs Bravo seemed annoyed that the faster horses were not put in the carriage.'

Said Mr George Harrison, second physician to arrive on the scene: 'I saw not the slightest sign of feigning or acting on the part of Mrs Bravo,' and, 'She seemed to be quite natural in her affectionate remarks to her husband.' He went on: 'I knew she had been unwell, and when she threw herself on the bed beside him, she said, "Do speak to me, Charlie, dear," and other endearing terms, and she became exhausted and fell asleep.'

Dr Johnson also spoke of the 'great anxiety' Florence showed concerning her husband's condition.

With regard to Florence's affection for her husband before the poisoning there are pictures presented by certain actions that took place: Florence making a pair of slippers for him: her insistence that he wore flannel for his touch of rheumatism; her buying for him a surprise gift of 'ties and things' in Oxford blue in preparation for the boat race; also, on the day of his collapse, her purchase of gifts for him in town.

With regard to the negative pictures of the marriage presented by Florence in her Treasury statement, it must be borne in mind that by the time she made her statement she had had to face the idea of

Charles's death and was by then having to fight for her reputation and her survival in the face of the sensational gossip that was circulating. Understandably her very real grief had become superseded by the need for self-preservation. The same situation was behind the picture she presented to Chief Inspector Clarke preceding his remark that she showed 'no grief at [Charles's] death'; by that time Charles had been dead for five weeks.

And she was surely speaking the truth at the inquest when she said she did not know that her Treasury statement was to have been made public. Not that the statement is all that shocking with regard to her relationship with Charles. The acts and words she attributes to him are not so very extreme when seen in the context of a quarrel. In her statement she said that following a quarrel he threatened to cut his throat. She also accused him of continually bringing up Dr Gully's name. She said that on another occasion when she protested about his mother's interference he struck her. But, she said later, 'he burst into tears immediately afterwards, and was very sorry'.

Another matter to be considered regarding the negative side of the relationship is her communication to Dr Dill regarding that 'particular line of conduct' in which Charles was apparently 'very persistent'. Even assuming that the conduct was indeed buggery there is no evidence that her communication was in the nature of a complaint, or that she was greatly upset because of it. She said she had gone to see Dr Dill about her health, so it seems reasonable to assume that her objection came as the result of some discomfort she suffered as a result of the act, and not of the act itself or from any stand regarding morals or the law. It was apparently only from Dr Dill that she learned that her communication to him constituted a 'grave charge'.

There is also reference – in one of Charles's letters – to the couple having had 'bitter trouble' – probably a reference to their quarrels over Florence's love affair with Dr Gully.

One gets the impression, all things considered and in spite of their occasional quarrels, that they were reasonably happy together, and that left to themselves, without the destructive influences from outside, mainly from Charles's mother, they would have settled happily. Their letters tend to indicate that they loved one another and that their respect for one another was growing – even though they might well have married for not altogether the right reasons.

Was Charles attracted to her money? – to an extent, very probably – just as Florence in all likelihood yearned passionately for respectability after being so long out in the cold, and saw in the young barrister a happy and secure future. Nevertheless, each also found in the other intelligence, personality and physical attraction – attributes which must surely have been endearing to a degree. It could also be argued that Charles's continual harping on Florence's past relationship with Dr Gully was, unwelcome as it might have been, one more manifestation of his love for her.

Certainly, when reviewing the various testimonies and looking at pictures of the couple's lives together, there does not appear in Florence's behaviour any sign of a great hatred that would lead her to kill her husband with an extremely painful poison. In the same way, when all is taken into consideration there is nothing in her behaviour to indicate during those days and nights of Charles's illness that she was ever anything but a distraught, loving and sorrowful wife. If she was, then she was a consummate actress.

There was one visitor to the house while Charles lay dying who, according to his later remarks, was not impressed with Florence's behaviour. He was Mr Joseph Bravo. Although he told the inquest that she and Charles 'were most affectionate to one another,' he later said that she did not appear to be 'particularly' grieved. It must be remembered, however, that Joseph Bravo was by this time very hostile towards Florence. Any affection he had once felt for her had long since gone. An indication that he had held her in affection before Charles's death was given by Mrs Cox at the first inquest, when she said that Mr Joseph Bravo had been 'kindness itself' to Florence while Charles lay dying.

In examination of Florence's behaviour on that Tuesday night her accusers invariably point to the fact that she did not respond when Charles shouted out: 'Florence! Hot water!' It is said that she was *feigning* sleep, and that with such a short distance between the two rooms she *must* have heard his cries.

The distance between Charles's door and the main bedroom was indeed very short, but the latter had an inner and an outer door, one of which was covered in green baize to act as a sound barrier. If this door was closed it would have blocked out much of the sound. Also, if Florence had in truth poisoned Charles there is no reason on earth why she should have feigned sleep; it could not have helped her case at all. She would have done better to have 'heard' him, and to have been 'surprised' at his cries.

Another factor in support of Florence's claim that she was asleep is her physical condition that evening. It must be remembered that she was still recovering from her miscarriage, and that Tuesday was the first day for some time that she had spent a long period out of bed. She returned from her trip to London utterly exhausted. In addition to her exhaustion she drank at least a full bottle of sherry and two glasses of Marsala in the two and a half hours before retiring. Following her consumption of wine *and* her exhausting day, it is hardly surprising that she was soundly asleep very soon after getting into bed.

Evidence of her physical exhaustion is given further testimony by the fact that as Charles lay unconscious on the bed and she lay beside him trying to coax him into wakefulness she fell asleep with her arms around his neck and had to be asked to get up as she was interfering with his breathing.

Does this appear to be the behaviour of a guilty woman – a woman described by John Williams as 'ruthless, self-centred, supremely unsentimental'? It is certainly not the behaviour of a murderous woman who is careful to watch every single move she makes lest she give herself away. Florence's falling asleep goes to indicate two things: one, her state of physical exhaustion, and the other her totally natural, unselfconscious behaviour.

There are certain other points that might be stated in support of Florence Bravo.

In her letter of 16 April (see p. 45), two days before Charles was poisoned, Florence wrote to her mother: '...Charlie is looking forward to a game of lawn tennis. I never saw him looking so well. The country is life to him and he walks about with a book under his arm, as happy as a king.' Are these the words of a woman who plans to kill her husband and is anxious to build up a picture of him as a likely suicide?

Also, in Mrs Cox's letter to Mr Harrison, written from Handsworth (see p. 97), she wrote: 'Mrs C. Bravo has told me several times that she thought had the stomach pump been used, Mr C. Bravo's life might have been saved.'

Through Mrs Cox's words Florence is seen as a woman who still cannot fully accept the fact that Charles could not be saved. Her words, harping on the 'if only' phrase, are not those of a wife who wanted her husband dead.

Another point: through her marriage Florence was just regaining the respectability she had been without for so long. She had a very shameful past to keep secret, and would surely have feared that any investigation might reveal that past.

On the same point there is the matter of her sending for Dr Gully's help when Charles lay dying. She risked her reputation in this instance, for if she had poisoned Charles she might have guessed that her action in sending to her former lover would surely come to light.

There are other factors concerning the events following Charles's collapse that go to indicate Florence's innocence. Apart from her shock on seeing his condition – which John Williams admits was genuine but was due to sudden remorse at her action – there is her desperate cry to Rowe to find a doctor who was closer than Mr Harrison – 'I don't mind who it is!', and then, later, her brief anger that faster horses were not sent for Royes Bell.

If there is still belief in Florence's guilt, then one must ask the question as to how she did it. While she had the opportunity, alone and unaided, to put the tartar emetic into Charles's water bottle without anyone being aware of it, she was not responsible for the revelation of Charles's alleged statement that he had taken poison because of Dr Gully. This came from Mrs Cox, and if she was lying it is impossible to believe that Florence inspired the lie, she would not have brought Dr Gully's name into it, knowing that the result might mean the exposure of her shameful past.

There again, the theory of Florence being guilty and being aided and abetted by Jane Cox is not supported by later events; surely a shared complicity would have tended to strengthen their relationship; Florence would never have severed all connection with her companion as she did.

At the same time, the question raises the further question of the relationship between Florence and Mrs Cox. Was it, as has been suggested, a homosexual one? The present authors do not believe that it was. There is no evidence of such a relationship, notwithstanding the fact that the two women sometimes slept together. Indeed, a study of the evidence shows that on the few occasions this is known to have happened there was generally a good reason for it:

i.e. that by having Jane Cox share her bed Florence could protect herself from the sexual advances from, in the first instances, Dr Gully and, in later times, from Charles. Furthermore, the very existence of her sexual relationship with Dr Gully – regardless of how it turned out – indicates that Florence was heterosexual; after all, she was not married to him, and therefore she need have felt no obligation to submit to his advances.

If the killer was not Florence Bravo then the question might be asked whether it might have been a resentful servant. Could it have been Rance the gardener, dismissed by Charles for unwillingness to do his work as required? Or Griffiths – dismissed for the quality of his driving? In spite of any grudges they might have borne, there is no indication that either one had the slightest desire or opportunity to commit the crime. As for a grudge held by one of the servants – in spite of claims by some writers that Charles was domineering and arrogant where the servants were concerned, the very opposite appears to have been the case. In their evidence to the court all the servants from The Priory spoke of Charles in the warmest terms, saying that he was very much loved. He was, they said, a very considerate man, always unwilling to cause them unnecessary work. Charles's relationship with his servants is illustrated by small events as he lay on his deathbed; one has only to look at his brief conversation with Mary Ann Keeber when she came in to tidy the room, and, further, his exhortation to Florence to 'be kind to Rowe'.

Having eliminated from suspicion Dr James Gully, Florence Bravo, and the lower servants from The Priory, one is left with one person, the guilty one.

From first to last, that guilty one was Florence's companion, Jane Cox.

21

Foundation for Murder

The writer and broadcaster Hugh Ross Williamson wrote in his book *Historical Enigmas* (1974): 'The first thing the historical detective (or, for that matter, any detective) has to learn is not to overlook the obvious...'

It is in this context that the Bravo mystery seems particularly to have suffered, for it appears that all the obvious indications of guilt are eschewed in favour of some more esoteric and surprising conclusion. It is as if a simple explanation will not do; as if the plain truth is just not good enough. An example of this is found in a comment on the case written by the late Agatha Christie and quoted in an article by Elizabeth Jenkins published in *The Sunday Times* in October 1968:

> ... I think it was Dr Gully who killed Charles Bravo. I've always felt he was the only person who had an overwhelming motive and who was the right type: exceedingly competent, successful, and always considered above suspicion.
>
> None of the other suspects is in the least credible...

It is absolute nonsense, as an examination of the evidence and the events shows. However, the fact that Agatha Christie supports her conclusion with the fact that Dr Gully was 'always considered above suspicion' gives her game away. She is not interested in the plain truth, but must needs have her real-life mysteries in the pattern of her own fiction, where nothing is as it seems and the least likely is sure to be the guilty one.

So it goes; and in the face of all the evidence the main protagonists are, in order to support some totally improbable conclusion, endowed with characters and characteristics that are often completely at odds with those that clearly appear through their court appearances and various testimonies. Thus Mrs Christie says: 'Mrs Cox is an obvious suspect at first glance, but not when you look into it – a timid and prudent character.'

But why, if Jane Cox is such an 'obvious suspect', does Agatha Christie dismiss her? The answer, of course, is *because* she is an obvious suspect – and therefore in Mrs Christie's eyes is not of sufficient interest. By this same token, of course, a man clutching a blood-dripping knife seen walking away from a lifeless body, and found to have inherited the victim's fortune, will be dismissed from the inquiries on the grounds that his guilt is too clear.

The plain truth is apparently not interesting to some writers, perhaps because the need for the complicated plot leading to the very startling conclusion in our detective fiction governs the approach to real-life mysteries of crime. Two and two must make three or five or there is no interest in the problem. It becomes a case of wanting nature to reflect art.

But real-life murder and its detection is not as it is portrayed in the popular whodunnit. For one thing, solutions to crimes do not depend on the happening-by of a world-famous Belgian detective or an astute little maiden lady from a picturesque English village. As often as not the investigation has to remain in the hands of a detective whose plodding progress shows little in the way of imagination, and who is rarely granted access to the kind of clues that Sherlock Holmes always found so readily available. Also, it is only in fictional detection that the suspects are lined up, and the motives of each one are catalogued, ending with the last, the guilty one – who is also faced with the accusation.

Unfortunately for devotees of fictional detection, in the matter of real-life murder the least obvious suspect is generally innocent of the crime. In the same way, the most obvious is usually found to be guilty.

So the present authors believe it to be the case in the murder of Charles Bravo. There all the available evidence points to one person and one person alone, Mrs Jane Cannon Cox. She it was who put the tartar emetic into Charles Bravo's drinking water.

Some writers have made no attempt whatever to explain Jane Cox's suspicious behaviour. Rather, they have tormented the facts out of all recognition in order to pursue a case against somebody else. However, it does not need much in the way of examination of the evidence to see that Jane Cox's behaviour is deeply suspicious.

It remains now to consider the case against her.

Examine first Jane Cox's motive for murder.

She had motive indeed – and the strongest of motives; that motive being the comfort – as opposed to poverty – of herself and her three sons. As Mrs Belloc Lowndes wrote in *Great Unsolved Crimes*:

> There are innumerable people to whom the death of some other human being may make the difference between carking care and the happiness which absence of money anxiety brings with it. This is why a man or a woman's urgent desire for what the possession of money can ensure has constantly in the past, and will constantly in the future, provide a motive which guides the hand of the secret poisoner.

The strength of Jane Cox's motive emerges clearly from her story, which, briefly recapitulated, is as follows.

After working as a governess following the death of her father, she married in 1858, bore her first son in 1860, then went with her husband to Jamaica where he took a government post as an engineer. Her husband's death in December 1867 left her without means, and in 1868 she and her three sons, Leslie, Henry and Charles, sailed for England. There, after an unsuccessful attempt to run a school of her own, she was forced to work as a governess again.

Yseult Bridges states that Jane Cox, whom she describes as an 'impecunious Creole', was born in Jamaica – 'Jane Edouard, while still in her teens, scraped up enough money to come to England.' However, like much of Mrs Bridges's 'factual' writing, such a statement is far from the truth. Jane Cox's antecedents will be gone into more fully a little further on in this book, but for the moment it must be stated that she was not born in Jamaica. It will be more readily acknowledged, therefore, that she had no natural affection for the place and did not necessarily wish to live there or, later, to return there.

It will also be acknowledged that packing up her home in the first

place and sailing with her sons to England shows a certain despera-
tion and also a determination to rise above her situation – so giving
an indication of Jane Cox's strength of purpose. Agatha Christie
describes her as timid. Timid she was not.

As already stated, with the failure in 1869 of her Suffolk dame
school she took advice from Mr Joseph Bravo and bought the house
at 150 Lancaster Road, Notting Hill. While collecting rent for it, and
with her sons away in school, she lived in lodgings while going out
as a daily governess – among others to the daughter of Mr Brooks of
Streatham. It was while working for the Streatham solicitor that she
met one of his clients, Mrs Ricardo, the result of the meeting being
that Mrs Ricardo offered her employment as a companion at the
extremely high salary of £80 a year.

At the time when Mrs Cox joined her service Florence was
involved in her affair with Dr Gully. Mrs Cox was later to claim –
although the affair was happening under her very nose – that she
knew nothing of it. There can be no doubt, however, but that she
must have been well aware of it, turned a blind eye to it and gave it
her subtle, and tacit, support.

And she had very good reason to do so. For it was out of
Florence's affair with Dr Gully that Mrs Cox's employment was
born, and, likewise, it was in the *continuing* of that affair that her
greatest security lay; for, should Florence be persuaded to give up
her elderly lover and marry, the companion's position would
become untenable. It was not an unlikely possibility. Florence was a
very attractive, very wealthy young widow, and constituted a great
catch to any number of ambitious and personable young men.
There can be no doubt that Mrs Cox must at least have toyed with
the possibility of her mistress's remarrying in the future – and of her
own position, as a result, becoming redundant.

It was Florence's affair with Dr Gully wherein lay Jane Cox's
strongest hopes – and with the doctor's wife still living the illicit
love affair could continue for many years – until, with the death of
Mrs Gully, the doctor and Florence would be free to marry. Then,
surely, Jane Cox, the one who had aided their affair throughout its
long duration, would be rewarded for her great loyalty and discretion, and would remain with the couple for the rest of their lives. On
the other hand, if after several years Florence eventually tired of her
affair with the doctor there was the likelihood that her reputation

would be so irretrievably ruined that marriage to any respectable man would be out of the question.

Unfortunately, however, the young barrister Charles Bravo suddenly came upon the scene, and all at once a courtship with him was proceeding at breakneck speed and Dr James Gully was out of the picture.

Mrs Cox must have seen the writing on the wall. She was not blind. The situation was clear to all the other members of staff at The Priory, and it must have been equally clear to herself: with Florence married to Charles Bravo there would no longer be any need to employ a companion. Jane Cox saw her dismissal looming – and with it the end of her very high salary and free board and lodging, and – and most important of all – the education and support of her beloved sons. And where would she find a similar situation? Before being employed by Florence she had, even with the help of numerous, continuing loans (mostly from Mr Joseph Bravo), failed to do more than merely scratch a living for herself and her sons. Now, with all three boys at school, her expenses were greater than at any time before.

Another factor to consider is that although Jane Cox was the mother of three growing sons, her employment with Florence meant that she did not even have the responsibility, or the cost, of providing a family home. Employment as Florence's companion gave to her the best of all worlds; she lived as a single woman, yet at the same time she was able to support her sons and to offer them a fine, luxurious place to visit on occasional brief vacations from school. All this would end with her dismissal from The Priory, added to which, as she was nearing the age of fifty, she would have been well aware that she was on the wrong side of the hill where any future employment was concerned.

Seeing clearly what was on the cards if the planned marriage went ahead, Mrs Cox did all she could to spoil the plans of the young couple, persistently urging Charles to tell his mother of Florence's shady past – for she knew full well what would be the result of such a revelation. Mrs Joseph Bravo was already ill-disposed towards her prospective daughter-in-law, and such a scandalous admission would have ended all hopes Florence and Charles had of marrying. As Charles told Mrs Cox when once she went too far in her insistence that he tell all: 'If I do there will be no wedding.'

The wedding took place, though it appears that afterwards certain anonymous letters were sent to Charles's mother and to Charles himself. The question must arise as to whether these letters came from Jane Cox herself in a bid to destroy the new marriage. Mrs Cox's own testimony shows that her situation had been a subject of discussion between Florence and Charles from the time of the marriage at the latest, so there is no doubt that she felt the uncertainty of her position most keenly. Whether she was indeed responsible for sending the letters we shall never know, but she certainly had a very powerful motive for doing so. Nor is it known what was the exact content of the letters purportedly sent to Mrs Joseph Bravo at Palace Green; all that is known is that very soon afterwards she accused Florence of having ruined Charles's life.

With the wedding having taken place, however, and surviving in spite of external influences – anonymous letters, parental interference – Jane Cox set out to make herself sufficiently useful in the eyes of her new master in the hope that she would be allowed to stay on. That she did all she could to ingratiate herself cannot be doubted; as Charles told a friend: 'Mrs Cox is very helpful and obliging.' Her position now, however, had become totally redundant. The one thing that Florence no longer needed was a companion and Mrs Cox had nothing else to do at The Priory. As Rowe testified, she had 'no particular duties to perform', only 'getting anything that Mrs Bravo wished for'.

The omens for Mrs Cox's dismissal were clearly there, of which she was well aware, just as were the other servants, among whom the situation had become common gossip. As Rowe said at the inquest: 'There had been talk among the servants as to the probability of Mrs Cox leaving when Mrs Ricardo was married, but it was said afterwards that she would stay for two years; that she had got two years' notice.'

With acknowledgement even among the servants that a companion is hardly a necessity for a newly-married woman, it is not surprising that Charles balked at Jane Cox's continued employment. Indeed, he probably expected her to have been given notice at the time of the wedding. He would have wanted Mrs Cox gone for several reasons. For one thing her continued presence was a constant reminder to him of the fact that although he was master of the house, the companion was an employee of his *wife's*, that where the companion was concerned Florence was calling the tune. Said Florence at the inquest, 'I did not hear [Mrs Cox] express gratitude to Mr Charles Bravo, because I do not think she thought she owed it to him. I think she thought she owed it to me.'

Another sore spot for Charles would have been Mrs Cox's very presence – when he would have probably much preferred to have Florence to himself. No matter how helpful she tried to make herself, Mrs Cox was always there – like a distant relative who has long outstayed the welcome. Charles and Florence were young and newly married, and where they should have had much of their time alone they often had to have the ingratiating middle-aged woman sharing their leisure.

A third, and probably most important, reason for Charles's resentment was the cost of Mrs Cox to the household budget.

Charles, being well aware of the value of money, saw the employment of Mrs Cox – with her salary of £100 and 'all found' – a totally unnecessary expense, and indeed spoke on the matter to several individuals, among them Florence, his family and certain of his friends. He had even worked out – with the additional cost of her frequent travelling and her upkeep – how much the companion was costing the household: 'After all,' he had told a friend, 'this Mrs Cox must be costing me £300 or £400 a year.' Further, when one realizes that Mrs Cox was costing the Bravo household more than Charles himself was earning one can even better understand his resentment of her presence in his home.

And the signs of his attitude towards her were there. As Rowe stated at the inquest, although Charles sometimes called the companion by her first name he usually addressed her as 'Mrs Cox'. Clearly Charles, apart from showing his resentment of the woman, was keeping his distance.

Nevertheless, in the face of Charles's objections, Florence continued to employ Mrs Cox, her actions probably deriving from a combination of reasons, among them her keen awareness of Mrs Cox's situation as the sole breadwinner for herself and her three sons, of whom Florence was very fond. She probably also felt a degree of obligation to Mrs Cox for her unwavering support during her affair with Dr Gully and its bitter ending. And there was gratitude also for Mrs Cox's unquestioning help during the illness following the abortion, with regard to which crisis Florence had told the court that she owed her life to Mrs Cox.

Even so, notwithstanding her gratitude, it is almost certain that Florence intended to dismiss the companion in time, and was only waiting for the right opportunity to come along. And Mrs Cox, on her part, must have lived in dread of receiving that notice of dismissal which she knew was to come.

She knew that it would not be long; she was already on borrowed time. She must have realized the nature of Charles's character by now, that he was not likely to be swayed for long by considerations of her personal situation. As Atkinson, one of his colleagues, said, Charles was a man of 'commonsense and very little sentiment'. Also, in the eyes of Mr Joseph Bravo: 'He was outspoken to a fault; more outspoken than was judicial' – a view shared by the elderly servant, Amelia Bushell: 'He was a very truthful and outspoken man.' Furthermore, Mrs Cox had seen how other servants had been dismissed since Charles had come on the scene – notably Griffiths the coachman and Rance the gardener. An indication of Charles's lack of sentimentality where Mrs Cox was concerned is illustrated in his letter of 15 March, when he wrote to Florence: 'By giving up the cobs and Mrs Cox we could save £400 a year.' She was categorized along with the ponies as a means of economising.

In her situation, there can be no doubt that Jane Cox must have felt a growing hatred for Charles. There he was, agitating for her removal, when he was only in a position to do so *because of her*. She it was who had introduced him to Florence, her fortune and her fine house; she it was who had urged his suit with Mrs Joseph Bravo. Indeed, she probably thought, had it not been for herself he would still be dependent upon his occasional barrister's fees and the generosity of his stepfather.

It is also possible that Jane Cox resented the close relationship that existed between Florence and Charles. For the previous four years she had been Florence's friend, confidante and trusted adviser; now, however, with Florence's marriage and intimacy with her husband, the companion found herself excluded and out in the cold. Unfortunately, just when she was in the most desperate need of something to help her now-weakened position at The Priory, there came the bombshell to all her hopes – the letter from her aunt in Jamaica,

urging her to travel there in connection with the property which
Margaret Cox planned to bequeath to Leslie, Mrs Cox's son.

Jane Cox was at a complete loss as to what to do. She was certain
that as soon as she left the country she would be dismissed; it would
be the ideal opportunity for such a move – a move which had shown
on the cards as soon as Florence and Charles had learned of the call
for Mrs Cox to return to Jamaica. Florence's mother made this clear
in her evidence; it was her understanding that Florence was only
keeping Mrs Cox on until she left for Jamaica – 'As Mrs Cox was
going to Jamaica and she had no home to go to my daughter kept her
more from kindness, I think.'

In that early March of 1876 Mrs Cox found herself on the horns of
a dilemma. If she ignored her aunt's summons she knew well that
Leslie would lose his inheritance. Mrs Margaret Cox had made it
very clear in her letters that she would not become the benefactress
to anyone who, she felt, was undeserving. She had told Jane two
years earlier how she had revoked a will made in favour of the sons
of John Cox (see p. 21), and there was no doubt but that she would
not hesitate to do the same again – 'My own money paid for these
properties, and I can leave them to whom I please.' Jane Cox knew
very well, therefore, that if she wished Leslie to inherit the properties in St Ann's Bay she had no choice but to sail for Jamaica. At the
same time she knew very well that if she went there would be no
position at The Priory to return to. Gone would be her yearly salary
of £100, her security, and the expensive education for her three sons;
gone her peace of mind and the hope of a happy, comfortable future.
As for finding another position, she could not begin to hope that one
as eminently desirable would ever come her way again.

It must be remembered also, that in the days before Social Security benefits, for those without work and without means the
prospect of the workhouse with all its attendant horror and degradation was very real. For Jane Cox, now accustomed to a luxurious
lifestyle, such a prospect would have been too unbearable to contemplate.

In a quandary, and not knowing what to do, she went to see Mr
Joseph Bravo, to ask his advice on her difficulty, telling him that for
one thing she could not leave her sons, and for another that she did
not have the money for her fare.

One wonders why she chose to consult that particular person,

Charles's stepfather, a man who was devoted to Charles, and was very careful of his interests. She probably hoped to find out whether Charles truly did intend to dismiss her, and if he did then she hoped to enlist the sympathies of Joseph Bravo – who had so often aided her in times past, and who might now offer to intercede with his stepson on her behalf. Her hopes came to nothing; Joseph Bravo was in full agreement with Charles that Mrs Cox's continued employment would be a mistake; as he was later to tell the court: 'I agreed with him that it was not a wise thing to subject the establishment to that charge.' Consequently he advised her to go to Jamaica. There was no future where she was, he told her, pointing out that it was her duty, not only to her aunt, but to her sons, to go. As regards her lack of funds for her passage, he would advance her the money. His words did no good; as he told the court, she told him she would not go.

There can be no doubt that Mrs Cox left Joseph Bravo's office a very worried woman, and, still worried, she went to Norwood to consult Mrs Harford. Her friend, however, gave her similar advice, saying that she had no choice but to go to Jamaica. As for Mrs Cox's sons, Mrs Harford assured her that she would look after them while their mother was away. What would become of her sons in her absence, however, was not in truth, of course, Mrs Cox's dilemma; it was what would become of them all when she returned from Jamaica to find that she had been dismissed from her well-paid position at The Priory and no longer had any home or any employment to go to. Clearly, therefore, something would have to be done.

Mrs Cox's visits to Joseph Bravo and Mrs Harford took place early in March while Florence was away at Buscot, and it was almost immediately afterwards that Charles, without any warning, was stricken by the illness which was later written of in *The Daily Telegraph* (see p. 86) and of which Mr Joseph Bravo spoke at the inquest.

As previously stated, Charles was suddenly taken ill one morning after breakfast as he was preparing to leave to visit his parents' house. Rowe gave him some brandy to relieve the acute nausea but on his way to Balham Station he began to vomit profusely. The sickness remained with him during the half-hour journey to Notting Hill and when he arrived at his parents' house in Palace Green he suffered a violent attack of diarrhoea. He was given a glass of Curaçao and after a while recovered sufficiently to make the journey to his chambers at the Temple. On his return to The Priory that evening he made light of his illness by telling Rowe that his reeling and vomiting must have given his fellow travellers the impression that he was suffering from a hangover.

The symptoms of Charles's mysterious illness, it will of course be seen – nausea, vomiting and purging – are the first three classic symptoms of antimonial poisoning, and there can be little doubt that the attack was the result of an attempt to poison him. Such a hypothesis has support in the testimony of Royes Bell, who stated at the inquest that the post-mortem had revealed 'the upper part of the alimentary canal [to be] quite free from inflammation', a condition which had much surprised him, for, he added: 'Supposing the poisonous dose was the very first one that Mr Charles Bravo had ever taken, I should have expected to find the stomach and small intestine *highly inflamed* . . .'

In *Suddenly at The Priory*, John Williams says of Charles's mysterious, unaccustomed and violent attack in March that it was 'the result of an ordinary stomach upset'. But of course, having named Florence as Charles's killer, Mr Williams is bound to find some innocuous means to account for the mysterious illness for, as was established, Florence was at Buscot at that time and could not have been responsible.

With regard to Mr Williams's description of the attack as 'ordinary', it must be stated that most certainly it was not that. Indeed, the very fact of its being *so extraordinary* was what marked it out for attention. As Joseph Bravo told the court, Charles had never before been known to suffer 'vomiting and purging' as occurred on that morning in March.

The present writers are quite sure that this was Jane Cox's first attempt to poison Charles Bravo. Whether she intended it to be fatal, however, or whether it was merely a trial run, cannot be known. Whatever her intentions, she would make sure that the next time it happened he would not recover.

22

'A Good Little Woman'

To continue the hypothesis in the presentation of Mrs Cox's guilt one has to try to imagine the scheme she had in mind with regard to the poisoning of Charles Bravo and her necessary journey to Jamaica.

It is not difficult to see her plans.

If Charles's death had been attributed to natural causes or to an accident, it would, at the time it occurred, have solved all Mrs Cox's problems. Following the funeral Florence would return to her family at Buscot for some weeks, at which time Jane Cox would have been free to return to Jamaica to complete her business there. On her return she would find herself in the situation that had prevailed before Florence's marriage to Charles – except that now Florence would need her support and companionship more than ever. Furthermore, there might also be a chance that Florence, in her sorrow, would patch up the ruptured relationship with Dr Gully – with which possibility in mind Mrs Cox had sustained contact with the doctor. Should this turn out to be the case, then it is very unlikely that Florence would ever contemplate marriage for a third time. Regardless of any part which Dr Gully might play, however, the chances were that following Charles's death, Jane Cox would have remained with Florence for the rest of her life, or for as long as it suited her.

With regard to Mrs Cox's determination to kill Charles, her safest means would probably have been by a slow method – by feeding him a little of the poison at regular intervals. Although antimony was not a commonly-used means of poisoning in Britain, there

were a few well-documented cases of deaths caused by it. Eleven
years earlier, in 1865, Dr Edward Pritchard had been hanged in
Edinburgh for poisoning his wife and mother-in-law with antimony. Both women had suffered vomiting and diarrhoea, symptoms which to some had indicated gastric fever. Post-mortems had
revealed, however, that the victims were impregnated with antimony, though there was no trace of the poison in their stomachs –
which indicated poisoning over a long period. Pritchard's mother-
in-law was the first to die, and there is no doubt that he would have
got away with her murder had he not dispatched his wife less than a
month later. It was the latter's death, after suffering the same
symptoms, that created the suspicion that led to his downfall.
(Similarly, later, in 1903, George Chapman was to be executed for
the murder of three women whom he had bigamously married –
only the third death arousing the suspicion that led to his arrest.)

If Jane Cox had wished to poison Charles Bravo over a period,
therefore, perhaps a few weeks, it is possible that she could have
succeeded without arousing any great suspicion; any persistent
vomiting and diarrhoea might well have been accepted as symptoms of some natural gastric disorder. And it is possible that
Charles's attack in March was part of some plan in that direction.
Whatever her intentions, however, the likelihood is that come
mid-April Jane Cox saw that her time was running out and that she
would have to act quickly; as a result on the evening of the 18th she
gave Charles Bravo enough tartar emetic 'to kill a horse'.

Jane Cox's dilemma over the journey to Jamaica had been on her
mind all that day while she was on her errand to Worthing and
seeing her son in Brighton. Then, later, on returning to The Priory,
she encountered the factors that prompted her determination to act
at once.

One thing she learned was that during the afternoon one of the
cobs had bolted with Charles and he had returned to the house very
shaken; indeed he was still in great discomfort from the ride by the
time dinner was served. In addition – and also very importantly –
over dinner he stated that he would not be accompanying the two
women to Worthing on the Thursday.

Another likely factor in bringing about Mrs Cox's decision was
Charles's behaviour at dinner. He was in a very bad mood, surly and
uncommunicative, and not only because of his physical discomfort

but also because he had received notification of a loss on the stock market – which had come with a reprimand from his stepfather for making the speculation. In addition, as Rowe testified, a cheque for one of the tradesmen had gone missing, a cheque which Mrs Cox said had been in a letter which she had given Rowe to post.

As well as Florence and Rowe being aware of Charles's bad mood, Mrs Cox was also well aware of it – and not least aware that much of his anger concerned money, a matter with which she was very much connected in his mind. She later told Chief Inspector Clarke that Charles 'appeared in his usual health and spirits at dinner', and that she 'noticed nothing unusual'. But this was a calculated lie. Florence said, 'His face worked all evening', while Rowe also spoke of Charles's dark mood. Rowe was later to tell the court, his account being very revealing:

'When Mrs Cox first came into the room Mrs Bravo asked her whether she had taken a house for them at Worthing. Mrs Cox then described what sort of house it was. Mr Bravo, referring to someone at Worthing, asked Mrs Cox whether they knew his name. Mrs Cox appeared to laugh at that. He seemed to know Worthing. He appeared, I thought, rather dissatisfied about the house, and threw a photograph of it which Mrs Cox had brought on to the table. There was a picture including a man with a horse and cart, and he said it was "the usual trap", appeared disgusted and threw the picture down. He looked round the room and said, "I shall not be there." He seemed to mutter the words. He appeared out of sorts with everything that night. I thought he was in pain, and all was going wrong. They had been talking before about going abroad. Mrs Bravo did not appear to notice what Mr Bravo said, but Mrs Cox looked all at once above her glasses and said, "Oh", as if she was scolding him . . . She seemed to be trying to think what he had said, and then it struck me that she was scolding him. She only said, "Oh", and looked above her glasses.'

Florence was later to say that Charles regarded the planned trip to Worthing as 'an unnecessary expense'; and Jane Cox would certainly have known of his feelings – just as she knew that he felt the same way about her employment. All in all, through the missing cheque, his obvious dissatisfaction over the Worthing house and her continuing drain on the household expenses, Mrs Cox was made obliquely but acutely aware at the dinner table that she was the cause

of much of his resulting resentment and anger. 'Oh', she said, looking at him over her spectacles. And was that 'Oh', accompanied by
the long, 'scolding' look, her assessment and her decision?

It was the sum of all these factors that prompted Mrs Cox to carry
out her intention – for apart from the need to do so, the time
appeared propitious. If Charles truly intended not accompanying
Florence on the trip to Worthing then Mrs Cox would have to act
now; by the time she and Florence returned to The Priory it might
be too late. Secondly, with Charles suffering from his experience on
the cob, she suddenly realized that she was presented with a situation wherein his sudden death might not give rise to suspicion.

Having made her decision, she acted.

After dinner, while Charles was downstairs smoking and pacing,
Florence expressed a wish for more wine. Saying that she would not
disturb Mary Ann, who was at dinner, Mrs Cox offered to get it
and, leaving Florence undressing for bed, went down to the dining
room. After pouring the wine she carried it upstairs, but instead of
going into Florence's dressing room she went quietly on up to her
own room on the next floor, and there to her chest in which she kept
the tartar emetic, already dissolved in water – perhaps in the bottle
that had once held the laurel water. (If so, this would explain her
refusal to hand over the bottle – ostensibly *untouched* – when asked to
do so by Mrs Campbell; insisting that *she* would throw it away, she
knew that it was already empty.) She later denied visiting her room
during this period, but she inadvertently intimated that she might
well have done so. When Mary Ann Keeber later asked after one of
the little dogs Jane Cox told her to look upstairs: 'I believe he has
gone up to my room.' Anyone familiar with dogs as pets knows that
they do not choose to sit alone in cold rooms away from the comfort
of their owners' sides – a trait even more applicable to lap-dogs.
Therefore Mrs Cox's words to Mary Ann might be taken as an
indication that she had gone upstairs and that the dog had followed
her and had accidentally got shut in.

Taking the bottle containing the poison, Mrs Cox quickly slipped
down to Charles's room, poured out some of the water from his
water bottle into the water in his bathtub and replaced it with the
solution of tartar emetic. Quickly then she returned to her own
room, rinsed the empty bottle and replaced it in the chest. The
whole operation took only a couple of minutes, and with Charles

downstairs and the servants at supper she was not detected. Very quickly she was back in Florence's dressing room, handing Florence her glass of wine and then helping her to finish undressing.

Florence, having had her first day out since her miscarriage, and also having drunk a very large quantity of wine, was extremely tired, and once in bed was soon asleep.

Mrs Cox, however, made no attempt to join her in the bed, but sat beside it, waiting. Unlike Florence, she was *fully dressed* – which is a positive clue to her guilt, for clearly she knew that tragedy was about to strike and she was prepared for the emergency. Not only was there the chance that she would have to face a stranger that night – the doctor – but when the time came there would be certain things to do at the immediate scene which would have to be done *at once*; consequently there would be no time to waste and she had to be ready.

In the meantime in the next room Charles was finishing preparing for bed. After changing into his nightshirt he brushed his teeth and then took a long draught from the water bottle. That done, he treated his neuralgia by putting some laudanum on his finger and rubbing it into his gums. Then, just as he was about to get into bed he was gripped with violent nausea, and dashing to the door he flung it open and cried out, 'Florence! Florence! Hot water! Hot water!' Turning, he rushed across the room to the window.

There can be no doubt that Mrs Cox, sitting in the master bedroom, heard the cries. Later she denied hearing them, but soon after the event she told the doctors that she had done so. Said Dr Johnson: 'She told me she heard him cry out very loudly.' From Dr Moore: 'Mrs Cox told me she heard him calling out.' She also gave herself away when asked why Mary Ann Keeber had not heard Charles speak of having taken poison. 'He called out very loudly for hot water,' she said, 'but he spoke softly to me about taking poison.'

However, in spite of the fact that she clearly heard Charles's cries she did not run to his aid but continued to sit there until Mary Ann came to fetch her – further evidence of her guilt. Said Mary Ann later: 'Mrs Cox was just sitting there beside the bed.'

At Mary Ann's frightened words that Mr Bravo was ill, Jane Cox got up and hurried into his room, reaching him as he vomited out of the window. Then, as he collapsed on the floor at her feet, she turned to Mary Ann and told her to fetch hot water.

As soon as the girl had gone from the scene Mrs Cox picked up the water bottle containing the remains of the tartar emetic solution, and either threw it out of the window or else emptied it into the bathtub containing Charles's used bathwater. That done, she could give her attention to Charles himself.

That he was alive probably came as a great disappointment to her, for it was her fervent hope that the whole business would be over very quickly and that there would be no complications. One of the more dynamic symptoms of acute antimonial poisoning is heart-failure, and, knowing this, she had hoped that Charles would swiftly succumb to such an attack, dying almost immediately after swallowing the tartar emetic. This being the case, and with the doctors searching for the cause of heart-failure, she hoped they would attribute it to his experience on the runaway cob. (When the time came both she and Florence would suggest to Dr Moore the experience with the cob as a possible cause of Charles's illness.)

It was probably in accordance with this scenario that Mrs Cox neither awakened Florence nor sent immediately for a doctor. Florence would of course have to be called eventually, and a doctor summoned, but not yet; it would be better for Jane Cox if Charles were already dead by the time they appeared on the scene. In the meantime she had to give every appearance of doing all she could to save his life.

So it was that by the time Mary Ann got back with the hot water Mrs Cox was sitting on the floor with Charles propped up against her while she rubbed his chest. As soon as the maid had set down the water Mrs Cox sent her running off to the kitchen again, this time to fetch mustard. When the girl returned with it Mrs Cox mixed some with water, stirring it with her finger; then with the maid's help she managed to pour a little down Charles's throat. After Charles had vomited into a basin, however, his jaws locked, and he could swallow no more. Mary Ann was then sent to throw away the vomit. Regarding the vomit on the leads beneath Charles's window there was nothing that Mrs Cox could do, so for the time being she kept silent on the matter.

When Mary Ann had brought back the clean washbasin she was sent off again, this time to make coffee. That done she was sent scurrying off for a bottle of camphor which, she was told, was in the medicine chest in Mrs Cox's room. She came hurrying back to report that it was not there, whereupon Mrs Cox told her to look in Mrs Bravo's dressing room. Mary Ann looked and could not find it, and Mrs Cox told her to look in her room again, this time on her table. There the camphor was found.

During the early stages of Charles's illness Mary Ann Keeber was sent on a variety of errands, and while they might well be regarded as necessary in view of the situation they also had the effect of keeping her out of the bedroom for most of the time, so enabling Mrs Cox to carry out any particular tasks – tasks which were essential, not to Charles's preservation but to her own. For one thing she could rinse out the water bottle and refill it with the water brought by Mary Ann; it would cool soon enough; indeed, it could not have been very hot anyway, for she had stirred the mustard and water mixture with her finger. All of her acts could have been carried out without there being any witnesses; the only other person in the room for much of the time was Charles, and he was in no state to be aware of anything that was happening. It should also be noted that before Dr Moore arrived Mrs Cox instructed Mary Ann to empty the water from the bathtub – so ensuring that whatever else had been added to it, it would never be discovered.

What went on in Charles's room while the maid was absent we have no way of knowing. We only have Mrs Cox's word for what took place, and for all that is known she might well have been working to hasten the man's death instead of, as it appeared, trying to save him.

One thing that is apparent on considering Mrs Cox's behaviour when she first went to Charles's side is that she appeared to be in control of the situation. There was no sign whatever of panic, of her becoming hysterical, or being at a loss as to what to do. Her actions give the impression of one who is in command as, to all appearances, she worked desperately to save Charles's life.

One remarkable fact, were Jane Cox innocent, is that although she seemed to be so in command and appeared to be thinking of everything that was necessary to help the stricken man, *she never sent the maid to awaken Mrs Bravo – even after a doctor had been summoned*. For a servant to take it upon herself to summon a doctor to her master without apprising her mistress of the fact constitutes an act that is truly astonishing. And to this must be added the fact that even though Charles had been vomiting profusely and was now lying totally insensible on the floor, his jaws locked, Mrs Cox still left Florence sleeping soundly in her bed.

Such an omission can only be understood in terms of Jane Cox's guilt, and it is remarkable that she was never questioned in court on the matter. Chief Inspector Clarke was to report that Mrs Cox stated that '[Mr Bravo] became very ill and she sent for medical assistance and informed Mrs Bravo'. This latter was another of her lies. She most certainly *did not* inform Mrs Bravo; Mary Ann Keeber did, as she made very clear at the inquest. And the very fact that Mrs Cox lied about it is further indication of her guilt, for it shows that she was very much aware of the fact that she *should* have informed Florence.

Notwithstanding that she did not wake Florence from her sleep, Mrs Cox's actions were nevertheless an acknowledgement of the seriousness of Charles's condition. Her sending Parton to fetch Mr Harrison is proof of that. And it was after Parton had gone from the house that Mary Ann Keeber, believing that her mistress should be informed of the master's collapse, took it upon herself to rouse Florence. And Charles's appearance must have presented a very shocking, horrifying spectacle for Florence, for on seeing him she burst into tears. Then, on learning that Mrs Cox had sent for Mr Harrison she asked why Dr Moore, who lived closer, had not been sent for. Without wasting any further time she hurried downstairs, in her dressing gown and with her hair loose, crying out loudly for Rowe to go and fetch Dr Moore. Said Rowe: 'She was running screaming along the passage with the housemaid.'

The fact that Mrs Cox sent for Mr Harrison when it was obviously necessary to call in someone nearer emphasises the point that she wanted Charles to die before medical aid and expertise arrived on the scene. Her hopes in this respect were of course thwarted by the fact that Florence sent for Dr Moore who lived so much closer. Had not Moore arrived and given immediate treatment, Charles would probably have been dead by the time Mr Harrison got there. As it was, Dr Moore found Charles lying at the very brink of death, but by administering an enema of brandy he managed to effect some temporary recovery. By the time Mr Harrison arrived Charles's pulse had begun to improve slightly.

It was probably at some time just before Dr Moore's arrival that Mrs Cox threw the contents of the chloroform bottle out of the window – the liquid would very swiftly evaporate – and replaced the empty bottle on the mantelpiece.

Her hopes being dashed of a doctor appearing on the scene too late to help had prompted her to find some other means of accounting for Charles's violent, mysterious attack. Had the doctor been faced with a dead man there would have been no symptoms to examine. Finding him alive, however, albeit unconscious and with his jaws locked, changed the situation dramatically; he might at any time manifest symptoms which would clearly indicate the cause of his illness, that he had in fact been poisoned. (As it was, the bloodied vomit and stools that came not long afterwards fully confirmed this.) So it was that Mrs Cox, seeing the blue, fluted chloroform bottle on the mantelpiece, saw in it a possible answer to her dilemma. In the event that it was too late to hope realistically for the acceptance of a 'natural' death, she hoped to promote the notion that Charles, in treating his aches and pains – his neuralgia and his stiffness from the ride – with chloroform, had somehow swallowed some and accidentally poisoned himself.

Even so, she made no mention of it to Dr Moore but waited until Mr Harrison appeared. Only then did she say, 'I'm sure he has taken poison, and the chloroform bottle is empty.'

Much has been made of the precise time at which Mrs Cox first spoke to Mr Harrison about Charles having 'confessed' to taking poison, but no one, it appears, has seen any significance in the fact that she made no mention of chloroform to Dr Moore who was first on the scene. If indeed she *had* detected chloroform on Charles's breath and so suspected that he had poisoned himself she would surely have mentioned it to Dr Moore at once. She did not; she waited until Mr Harrison had arrived.

Another, and vital, question arises with regard to the chloroform; one which, it appears, has not before been addressed – and the answer to it gives further indication of Mrs Cox's guilt. The question is: how did the chloroform bottle come to be empty if Jane Cox did not empty it herself? She herself was the first on the scene and she testified that after smelling chloroform on Charles's breath she noticed that the chloroform bottle was empty. However, the medical men who attended Charles testified that he had *not* swallowed any – which in fact was borne out by the post-mortem. If Charles, therefore, did not empty the bottle then there is no question but that

Mrs Cox must have found it full and emptied it herself in order to support her story.

As it turned out, however, in spite of all Mrs Cox's hopes the two medical men made it very clear that chloroform was not responsible for Charles's attack; nor, they said, could they detect any smell of chloroform about him.

Disappointed for the second time in her wish to account for Charles's illness, and knowing that the medical men were desperately searching for the cause of that illness, Mrs Cox kept silent about the vomit lying on the leads. Had she pointed it out at once, or saved the vomit in the basin, Charles might have been saved. She could not allow that to happen, though, for she knew that the vomited matter would show that he had been poisoned with antimony. Further, if he were saved he would of course make it very clear that he had not taken the poison voluntarily, in which case someone – herself, she feared – would be charged with *attempted murder*. So, she must needs go on and let the man die, in the knowledge that as he could then never speak for himself she had a chance of escaping any charge at all. Which is exactly what happened. So she cruelly perpetuated his destruction by allowing the poison to become absorbed into his system while he lay unconscious. Any other course was fraught with greater peril for her own position.

The dilemma which she then faced was how to account for the antimony that would be found in his body once he was dead. So, improvising again, as she had done repeatedly from the moment when he had first cried out from his bedroom doorway, she told Royes Bell that Charles had confessed to having *deliberately* swallowed poison. The idea of Charles being stricken with a natural illness had not been accepted, nor had the idea that he had swallowed chloroform by accident. Now, with her words, supposedly spoken by Charles – 'I've taken poison; don't tell Florence' – she hoped to provide a convincing theory of suicide.

Understandably the doctors were scandalised, particularly Mr Harrison who, Mrs Cox stated, had been the recipient of this information on the moment of his arrival at the house. Of course he vehemently denied it; and he had no reason to lie – as did none of the other medical men. Indeed, they would have given very great attention to such words, for such a revelation was associated with the question that was bedevilling them all – the question of what Charles had taken. They had pleaded with him enough times – 'Tell us what you have taken' – so they would not have ignored or forgotten such vital information offered to them on that very matter.

Mrs Cox did *not* tell Mr Harrison: of that there can be no possible doubt. For a start, Charles Bravo did not kill himself; he was murdered, and men dying at the hands of assassins do not say they have taken their own lives.

Long after Mrs Cox's 'revelation' to the medical men in Florence's dressing room Sir William Gull was summoned. After he had examined Charles he met Mrs Cox on the landing and there told her that the patient was dying. Only then did she decide that it was safe to speak of the vomit on the leads. She now had it confirmed that Charles was too near death to benefit from any analysis the doctors might make. Later, at the second inquest, she would insist that she had told Mr Harrison *much earlier* that Charles had vomited out of the window. Mr Harrison, however, would remain adamant that she had not done so.

Much later, of course, long after Charles's death, and whilst making her Treasury statement, Mrs Cox embellished her words about Charles's admission, saying he had told her that he had taken the poison *'for Dr Gully'*. Also, she told the court that when alone in the sickroom later with the dying man he had gently criticised her for revealing his secret, saying, 'Why did you tell them? Does Florence know I have poisoned myself?'

To this she said she replied: 'I was obliged to tell them. I could not let you die.' And then, 'What have you taken, Charlie?'

At these words, she said, 'He turned his head round impatiently and said, "I don't know." Immediately after that his wife came into the room.'

Asked by Mr Muir whether she had mentioned this second conversation to any of the surgeons, she replied: 'No, I did not.'

'Or to anybody?'

'No.'

'Why was that?'

'Because I thought he would not wish me to.'

'Did the doctors at any time say anything to you to the effect that Mr Bravo had no recollection of any conversation with you?'

'Mr Royes Bell said he would not acknowledge anything.'

'Was that all he said?'

'Yes – that is all I remember.'

'Was it ever suggested that you should be brought face to face with Mr Bravo to have this matter explained, if there was anything to explain?'

'No, I only wish it had been.'

'Did the doctors ever, from first to last, say they doubted the accuracy of what you said?'

'No, never for a moment.'

The reason for Mrs Cox not repeating Charles's alleged words to her as he lay on his sickbed was, of course, because he had never uttered them – and clearly, judging by his words, the assessor, Mr Muir, doubted that he had. Like so much of Jane Cox's testimony there was no truth in her words. Much of her testimony gives the impression of being cobbled together to suit the needs of the moment, as and when those needs arose. Her statements suggesting that Charles would choose *her* to confide in are frankly ludicrous. Before he died he had four individuals at his side whom he loved very much – his mother, his stepfather, his cousin and his wife – and in the face of that fact one is expected to believe that he would ignore these people and choose to confide in a woman with whom he was rarely even on first-name terms, whom he saw as a drain on his resources, whom he could not wait to get out of his house, and for whom he had no affection whatsoever.

With regard to the last, the only words testifying to any affection he had for her came from Jane Cox herself – mainly in her Treasury statement, in which she positively harped upon it.

That statement was yet another means she employed to further her aim – which was to have Charles's death attributed to suicide and at the same time to divest herself of any possible responsibility in his death and to show, almost incidentally, that she had no motive for wanting him out of the picture.

A very interesting piece of work, her Treasury statement should be examined briefly here. It is notable, not only for its references to Charles's affection for her, but also for her testimony as to his appreciation of her efforts on behalf of Florence and himself. Clearly she was trying to present a picture of a man who not only liked her enormously, but also found her a very useful addition to his household; i.e. a woman he was not likely to dismiss.

One thing is certain – Mrs Cox's Treasury statement gives a view of a relationship between herself and Charles that has no support whatever from any other source; indeed, it is contradicted by all the independent evidence.

On first looking at the statement one receives a general impression of great unrest, conflict and unhappiness existing between Charles and Florence. However, on closer examination one sees that there are in fact only two incidents occurring between Florence and Charles that relate to any disharmonious confrontations between them. Says Mrs Cox:

> On Good Friday, the first day she [Florence] had come down after her illness, he was annoyed with her for lying down after luncheon and not wishing him to remain in the room. He was so restless, she could not rest. He got very angry and went out of the room and I put a match to the library fire, and he went and sat in there.

And later in her statement:

> Three or four weeks before that there was a quarrel between them, I believe through a letter from his home, and he was very violent and said he would go.

Most of the rest of Mrs Cox's statement is concerned with incidents *occurring between Charles and herself*, incidents which neither Florence nor the other servants seemed to be aware of, so could not verify or deny.

During these scenes Mrs Cox has Charles continually threatening to kill himself or leave Florence and return to his mother. In fact in her Treasury statement Mrs Cox has Charles speaking of leaving or wishing he were dead no fewer than *thirteen times* (Florence, on the other hand, does not mention his leaving the house once), and each time, according to Mrs Cox, it was only by her own sensitive and tactful mediation that he was prevailed upon to remain.

Not only did she act as mediator between Charles and Florence, so Jane Cox would have one believe, but Charles also showed great gratitude and affection for her in respect of her work. In a particularly nauseating and sanctimonious strain, she writes:

. . . I again reasoned with him for a long time but he seemed quite determined and shook hands, saying, 'You are a good little woman. I will always do what I can for you.' He turned and kissed me on the cheek and said, 'Goodnight.' He thanked me again, saying, 'You love Florence and you do the best you can for me. I thank you for it.'

This 'good little woman' was a clever little woman indeed, for in this one paragraph she not only attempts to demolish the notion that he might have been planning to dismiss her – 'I will always do what I can for you' – but also shows his great affection for her and appreciation of her efforts – 'You love Florence and you do the best you can for me. I thank you for it.'

Charles, however, had made known to several people his wish to get rid of Mrs Cox, and quite a number actually testified to his sentiments, among them Florence, Mrs Campbell, Joseph Bravo and Frederick MacCalmont. It is a singular point that, in spite of many people – even the other servants at The Priory – being aware of Jane Cox's impending dismissal, she should insist that Charles wanted her to stay – notwithstanding her interview with Mr Joseph Bravo when he told her to her face that she was no longer required at The Priory.

There can be no doubt at all that she was very conscious of Charles's fervent wish to get rid of her – and this is proved by her constant denial of it.

One notable example of that denial came at the inquiry when she was asked about a quarrel that had taken place between Florence and Charles. She said: 'He wanted her to put down the horses and cobs, to dispense with a lady's maid, and retrench expenditure.' Mrs Cox, of course, was again altering the truth to suit her case. Charles had not only wanted Florence to dispense with the cobs and her maid, but *also with Mrs Cox*, which his letter of 15 March makes clear (see p. 39). Mrs Cox could not admit that, however, without admitting her motive for murder. Which is why, of course, she went to endless effort throughout the whole business to give the impression that Charles was delighted to have her in the house.

On this same matter the Treasury statements of Jane Cox and Florence Bravo differ in one very particular and very significant respect:

Florence spoke of Charles wanting to get rid of Mrs Cox; Mrs Cox spoke of Charles wanting her to stay.

It was in her Treasury statement, too, of course, that Mrs Cox introduced into the mystery the startling concept that Dr Gully was the direct reason for Charles's alleged suicide. The hypothesis could not be seriously entertained by anyone who looked closely at the circumstances, but nevertheless his being named as the cause created a very successful smoke screen. Without Mrs Cox's words here the suicide theory would not have had even a chance of being accepted.

Florence herself had spoken of Dr Gully in her Treasury statement, but it was Jane Cox's introduction of his name into the inquiry, of course, that led to Florence's disgrace. And Mrs Cox, for all her apparent reluctance to reveal Florence's past, knew that it would; but if a woman will not stop at murder to get what she wants she will certainly not hesitate to ruin another socially for the same purpose.

Notwithstanding Jane Cox's successfully managing to avoid being charged with murder, there were many who regarded her with great suspicion – which is made clear in the reports of the inquest as they appeared in the newspapers. Some of the interrogators were obviously of the opinion that she was guilty of Charles's murder, as the questions they asked indicate. Certain journalists also made known their suspicions. Said *The Lancet* shortly after the second inquest ended:

> It is remarkable that previous to the arrival of the medical men, the patient was treated for poisoning, as a mustard emetic had been administered. Supposing a person to be suddenly attacked with vomiting, that is by no means a remedy likely to be instantly applied, least of all in a family with homeopathic proclivities. It is necessary to assume, therefore, that either the patient did make a statement as alleged to the effect that he had taken poison, or it was known by the person directing the use of the mustard emetic.

It is not difficult to read between the lines.

Having established that Jane Cox had the *motive*, it is clear too, that she had the *means*, as much as anybody had. It has been demonstrated that tartar emetic was not difficult to obtain, though it is quite possible that she procured the poison at an earlier time, from the stables, when Griffiths was coachman at The Priory.

In addition to the means, she certainly had the *opportunity* to carry out the murder. As has been shown, she could have put the poison in Charles's water bottle while the servants were at supper and while Florence was getting undressed for bed. Alternatively, an earlier opportunity was on her return from Worthing, when she looked into the morning room and saw Charles there sitting in a chair.

The hypothesis of her guilt is further strongly supported by her *behaviour subsequent to the event.*

As pointed out, her conduct after Charles was poisoned gives cause for great suspicion. By her own admission she lied repeatedly about the statement regarding poison that Charles was alleged to have made. And surely this implies guilty knowledge. In addition to this one must add the other points indicating her guilt.

Why did she not respond to Charles's cry for help? And why did she later lie about hearing him cry out? At the inquest she denied that she had heard him, saying the first she knew of his illness was when the maid came into the room, yet by her own words to several of the medical men she made it very clear that she had indeed heard his cry.

If, however, she did *not* hear him, then *why* did she not? She was not asleep; she was sitting awake in a chair. And this last factor raises the question: why had she made no attempt to prepare for bed for the night?

Once summoned to Charles's side and seeing how ill he was, why did she not wake Florence immediately? Why, also, did she not send for the nearest doctor?

Why did she throw away the vomit?

Why did she not point out the vomit on the leads as soon as the doctors arrived?

Why did she lie in saying that she had informed Mr Harrison of Charles's alleged poison statement?

Why did she lie in saying that she had smelled chloroform when Charles was vomiting? She could not have done, as he had not drunk any.

Why did she lie about finding the chloroform bottle empty?

Frederick Veale, in his excellent slim volume on the case, *Verdict in Doubt: The Bravo Case*, points out that the one weakness in a prosecution's case against Mrs Cox – whom he believes was guilty of the murder – would be lack of proof that she had ever possessed poison, and lack of proof that she gave Charles Bravo anything to eat or drink on the day he was taken ill. However, says Veale, these would not have been serious obstacles to a conviction, and cites the case of the Crown *v.* Frederick Henry Seddon in 1911. In spite of being defended by the great Marshall Hall, Seddon was convicted of murder by administering arsenic, even though it was never proved that he had ever possessed poison or had ever administered anything to the victim. It was found sufficient to prove that, Seddon's little daughter having recently purchased fly-papers, from which arsenic could be extracted, he had *access* to poison. There was also the fact that the victim occupied a room in his house, therefore giving him the opportunity. Added to these factors was Seddon's suspicious conduct and the surrounding circumstances, all of which convinced the jury of his guilt. Seddon's conviction was solely due to his actions after the fact.

It may well be thought that today, faced with a determined and sharp prosecutor, Jane Cox would have a very hard time convincing a jury of her innocence. In 1876, however, she could not have been examined in the witness box, the testimony of accused persons in their own defence not being allowed until the Criminal Evidence Act of 1898. However, says Veale:

> . . . On the other hand there were flourishing in the eighteen-seventies a number of strong-minded judges little disposed to take the merciful view in favour of the prisoner. If it had been Mrs Cox's fate to have come before the notorious 'hanging judge', Mr Justice Hawkins, we may be confident he would have made as short work of her as remorsely as he made short work of the wretched Stauntons.*

Not that everyone believed Mrs Cox to be guilty, however. Sir Harry Poland, who as Mr Poland had represented the Crown, later gave his opinion to the effect that the fact that Mrs Cox was faced with losing her job was 'scarcely sufficient' as a motive. It was

---

* In 1877 Louis, Patrick and Elizabeth Staunton, along with Alice Rhodes, were convicted of the murder of Louis Staunton's wife Harriet. Sentenced to death, they were later reprieved.

obtuseness of this kind that helped the killer to escape, a refusal to see that the fact of being faced with losing her job, and with all the ramifications of that loss, in truth constituted the most real and powerful motive. Added to this is the fact of Mrs Cox's lies and highly suspicious actions – lies and actions that cannot be accounted for except in the context of her guilt. Perhaps, where Sir Harry was concerned, the motive was – as it was later for Agatha Christie – just too obvious.

Surely there can be no doubt – certainly the present writers are convinced of it – that Jane Cannon Cox was the murderer of Charles Bravo. In examining the story surrounding the case in the light of a supposition of the guilt of Florence or Dr Gully one quickly sees that inconsistency treads on the heels of improbability. Examining the story in the light of a supposition of the guilt of Jane Cox, however, one finds that it makes sense at every step of the way.

Sadly for justice, in the Bravo case its process was hampered by several factors which enabled Mrs Cox to escape an encounter with the hangman. First and foremost she was helped enormously by the mismanagement of the two inquests – at the first inquest when evidence was in fact suppressed, and at the second when nothing was held back and vital information was allowed to be swamped in a morass of irrelevancies. Mr Carter, the coroner, has to bear much of the responsibility for Jane Cox's getting away with murder. Single-handedly he did as much to thwart the cause of justice as did the inadequacies of the police investigators, though it must be mentioned that by the time the police came on the scene the trail was very cold. Even so, with the inquiries under the direction of Chief Inspector Clarke, the investigators do not appear to have done all they might, and, as stated earlier, Clarke's reports do not even indicate a suspicion – except in his stated disbelief of Mrs Cox's 'poison' statement. Clarke, unfortunately, was entirely inadequate to the situation; what was needed was someone of the calibre of Jonathan Whicher.* He, one feels, with his sharp eye for detail and human nature, would have got to the bottom of the affair.

And what of those in court who *did* believe in the guilt of Jane Cox? Among those present in a professional or official capacity

* The celebrated Scotland Yard detective whose name became well known through his involvement in the Constance Kent case, 1860–5, and in the case of the Tichborne Claimant, 1870.

there were many, as there were among the spectators. Mrs Belloc Lowndes, in her short, but telling, account of the case, writes of an acquaintance's impressions gathered during the inquest:

> Among those present at the second inquest was the late Sir Douglas Strait. That famous lawyer once told me that he had never seen so intelligent and composed a witness as Mrs Cox during the hours when she was engaged in swearing away her generous friend and kind employer's reputation, and, it might almost be said, her very life.
>
> While apparently willing to say anything that would injure Mrs Bravo . . . she refrained from making a single admission that told against herself.
>
> When she was subsequently reminded of the lies she had told, both during Bravo's illness and at the first inquest, she wisely remained silent and 'stood as if deeply thoughtful and perplexed'.

Belief in Mrs Cox's guilt is also demonstrated by many of the questions asked at the inquiry and from the jury's verdict. By bringing in a verdict of murder the jury stated plainly that they regarded Mrs Cox as a liar, and did not accept for a moment her story of Charles's alleged confession to suicide. Further indication came in their rider to the body of the verdict, that there 'was not sufficient evidence to fix the guilt upon any person or persons'. It was not necessary for them to add this, but in doing so they indicated their suspicions. Add this to the fact that they discounted Mrs Cox's evidence and the conclusion must be inescapable.

Among the learned counsel who were convinced of Mrs Cox's guilt was Mr George Lewis, the fearsome interrogator who represented Mr Joseph Bravo, a man not kindly disposed towards Florence. In an interview in the *Strand Magazine* in 1893 Sir George, as he became, said, speaking of the case many years after it had ceased to be headline news:

'There was the Balham mystery. I represented the family of the late Mr Bravo . . . The jury found a new verdict of wilful murder against some person or persons unknown. Now listen – it is much to be regretted that at an inquest the advocate is not allowed to make a speech to the jury. Had I been able to do so, I could and should at

once have relieved both Dr Gully and Mrs Bravo from any suggestion that they in any way participated in the crime. You are at liberty
to say – and I am publicly expressing this for the first time – that I
[did] then and still do believe them *not guilty*.'

Said his interviewer: 'Then who poisoned Mr Bravo?'

'Who?' repeated Sir George . . .

And, said the interviewer: 'He told me the name.'

23

Finale

As soon as the pressures of the investigation and the publicity permitted, the three main protagonists in the Charles Bravo murder inquiry went their separate ways.

Dr Gully remained at Orwell Lodge on Bedford Hill where he continued to be served by his faithful butler Pritchard. He was harshly penalised for his part in the scandal, however, being denied membership of several clubs and associations, the reason given being that his address could not be correctly ascertained. Fortunately he was supported during his trials by his family (with the exception of his daughter Susanna), his elderly sisters eventually going to live with him once more. On 21 October 1879 his aged wife died. Four years later, on 27 March 1883, Gully himself died. In his will he left £500 and all his clothes – on account of 'long and upright service' – to his loyal butler, Pritchard, who had remained with him to the end.*

Unlike Dr Gully, Jane Cox soon left the scene of the crime, and in *The Illustrated London News* of 14 October came the announcement: 'Mrs Cox, who gave evidence at the recent inquiry into the death of Mr Bravo, has sailed for Jamaica.'

In an attempt to discover what became of her afterwards we, the present authors, thought it advisable to find out as much as possible about her antecedents, in that her earlier history might give some clue as to her later movements. We must say at once that we have

* Dr Gully's son William later went into politics. It is not known whether any irony was intended, but in 1895, when he took his seat as Speaker in the House of Commons, he was greeted with cries of 'Bravo, Gully!'.

not met with much success in tracing her later history, but what we discovered about her earlier years has a certain significance.

As stated, the only information available on Jane Cox's past before she went to work for Florence Bravo was that which came from the woman herself, from the legend she created – that her maiden name was Edouard, that her father was French and that she was born in the East Indies; she also stated that she married in 1858 and went to Jamaica with her husband in 1861, returning to England seven years later.

Yseult Bridges says Jane Cox was born in Jamaica, and with that invention goes on to invent an appearance to match such a background. Describing her as a Creole, she gives a vivid description of a woman with dark skin and jet black hair – altogether a very exotic picture, and one at odds with the English-looking woman whose face appears in contemporary newspapers. We, the present authors, felt that as far as our own researches went we should begin from scratch and not rely on secondary sources.

The results of our early efforts were, to say the least, unpromising. For a start, a careful search of the marriage records for Britain held at the General Register Office in St Catherine's House in London revealed no record of any marriage having taken place between a Mr Cox and a Miss Edouard at any time between 1855 and 1861.

Could it be, we wondered, that Jane Edouard's husband, like Charles's confession to having taken poison, was a figment of her imagination? The absence of a record of marriage could well indicate that she had not married Mr Cox, but had simply become his common-law wife and taken his name. Having already proved to our own satisfaction what a consummate liar Jane Cox was, we had to consider such a possibility.

The only possible lead we had was a report in one newspaper that Rowe the butler said that Mrs Cox had once referred to her late husband as 'Philip'. A consultation of the marriage register for 1858 showed among the records of the many Coxes an entry relating to a Philip Cox, but at the same time there was no escaping the fact that there was no entry for any Miss Edouard.

Ironically as it turned out, it was from an acknowledgement of Jane Cox's mendacity that we found what we were looking for. Supposing, we thought, she had not been Jane *Edouard* at all, but, through affectation and a wish to promote herself to advantage as a teacher, had Frenchified the very common, very English name of *Edwards*. It seemed a rather wild chance, but nevertheless seemed worth testing. And so it proved to be.

In the register for the last quarter of 1858, at the very top of one page devoted to seemingly numberless Edwardses, was an entry for *Jane Cannon Edwards*, with the information that her marriage had taken place in the Wirral. Beside it was the reference number *8a 646* – the same reference number relating to the marriage of the *Philip Cox* whose entry we had already seen. It appeared, then, that Jane Cox had indeed lied about her name.

Requisitioning a copy of the marriage certificate it was revealed that the marriage between Jane Cannon Edwards, spinster, and Philip Cox, bachelor, engineer, had taken place by special licence on 28 December 1858 in the parish church of Bebington, in the county of Chester. The father of Philip was named as John Cox, a clerk in holy orders; that of Jane as John Edwards, merchant. The age of both the bride and groom was given as twenty-one.

If they were both twenty-one then simple arithmetic told us that they had been born in 1837, which was the year in which records of births, marriages and deaths began to be registered formally and centrally. However, as those records only began half-way through the year we had to hope that Jane Edwards and Philip Cox had been born during the latter half.

A study of the birth registers for the second half of 1837 turned up an entry for a Philip Cox born in Brixworth, Northamptonshire, and happily this turned out to be the right one. There he was, born 15 September 1837 in Walgrave, the son of John Cox, curate of Walgrave (contradicting Yseult Bridges's statement that Jane Cox's husband was also a Jamaican).

Where Jane Cox was concerned we had no similar luck. We could find no record of her birth in the second half of 1837 and therefore could only conclude that, if she had been born in that year, her birth had occurred during the first half. However, an assumption of her birth during *any* part of 1837 did not sit comfortably, for it meant that in 1876, the year of Charles's death, she would have been only thirty-nine, and judging by the various drawings of her that appeared in the illustrated newspapers that summer she looked considerably older than this. At the same time, we had at least to bear in mind that Yseult Bridges gave Jane Cox's age as 'only some six or seven years older than Florence herself'.

In a further effort to find more information on Jane Cox's background we turned to the 1861 census entry for Lower Bebington, Chester, from where she had married. The rest of her family, it appeared, were still living there in April of that year: her mother, Martha, age sixty, born in Brough, Westmorland, and her three sisters: Catherine, twenty-nine, Mary, twenty-one, and Adria Elizabeth, nineteen. (Adria's name appears on Jane's marriage certificate, as a witness.) Also resident with Mrs Martha Edwards was the latter's younger brother, George Forrester, fifty-eight, a tobacconist, indicating that on Jane's mother's side also her ancestors were English. According to the census entries, Mrs Edwards was the principal of a ladies' seminary, at which her three daughters were teachers. It was interesting to note, also, that all three girls, Catherine, Mary and Adria, had been born in the East Indies – which vaguely defined area had also been given as a birthplace by sister Jane.

Having found the record of Jane Cox's marriage it turned out to be a simple matter to find the record of the birth of her first son. He was born John Leslie Clarke Cox on 17 March 1860 at 6 King Street, Higher Bebington. With this information it was a simple, though tedious, matter to find in the 1871 census the record of his presence at his school, the Royal Asylum of St Anne's Society, Streatham Hill. His age is given as eleven; that of his younger brother, Henry – 'born in St Ann's Bay, Jamaica' – as eight.

Returning to the search for some more positive indication of the year and place of Jane Cox's birth, we found in one part of her testimony a statement that before joining Florence Ricardo at Stokefield she had gone in January of 1871 to live in Eastbourne Terrace, West London. Immediately then we set out to find the census records for Eastbourne Terrace to see whether she was still there in April when the census was taken.

She was.

In the entry for 2 Eastbourne Terrace, which was a lodging house alongside Paddington Station, she is listed as one of its tenants. The entry regarding her reads:

NAME: Jane C. Cox.
RELATION TO HEAD OF FAMILY: Head.

CONDITION: Widow.
AGE: 43.
OCCUPATION: Annuitant.
WHERE BORN: Liverpool.

Where her youngest son, six-year-old Charles Forrester Todd, was at this time we have not yet discovered. He was very probably at some preparatory school, for according to Jane Cox he did not go to school at St Anne's in Streatham Hill until 1872. Incidentally, the full name of this youngest Cox boy was only recently found by the authors – as indeed were the full names of the twins, Henry Philip Robertson and Sarah Evelyn Major.

Not that this is of great importance, however. More significant is the information unearthed in the census regarding Jane Cox herself, and what it says of her honesty.

Having already lied as to her name and the nationality of her parentage, she was now seen to have lied in her census entry when she described herself as an annuitant (one who lives on an annuity); she and her sons were in fact solely dependent for their living on her earnings as a teacher, the rents from the house in Lancaster Road and the frequent loans she was granted by, among others, Joseph Bravo. Not only that, the age she gave, forty-three, gives the lie to her age given on her marriage certificate. If she was already forty-three in April of 1871 then she was born at some time in the year following April 1827. This would have made her thirty or thirty-one when she married the twenty-one-year-old clergyman's son by special licence in 1858 – not twenty-one as she stated in the marriage register. Also, an assumption of her birth in 1827 gives her an age approaching forty-nine at the time of Charles's death in 1876 – an age far more in keeping with the pictures of her that appeared at the time, and the rather unflattering descriptions of her as 'the old lady'.

It is clear now that almost all of the known history of Mrs Jane Cox, that 'good little woman', was a tapestry of lies. Just a little diligence has revealed a history quite different from the one which she perpetuated. Through our researches it is seen that Jane Cannon Edouard, born in 1837 in the East Indies of a French father, was in fact born Jane Cannon Edwards c.1827 in Liverpool, of, presumably, well-established English stock on both her paternal and maternal sides.

*

Having discovered something of Jane Cox's past, one wonders what became of her between the inquest and the time of her death. As stated, our researches have so far revealed no answers.

It is very likely that she did indeed return to Jamaica, as *The Illustrated London News* reported. In order to ensure Leslie's inheritance she had no choice but to go, though it is very doubtful that she took her sons with her. Considering the effort required to bring them to England in the first place, and that she was loath to take them back, it is almost certain that they remained in England while she was gone. Furthermore, as she had insufficient money for her own fare to Jamaica it is unlikely that she could have found the fares for three growing sons as well. In addition, her friend Mrs Hartford had testified to offering to care for the boys while Mrs Cox was out of the country, so it appears that the question of them accompanying their mother was never really considered.

It is reasonable to assume, then, that Jane Cox left her sons in England while she went to Jamaica, returning to them once she had sorted out the business affairs with her aunt. Perhaps she then tried to return to her old employment as a teacher – if not under her own name with all its concomitant scandal and opprobrium, then under another.

The writer Elizabeth Jenkins, following publication of an article she had written on the case in 1945, received a letter from a Mr Carmley, seventy-eight years old, who said that he had known Mrs Cox when he had worked as a bank clerk in Brighton some years after the inquest into the Bravo case. Describing her as 'very plain' and 'a poor little woman', he said: 'She often came to see me and brought fruit and things for my father, who was ill.' We do not know whether Mr Carmley's account is reliable, though it is conceivable that Mrs Cox might have lived for a time in Brighton following her return from Jamaica; she would have known the town well, for her eldest son had been at school there and she had stayed there many times.

It would be very satisfying to have knowledge of her career following the inquest – and also to know what became of her sons, those three shadowy figures who hovered on the fringes of the tragedy, of whom the two youngest were brought from school by Charles and Florence on that Easter Monday of 1876 and with whom Charles played tennis on his new lawn tennis court. Just over a day later Charles lay unconscious, poisoned with a massive dose of antimony. Had Mrs Cox, the proud mother, planned his death even as she watched the game from the sidelines?

Regardless of speculation concerning Jane Cox's later years, her earlier history must at least indicate that she would not have hesitated to lie and deceive in order to protect herself and her own. And there can be little doubt that somehow she managed to provide for her sons and furnish the rest of their education. For them, her boys, she had calculatingly murdered a young man in cold blood, a man who had shown her 'only kindness'. She would not be deterred for long in her efforts to provide her sons with their needs.

The only further information we have of her is of her death. With the invaluable assistance of a friend, actor and bibliophile David Simeon, we eventually found in the registers at St Catherine's House a note of the death in 1917 of a Jane C. Cox at the age of ninety. This proved to be the one we sought. It transpires that Jane Cox died in a village in the borough of Lewisham, now a part of southeast London. According to her death certificate, Jane Cannon Cox, widow of Philip Cox, Civil Engineer, died at 19 Cambridge Road, Lee. The cause of her death is given as 'Exhaustion and decay of nature'. The informant of her demise was her son, Henry Philip, who was living with her at the time of her death. She was buried, without a memorial stone, close by in Hither Green Cemetery.

There is not a little irony in the fact that while her victims died young, she who was the cause of their suffering and death lived to a ripe age.

And what of Florence herself, the central figure in the Balham drama?

Shattered by the ordeal of the second inquest, and shamed beyond measure by the exposure of her immorality, Florence Bravo sought comfort and oblivion in alcohol, visited in her unhappiness only by members of her family. She had been ostracised before her marriage to Charles, but after his death society's rejection of her was complete and irrevocable. As history shows, there are few judgements as harsh and inhuman as those meted out from a truly sanctimonious society acting in the names of Righteousness and Christian Goodness, and Florence Bravo would have been tailor-made as a target. She was a confessed adulteress and suspected of having committed a most terrible murder, and no Biblical stoning could have been more lethal, or as painful as the scorn and condemnation that was thrown at her.

On 20 February 1877, the year following the murder, Florence made a new will. Later, in August, having decided to give up the lease on her home, the furniture and effects of The Priory went up for auction at Bonham & Son, of Princes Street. Those members of the public who were sufficiently curious but could not afford to bid for any of Florence's possessions could settle instead for an auction catalogue – on sale at the Bedford Hotel, price one shilling.

It is not known where Florence went immediately on her departure from Balham, but in April of the following year, 1878, she went to live in Lumps Lane (now known as Eastern Parade), Southsea, in a large, secluded house called Lumps Villa, which she renamed Coombe Lodge. Now long since demolished, the house stood in spacious grounds looking past Lumps Fort to the sea. It is quite possibly the same house where she once stayed with Dr Gully when, chaperoned by Mrs Cox, she enjoyed a vacation in the the town a few years earlier. Now, with the local inhabitants unaware of her real identity, she called herself Mrs Turner – using Charles's true surname – and lived in social isolation with her staff: three female servants, a coachman (Parton) and a gardener.

Later that year came the startling news of her death. She died on 17 September at the age of thirty-three.

Evidence of the fact that rumour breeds rumour, the speculation concerning her death and its cause was so wild that an inquest was held. From the testimonies of the witnesses called, the sad story of Florence's last days emerged.

Florence had treated unhappiness and despair in the past with alcohol, and following the tragedy of Charles's death and her resulting disgrace her alcohol consumption increased. In May 1878, soon after taking up residence in Southsea, she summoned a local doctor, Dr Henry Robert Smith, who found her to be suffering 'from the effects of an undue amount of stimulants'. He later told the inquest that she was suffering from intense vomiting and prostration. However, he said, at his suggestion she managed to give up her dependence on alcohol, her symptoms abated and she recovered her health, adding that when he last saw her on 30 June 'she was in excellent health and spirits'. Since that time, the doctor said, he had 'seen her in a casual manner when she was out driving' but had not visited her professionally.

Sadly Florence's abstinence lasted only seven weeks, and shortly after Dr Smith's last visit to her she began to drink steadily again, with the result that her health once more began to deteriorate.

At the end of July her maternal uncle, James Orr, who was very fond of his niece (and with whom Charles had lunched on the day he was poisoned), arrived in Southsea with the express purpose of keeping an eye on her. Probably there partly at the instigation of Florence's parents, he took rooms at the Royal Beach Mansion Hotel and began to pay regular visits to Florence at Coombe Lodge, often calling on her twice in one day. She had no other visitors. Said James Orr at the inquest: 'She had offers of visits from some of the inhabitants but she declined them.'

He went on to tell the court, reluctantly, that on several occasions he had seen her much the worse for alcohol. He had seen her ill three times since his visits to her began, he said, and each time her illness was due to 'excessive stimulants'. 'She would be vomiting for hours,' he said, and added: 'Twice she recovered. The third time was the fatal one.'

The coroner asked whether the dead woman's drinking had been excessive during the last three weeks, to which James Orr replied: 'No, not different from usual. She took drink until it caused her these vomitings, and then she was obliged to leave off. Her drinking would last for several hours, then she would leave off, trying to recover herself, with the help of her maid, and her own good constitution.' Her confidential maid, James Orr said, was named Everett; she had been with her mistress about twelve months, and had tried to induce her to leave off drinking.

He went on to say that on the evening of Friday 13 September he called to see Florence with regard to arrangements they had made to go on a tour of Scotland together, leaving the following week. He found her, he said, 'not in right form', and pleaded with her: 'Florrie, keep straight, and let us start on Monday.' He begged her, he said, not to take any more brandy, added to which the maid, Everett, also tried to induce her to leave off drinking – 'Oh, ma'am, do promise Mr Orr you won't drink any more brandy tonight' – to which Florence replied that she would not make any such promise.

Later, said James Orr, Everett followed Florence upstairs and returned to tell him that she did not think her mistress would be able to leave for Scotland on Monday as planned.

Continuing with his testimony, James Orr said that later there was a dispute between Florence and Everett about the former taking so much stimulants, and that finally she discharged the maid. 'Instead of a month's warning,' he said, 'she gave her a month's wages and discharged her on the spot.'

On Sunday afternoon, he went on, he found Florence intoxicated, and when he called the following day he found that she had commenced vomiting during the night, bringing up a dark-coloured fluid from her stomach. 'After that,' he said, 'the two servants could hardly keep life in her.' Seeing how ill she was on the Monday evening he told the two servants to sit up with her. He went on:

'On Tuesday morning I called to see her at six o'clock, before I went to my sea bath. I went there at that early hour because I felt anxious about her.' In spite of her condition, she pleaded with him for alcohol – 'Oh, do give me a little, or I shall die.' He added, 'I carried a little flask of brandy in my pocket, and as I saw she was faint I gave her a little.'

He went on to say that he did not notice 'any particular change in her', adding, 'but she was very pale and breathing heavily, as was always the case after heavy vomitings. I saw what came off her stomach; it was heavy black fluid. This continued at times during the day. Her breathing was very bad. She said she was very tired, and remarked during the day, "I'm going, I'm going."'

James Orr told the coroner's court how he had tried to persuade her to summon her doctor, and how she had refused. 'I didn't think the case would be fatal,' he said, 'until the Tuesday afternoon. Then I began to have my doubts about it. I had thought that she would recover, the same as she had done before. The collapse was sudden.'

Said the coroner: 'When you saw that sudden collapse, then did you send for Dr Smith?'

'No, I did not,' said Orr. 'I asked her if I should send for him, but she shook her head and said, "No." I also asked her if I should send for her mother. Again she shook her head and said, "No." The last black vomit occurred about two hours before her death. Then she cried, "Oh, I can't breathe! Oh, save me, save me!" This was about two o'clock on Tuesday afternoon. I then went and got a spoonful of brandy and gave it to her. She died shortly before four o'clock, in the presence of myself and the two servants.'

Dr Smith, in giving evidence, said that he had carried out a post-mortem examination of the body and that he had found the heart, liver and kidneys to be in a degenerated condition, while much internal bleeding – through the stomach wall – had taken place. Asked to what he had attributed death, he replied:

'To haematemisis, or haemorrhage produced by intense vomiting, and accelerated by a weakened state of the heart.' Questioned as to the cause of the haemorrhage the doctor said, 'I believe it to be due to the excessive use of alcoholic stimulants, producing violent sickness, thereby straining the stomach and rupturing the vessels.'

Asked by the foreman of the jury, 'You think there were no symptoms of poison?' the doctor replied:

'No. There was no appearance of her having taken, or having had administered to her, any irritant poison.'

Before the jury brought in its verdict, which was in accordance with the doctor's findings, Mr James Orr was asked whether she had been of a nervous temperament.

'She was not nervous,' he replied, 'but I think she felt the uncharitable and persistent remarks made about the trial [sic] by a portion of the press.'

Notwithstanding the unequivocal verdict of the jury there were those who were intent on making a mystery of Florence's sad and sordid end and hinted strongly that she had been poisoned. Furthermore, with the discharged servant Ann Everett having gone from Southsea by the time Florence died, leaving no forwarding address, there were some journalists who made of her a rather sinister figure, even implying that she might even have been Mrs Cox. Another newspaper reported that Dr James Gully had been seen in the vicinity of Coombe Lodge shortly before Florence Bravo died. The rumours, the old feeding the new, flew thick and fast. *The Hampshire Post* got to the point, however, in saying that the cause of the deceased's death was 'transparent, and had not the deceased been Mrs Charles Bravo the word of her doctor would have been enough and there would have been no request for an inquiry into her death'. The same newspaper also had criticism for *The Whitehall Review* for implying that 'Mrs Bravo was a diabolical murderess, who went to the grave with the terrible secret in her own keeping' – which, said *The Hampshire Post*, considering the lack of evidence to support such a claim, was 'as cruel as it well could be'.

The words of *The Whitehall Review*, however, are representative of the calumny that circulated among an ignorant and cruel public and press following the Bravo affair, the calumny that was in truth – after the betrayal of Jane Cox – responsible for Florence Bravo's death. There are numberless similar instances throughout history. Thirty years later, in 1908, Major-General Luard would be driven by calumny to throw himself under a train, while ninety-four years earlier Marie Antoinette had gone to the guillotine because of it. 'Calumny kills people better than anything,' she had said, 'and it is by calumny that they will kill me.'

Now, however, with her death, Florence Bravo was beyond all the whispering and the shame that had caused her so much misery.

Following the closing of the inquest Florence went on her last journey – to the churchyard at Buscot, in which little church she had knelt in such happiness and hope at her marriage to Alexander Ricardo as a nineteen-year-old bride fourteen years earlier. Legend has it that the coffin bearing her body was carried by train not to Faringdon station, which would have been so much more convenient, but to Challow, seven miles from Buscot. Apparently the coffin arrived there in the small hours of the morning, after which it was carried at once to the churchyard and buried. The Campbell servants, it is said, were sworn to secrecy as to the nature of their work.

The legend is believable, for not even the smallest stone marks Florence's grave; it is clear, therefore, that her parents were intent on avoiding any further publicity connected with her. So it is that no one knows now in which part of the quiet, green churchyard her body lies.

In her will Florence left £1000 to her young god-daughter, Florence Julia Gully (James Gully's grand-daughter), and to members of her own family various items of fine jewellery, fur and lace. To her sister-in-law Augusta she left her pictures, glass and silver. To William, her much loved brother who had supported her throughout her ordeal, she left the residue of her estate – amounting to a little less than £60,000 – in trust for his descendants. Mrs Cox was mentioned merely in the context of being mother to the three Cox boys, to whom Florence left £100 each. To Jane Cox herself she left nothing, which is hardly surprising, since her former companion had caused her so much grief. Whether Florence ever realised that Mrs Cox had murdered Charles we shall probably never know, but that she had, through her revelations about Dr Gully, brought about Florence's public shame and humiliation there was never any question.

And what of the scene of the Bravo murder?

The Priory still stands. After many years of being derelict its crumbling walls have been carefully restored and its interior restructured. Divided into a number of flats it now, anachronistically, stands cheek by jowl with modern red-brick blocks of flats that have all the attractiveness of something created from a child's Lego set, and which stand so close that it is difficult to see The Priory in its entirety. As to the rural land that once formed a part of The Priory's attraction, little remains of it. There are small areas of green lawn surrounding the house, out of which, before the front door, Florence's oak tree is still allowed to rise. The rest of the ten acres that made up the 'estate', as Charles liked to call it, has long since gone to urban development.

Two miles to the east lies West Norwood Cemetery, the site of Charles's grave.

The grave proved difficult to find, and it was only after considerable searching on a second attempt one early May afternoon, almost exactly 111 years to the day after his burial, that we, the present authors, came upon it.

Most of the graves in the area where Charles lies date from about the same period, though the appearance of the site must have changed a great deal since he was buried there. The graves now are neglected and falling to ruin, and subsidence over the past century has moved the stones so that not only the standing stones are tilting but even many of the horizontal slabs have been shifted from their original positions. Now the gravestones lie at crazy angles, lying as if scattered there by some giant hand.

A few feet to the north of Charles's grave tall sycamores and limes

stand, while the earth all around the grave itself is thickly over-
grown. The time of our visit, the spring, was the best time, we
realized, for in the summer the area would be choked by brambles
and practically impassable. On that May day of our discovery of the
grave, though, there was room for primroses and bluebells to grow.
It was peaceful too; only the sound of birdsong and the rustling of
the leaves disturbed the quiet.

Even in its melancholy setting, amid the other graves – the
crumbling mausoleums and tombs almost hidden beneath creeping
ivy – Charles's grave has a particularly forlorn appearance. It has
deteriorated more than most in the area, and it is difficult to imagine
exactly how it originally appeared, although the crumbling remains
show that it comprised a stone surround with a low iron fence, at its
head a tall stone carved in the shape of a Maltese cross. Over the
years the iron has rusted away, only the sockets in the stone surround showing it was ever there. Part of the surround itself has
gone, too, while the cross itself no longer stands but lies full-length
upon the grave, its time-eroded surface showing the inscription:

SACRED

TO THE MEMORY OF

CHARLES D TURNER BRAVO

BORN ON 30TH MAY 1845

DIED ON 21ST APRIL 1876

It will not be long before Charles's grave has deterioratd beyond
repair and beyond recognition; then, as it is for Florence, his resting
place will be unknown.

There is the stuff of tragedy in the story of Charles and Florence
Bravo. Two young people, seeking happiness, found that their
meeting, so full of promise, was a swift path to destruction. And
they were destroyed by one whom they trusted, while – and irony
of ironies – the guilty one went unpunished. And now they lie apart,
and each beneath the weight of the most dreadful calumny – for
Florence that of murder; for Charles that of attempted murder. But
perhaps with this book the truth will be acknowledged and they will
be granted the benefit of those doubts that have touched their names
over the years. It is time.

SELECT BIBLIOGRAPHY

BOOKS

Bridges, Yseult, *How Charles Bravo Died*, Jarrolds Publishers (London) Ltd, 1956.

Hall, Sir John, *The Bravo Mystery and Other Cases*, John Lane, The Bodley Head Ltd, 1923.

Jenkins, Elizabeth, *Six Criminal Women*, Sampson Low, 1949.

Roughead, William, *Malice Domestic*, W. Green & Son, 1928.

Sayers, Dorothy L., *et al.*, *Great Unsolved Crimes*, Hutchinson, 1938.

Veale, F. J. P., *The Verdict in Doubt: The Bravo Case*, The Merrymeade Publishing Co. Ltd, 1950.

Williams, John, *Suddenly at The Priory*, William Heinemann Ltd, 1957.

JOURNALS

Balham Mystery, The (broadsheet issued in seven weekly parts, 1876)

Daily Chronicle, The
Daily News, The
Daily Telegraph, The
Graphic, The
Hampshire Post, The
Illustrated Police News, The
Illustrated London Clipper, The
Penny Illustrated Paper, The
Pictorial World, The
South London Press, The
Strand Magazine
Swindon Advertiser, The
Vanity Fair
Wandsworth & Battersea District Times
World, The

Anonymous pamphlet: *The Gay Young Widow of Balham*, 1876.

OFFICIAL PAPERS

Metropolitan Police File
Treasury File

Index